PATRONS, DEVOTEES AND GODDESSES

Patrons, Devotees and Goddesses

RITUAL AND POWER AMONG THE TAMIL FISHERMEN OF SRI LANKA

MASAKAZU TANAKA

MANOHAR
1997

First published in Japan, 1991
Published in India with corrections, 1997, by
MANOHAR PUBLISHERS & DISTRIBUTORS
under arrangement with
THE ASSOCIATION OF JINBUN

ISBN 81-7304-183-0

Published in India by
Ajay Kumar Jain for
Manohar Publishers & Distributors
2/6, Ansari Road, Daryaganj
New Delhi 110002

Printed at
Rajkamal Electric Press
G.T. Karnal Road
Delhi 110033

CONTENTS

ILLUSTRATIONS

Plates

Figures

TABLES

GLOSSARY

Where both Sanskrit and Tamil words are listed, the latter always appear in parenthesis.

abhiṣeka (*apiṣēkam*).	consecration
acuttam (Tam.).	impure
Agni.	Fire God
Aiyaṉār.	village god, son of Śiva and Viṣṇu
akkiṉiccaṭṭi (Tam.).	a fire pan or the procession of one
ampā (Tam.).	songs
āratti (Tam.).	waving of light
arcanā (*aruccaṉai*).	private offering
Arjuna.	one of the heros in the *Mahābhārata.*
aruḷ (Tam.).	divine grace
aṟuva (Tam.).	sand bar
asura (*acuraṉ*).	demon, evil being
āvi (Tam.).	ghost
balipīṭha (*palipīṭam*).	sacrificial altar
Bhadrakālī.	village goddess
Bhairava (Vairavaṉ).	a fierce form of Śiva, guardian god
bhakti (*pakti* or *patti*).	devotion, love to deities
Bhīma.	One of the heros of the *Mahābhārata*
cāmi (Tam.).	a lord, deity or priest
cāmi āṭutal (Tam.).	fierce possession
caṉṉatam (Tam.).	modest possession
cūrapuli.	Bhadrakālī's attendant
Cuṭalaimāṭaṉ.	Śiva's lower form
cuttam (Tam.).	clean, pure

dakṣiṇā (taṭcaṇai).	a fee to the priest
darbha (*taruppai*).	sacred grasses
Dhṛtarāṣṭra.	king and father of the Kauravas in the *Mahābhārata.*
dīkṣā.	the liminal phase of a sacrificial ritual or initiation
Draupadī.	the heroine of the *Mahābhārata*
Drupada.	father of Draupadī
Duryodhana.	the eldest brother of the Kauravas
Gaṇeśa.	Śiva's first son
grāma śānti (*kirāma cānti*).	the propitiation of a village
Gramodaya Mandalaya.	government office for local development
Hanuman.	Monkey God
homa (*ōmam*).	fire sacrifice
jajmāni.	caste division of labour
kāḻāñci (Tam.).	halved coconut shell
Kantacāmi.	Murukaṉ, or Śiva's second son
kāppu (Tam.).	protective cord
karakam (Tam.).	parading pots representing gods
kaṭṭumaram (Tam.).	raft for a beach seine
kāṭu (Tam.).	forest
kāvaṭi (Tam.).	votive ritual
kontaṉ (Tam.).	cross-cousin
kōyil (Tam.).	a temple or shrine
Kṛṣṇa.	one of Viṣṇu's incarnations
Kṣatriya.	a class of royals and warriors
kumbha (*kumpam*).	a pot or image
kummi (Tam.).	a dance
Lakṣmī.	Viṣṇu's consort
mahākumbhābhiṣeka (mahākumpāpiṣēkam).	temple consecration
maṇḍalābhiṣēka (maṇṭalāpiṣēkam).	consecration for forty days
mantra (*mantiram*).	sacred verses
mantra śakti (*mantira catti*).	power of sacred verses
Mohinī.	female form of Viṣṇu
Murukaṉ.	Kantacāmi, or Śiva's second son
Muttumāri.	village goddess
naivedya (*naivēttiyam*).	public offering
Navagraha.	nine planetary gods
neṟṟi (Tam.).	a vow

ōmappoṭi (Tam.).	the powder from fire sacrifice
Pāṇḍavas.	hero brothers in the *Mahābhārata*
Pāṇḍu.	father of the Pāṇḍavas
Panṭāram.	non-vegetarian priestly caste
pāṟkāvaṭi.	a votive ritual
Pārtasārati.	a form of Kṛṣṇa
pātai (Tam.).	beach seine boat
pavaṉi (Tam.).	a procession
Pēcci.	a minor village goddess
pēy (Tam.).	an evil spirit
pīṭha (*pīṭam*).	a small table, sacrificial altar
poṅkal (Tam.).	rice gruel, or ritual of cooking it.
poṭṭu (Tam.).	the mark of the Śaivites
prasāda (piracātam).	consecrated left-overs
pūjā (*pūcai*).	worship
puṇyakumbha (*puṇṇiyakumpam*).	the holy pot for a purificatory rite
puṟattār (Tam.).	sub-group of the higher sub-caste of the Karaiyar
Śaivite.	a follower of Śiva
śakti (*catti*).	divine power, or energy
Śakti.	female deities, Śiva's consorts
śaṅkhābhiṣeka (*caṅkāpiṣēkam*).	consecration with conches
śānti (*cānti*).	appeasement ritual
Śiva.	main god of Hinduism
snānābhiṣeka (*snanāpiṣēkam*).	consecration
tāli (Tam.).	wedding necklace
tāmbūla (*tāmpūlam*).	set of betel leaves and areca nuts
tēṅkāyppali (Tam.).	coconut sacrifice.
teppam (Tam.).	raft
tēvatai (Tam.).	a demon
teyvam (Tam.).	a deity
tīrtha (*tīrttam*).	sacred water
upayakkāraṉ (Tam.).	patron
upayam (Tam.).	an endowment
ūr (Tam.).	village
Vaiṣṇava	a follower of Viṣṇu
vaḷḷam (Tam.).	beach seine boat
Vāstu.	god of house or temple site
Vāstu *śānti* (*cānti*).	appeasement of Vāstu
vēḷvi (Tam.).	blood sacrifice
Vīrabhadra (Vīrapattiraṉ).	a fierce form of Śiva, guardian god

Viṣṇu.	main god of Hinduism
vrata (*viratam*).	a vow
yāgaśālā (*yākācālai*).	the place for fire sacrifice
Yudhiṣṭhira.	the eldest brother of the Pāṇḍavas

PREFACE

This book is about *śakti*. The general concept of the word concerns divine power, but the term is generally personified, and *śakti* also refers to goddesses as entities. Soon after arriving in Cattiyur, I realised that goddess cults were very important in village life, especially among the dominant Karaiyar. Subsequently I centred my investigations on the role of goddess festivals in the life of the village and the villagers' attitudes concerning the goddesses.

The fieldwork was carried out in Sri Lanka between June 1982 and November 1983. I lived with my wife in Adipetti for the first five months, then at the start of the fishing season, we moved to Cattiyur. It was not until I started visiting each house, for the purpose of making a complete census in November 1982 that I became familiar with the people of Cattiyur.

Although a subsequent brief trip in 1991 increased my understanding of Cattiyur social life, the ethnographic content of the book refers to the 1982-83 period.

Most of the data on religious matters were collected through participant observation, extensive interviews with the people concerned, and with some key informants—religious specialists and village elders. Their explanations were generally more elaborate than those of ordinary fishermen. But I also tried to ask my landladies, my assistants and other people about the same matters. When the only significant difference between the key informants, who conducted rituals, and ordinary people was one of the degree of elaboration, I present the data with the explanations given by the former without further qualifications. For example, chapter 5 is dependent on interpretations given by Paṇṭāram caste members, and chapter 6 on those by Brahman priests. But this does not mean that the ordinary people did not contribute to the present work. For example, interesting interpretations of *poṅkal* (ceremonial cooking of rice gruel), possession, songs called *ampā* and votary rituals were originally suggested by conversation with ordinary fishermen and women. Statistical data were collected by making more formal and structured interviews with householders or their wives, and with the various kinds of fishermen.

The principle of transliteration is as follows : for readers' convenience, deities found all over India are mostly expressed in Sanskrit, so are general terms concerning rituals (*homa*, for example, not *ōmam*). Proper names for places and persons follow established Anglicised usage without diacritical marks. At some stages of my exposition I have employed pseudonyms. Tamil transliteration in this work follows that of the *Tamil Lexicon*.

The value of Sri Lanka Rupee was Rs 100.00=U. S. $ 4.9 in June 1982.

Funding for the first resarch in Sri Lanka was provided by the London University Central Research Fund, and the Wenner-Gren Foundation, Anthropological Research Inc. (grant-in-aid 4284). The thesis from which the present work has been developed was entitled *Sacrifice and Divine Power : Temple Rituals and Village Festivals in a Fishing Village, Sri Lanka*, and submitted to the University of London in July 1986. For the writing-up of the thesis, I received grants from the Radcliffe-Brown Memorial Fund (Royal Anthropological Institute) and Malinowski Memorial Fund (Department of Anthropology at the London School of Economics and Political Science). My first year at the LSE was funded by the Japanese Government (International Student Exchange Program), and the two years after fieldwork were funded by a Honda Award administered by the LSE, and a graduate scholarship of the school. In 1987 I had an opportunity to receive financial support from Nanki Foundation. The visit to Sri Lanka in 1991 was made financially possible by the Japanese Ministry of Education, Science and Culture. I am grateful to these agencies for the support given to my studies.

Professors M. Kusunoki, K. Sugiyama, and T. Yamaori guided and encouraged me in the study of Hindu society and religion while I was an M. Phil. student in the Department of Religious Studies at Tohoku University in Japan.

In preparing for fieldwork, Dr. John Marr at the School of Oriental and African Studies, S. Selvakumar and Somasegaram, both from Jaffna, taught me Tamil language and much about Tamil culture. In Sri Lanka Dr. W. M. Sirisena kindly accepted me as a research student at the Department of Sociology, University of Peradeniya.

In Cattiyur and Adipetti my wife and I received a great deal of hospitality from countless villagers. To mention them all by name would be impossible, but special thanks are due to Mr S. Sivajody, and Mr. Ponnampalam and their families. I received invaluable help from my field assistants, interpreters, and friends ; Mr. Ramanathan, Mr. K. Dayanandan, Mr. K. Mayandy, Mr. S. Tangaraja and Miss Devi. I express my thanks to my key informants ; Mr. M. Parandaman, Mr. Kumaracami and Mr. Kesavamurty.

During the period of writing, I received helpful comments at thesis writing seminars from my fellow graduate students, and I have incorporated some of them without further acknowledgements. Mr K. Gnanasooriyan, while helping me with some local documents, especially the translations of festival songs, provided me a comprehensive knowledge of Śaiva tradition. I would like to acknowledge the patience and understanding of some of my friends who kindly read the original thesis, Liz Nissan, Debbie Rutter, Rob Jones and Eric Hirsch. I would like to acknowledge my debts to Maurice Bloch, Chris Fuller, Jock Stirrat, and the late Sir Edmund Leach.My supervisor, Jonathan Parry, was a continuous source of encouragement throughout the period of my stay, both in England and in Sri Lanka.

My former employer, the National Museum of Ethnology provided me with good facilities and I received much stimulation from seminars there organised by Drs. Y. Nagano, S. Tanabe, and S. Einou. I express my thanks to its Director-General, Dr. Tadao Umesao and Professor Komei Sasaki. Professor Yutaka Tani, Director of the Institute for Research in Humanities at Kyoto University has provided this opportunity to publish the present work. I also acknowledge my long term debt to Professor Y. Ikari of the Institute. I express my thanks to Dr. Hiroshi Yamashita, who has kindly read the final draft and given me some valuable advice. Both Tim Fitzgerald and David Eunice have patiently read the final draft and corrected my English. Yumiko Itami and Hong Funja kindly typed the final draft and prepared some of the figures and tables.

I would like to acknowledge my parents' financial and moral support at several critical periods. This book is dedicated to them. Finally, I must thank my wife, Noriko, who selflessly assisted me in England, Sri Lanka and Japan.

Kyoto, March 1991 M. T.

CHAPTER ONE
INTRODUCTION

The present work is based on data collected during my fieldwork in a Tamil fishing village in Sri Lanka. Consequently, the following discussion is restricted to so-called "popular Hinduism" or "village Hinduism" in a particular region, and to only some aspects of it : temple rituals and village festivals. In spite of this obvious restriction, I hope that my argument on Hinduism has some relevance beyond my research area, and will be of heuristic value for further studies of Hinduism. To this end, I choose fairly general theoretical issues for the following discussion in order to facilitate the reader's understanding, and to put the following chapters in a theoretical and comparative perspective.

First, I will try to pick out some broad developments in anthropological studies on Hinduism over the past thirty years, then present the perspective adopted in this work. Finally I outline the plan of the book.

For a Sociology of Hinduism

Introduction

This section aims to examine the main trends of anthropological studies on Hinduism. Although not exhaustive in any sense, even a cursory look at the relationships between the anthropological studies of Hinduism and more general analytical frameworks, which have implicitly or explicitly influenced them, will provide us with insight into the shortcomings of these studies.

It is often pointed out that as the gaze of anthropology shifted from relatively isolated, small, and self-sufficient societies—say in the South Pacific—to those of Africa and Asia, which have more complex systems, anthropologists had to face several hitherto unknown problems (Fortes 1953 ; Gluckman 1967 ; Redfield 1956 : 5-34). One of these concerned the theoretical proposition of holism. Holism is a proposition that socio-cultural facts are closely interrelated and integrated into "a whole," and should be analysed in relation to it—that is, within the contexts they are found in, and not in isolation (Cohen 1968). It became, however, increasingly difficult for anthropologists to discern the boundary of the whole.

The modern holistic standpoint emerged with functionalism in the 1920's, as the primary criticism of the then dominant diffusionism, which tended to take cultural elements arbitrarily out of context in order to reconstruct supposedly original cultural circles and their historical contacts. At this stage anthropology was mainly preoccupied with small and isolated societies, which were easily observed as discrete units. The ideal of holism was not conceived to be dissociated from empirical reality.[1] The problem of relevance of holism, however, was acutely felt by anthropologists who started studying so-called "peasant societies" or "communities," which could not be considered as self-sufficient sociological units, but as part of states and had been influenced by world civilizations for more than a thousand years. Since these are self-sufficient in neither politico-economic nor cultural terms, anthropologists found it difficult to view their objects as a whole. Without considering socio-historical influence from the outside world and ongoing interactions with it, the study of peasant societies would remain superficial. As a result, there was a partial retreat into a diffusionist view of the relationships between peasant societies and the outside world.

Before discussing anthropological studies of Hinduism, I propose to distinguish two types of holism. One is the structural-functional, or empiricist, holism of Radcliffe-Brown, where every part is held to be functionally integrated into a society as a whole in service of its solidarity. In this way, religious phenomena, especially rituals, are explained as integrating factors. The other is an idealist holism, which puts emphasis on "ideology" (a system of indigenous ideas) rather than on behavior and function. I see the main development in the anthropological study of Hinduism as a shift from empiricist holism (function) to idealist holism (meaning).

The Limits of Empiricist Holism

M. N. Srinivas's monograph, *Religion and Society among the Coorgs of South India* (1952), has been one of the most influential books in the anthropological literature on South Asia. Under the influence of Radcliffe-Brown's structural-functionalism he was able to make several contributions to our understanding of Hinduism and its relationship to the social structure of the Coorgs.[2] One of Srinivas' main contributions to our knowledge of Hinduism is his attempt to understand its diversity and uniformity.[3]

According to Srinivas, Hinduism among the Coorgs can be classified into four levels : "All-India Hinduism," "Peninsular Hinduism," "Regional Hinduism" and "Local Hinduism." All-India Hinduism has features observable all over India. As we move from All-India Hinduism to Local Hinduism, geographical universality gradually diminishes and particularity increases. Local Hinduism is therefore that found only in geographically restricted areas.

"Spread" is Srinivas's key concept for understanding the above four levels. There are two types of spread. One is "horizontal," that is the geographical spread of a particular form of Hinduism. The other is "vertical," that is, the penetration of a specific complex of beliefs and rites up and down castes within a particular language zone. Srinivas believes that Sanskritic and non-Sanskritic beliefs and rituals are disproportionally distributed among various castes. As we move down the caste hierarchy from the Brahman to the Untouchable, the Sanskritic elements gradually diminish. According to him,

> Each caste has both Sanskritic and non-Sanskritic rituals and beliefs, but the proportions in which the two are found together vary from caste to caste (vertical spread), and also from region to region (horizontal spread) (Srinivas 1952 : 213, parentheses mine).

All-India Hinduism is geographically spread all over India, and is epitomised by the upper castes, especially the Brahman. More specifically, Srinivas identifies it with the "ritual and cultural forms" of Sanskrit literature, which is the epitome of Brahmanical civilization. Understandably, he calls All-India Hinduism "Sanskritic Hinduism" and the historical process of the spread of Sanskritic rituals and beliefs "Sanskritization." In other words, the main distinguishing criteria of All-India Hinduism—and accordingly of other levels of Hinduism—depend on whether a particular religious element is or is not present in

Sanskritic literature. If it has a basis there, it is assumed to be observable among upper castes in other parts of India and is considered to be one of the attributes of All-India Hinduism.

Srinivas adopts the structural-functionalism of Radcliffe-Brown in order to explain rituals at the village and local level. For Radcliffe-Brown, religion, by which he primarily means ritual, serves the solidarity of a social group. One of the tasks of social anthropology is to elucidate these functions of rituals.[4] Certainly, Srinivas shows us the socio-functional aspects of rituals serving the unity of different levels of social groups; such as the family, lineage, and village. His structural-functionalist approach, however, does not go beyond a regional level, and he appeals to cultural elements rather than social functions to account for unity at higher levels of Hinduism. As we have observed, the criteria of the four levels of Hinduism depend on religious and cultural *forms*, having both horizontal and vertical distribution. The very concept of "spread" reminds us of diffusionism. The problem of the analytical inconsistency between a functionalist holistic approach to the village level, and an explicitly diffusionist approach to the levels beyond it, seems to indicate the limits of structural-functionalism itself. This central problem becomes clear, when a complex society such as an Indian village is considered.

It should be remembered that, for Radcliffe-Brown, the social structure is a concrete and observable entity (Lévi-Strauss 1953 : 542; Radcliffe-Brown 1940 : 4, cf. Leach 1976b). His functionalist approach to religion is relevant only if a concrete and observable social entity (group) with a clear-cut boundary can be identified (Radcliffe-Brown 1940 : 17), and its "social solidarity" takes on the visible form of a collective ritual. In the absence of such a social group, structural-functionalism simply fails to explain religious phenomena in a holistic perspective.

To be sure, Srinivas recognises the importance of the caste system and considers the Brahman caste as a social group which represents All-India Hinduism. But he cannot apply the same functionalist approach to this level as he did to the village level. Rather, he appeals to cultural elements in Sanskritic literature, which are the only concrete and observable things he can find. The use of such elements as evidence for All-India Hinduism fails to convince.

In a similar vein, M. Marriott applies the dichotomy of "Great and Little Traditions" to Hinduism in his article "Little Communities in an Indigenous Civilization" (1955). This dichotomy was originally developed by R. Redfield in his long-term study of a peasant society. According to the latter, civilization has two types of traditions, "a Great Tradition" and "a Little Tradition." The former is nourished and maintained by a small elite and based on a literary tradition, while the latter is maintained by the illiterate masses. Geographically, the former is represented by the urban centres, and the latter by rural areas (Redfield 1956 : 67-104).

Marriott's study starts with the recognition that an Indian village is "a part society" which can only be fully understood in reference to its interaction to the outside world. In this sense, he has a more sound comprehension of the Indian village than his predecessors, and is careful not to cut it off artificially from the outside world. On the other hand, he has totally relinquished any holistic analysis of village Hinduism, and consequently he ends up speculating about the historical transformation and transmission of religious elements (rituals, divine beings and so on) from one level to another. This dichotomy between the Great (literary) Tradition and various Little Traditions of the village more or less corresponds to Srinivas' All-India Hinduism (Sanskritic Hinduism) and Local Hinduism. We must appreciate Marriott's work for substantiating Srinivas' concept of Sanskritisation and the opposite process of localisation, and for its emphasis on the interaction between Sanskritic and non-Sanskritic elements. But although I do not deny the relevance of introducing the levels into Hinduism, in so far as he identifies the Great Tradition with the Sanskritic tradition of the texts, Marriott fails, in the same way as Srinivas, to understand Hinduism in a more comprehensive perspective.

To sum up, both Srinivas and Marriott take empirically observable elements as their analytical objects, and consequently fail to maintain a holistic approach to Hinduism. One possible solution to the problem of maintaining this holistic perspective is to shift the focus from the concrete level to a more abstract and ideal level, that is, to the ideology of Hinduism and perception of Hinduism by the Hindus themselves.[5] In South Asian ethnography, this idealist tendency is epitomised in the work of Louis Dumont, especially *Homo Hierarchicus* (1980, first published in French 1967).

The Encompassing Nature of the Pure-Impure Ideology

Although the present book is mainly concerned with Hindu beliefs and rituals and not with the caste system, it is necessary—given the breadth of Dumont's influence on South Asian ethnography—to discuss his work carefully at the outset. Dumont sums up the tendency of past works on the caste system as follows :

> We have seen that its chief manifestations are : the reduction of the religious to the non-religious ; the tendency to take the part for the whole, either *the* caste instead of the system, or one aspect (separation *or* hierarchy) instead of all the aspects together ; finally and especially at this time, the underestimation or the reduction of *hierarchy,* the failure to consider it or the incapacity to understand it (Dumont 1980 : 32, emphasis author's).

This criticism shows Dumont's stance clearly : he stresses a holistic view that includes religious and hierarchical elements. Dumont starts his analysis of the caste system by considering the ideology through which Hindus themselves are assumed to recognise the rationale of their world.[6] Fundamental to their understanding is the religious concept of purity and impurity (pollution). For Dumont, prevalent values of hierarchy in Hindu society are essentially holistic : emphasis put on the whole is always religious. Thus, his holism is not just a methodological device : holism, religion and hierarchy are all closely integrated in his argument (ibid., 65, 108).

Dumont goes on to offer an explanation of how the ideas of purity and impurity have come to play a central role in the caste ideology. According to him, temporary (organic, bodily) pollution is of the same nature as permanent (caste) pollution. So, those castes specialising in tasks concerning the temporary pollution of the high castes are considered impure as a group (ibid., 47). His theory of purity and pollution does not explain why—in the middle ranges of the hierarchy—a particular caste occupies a particular rank. Here ranking is influenced to a greater degree by politico-eonomic factors than by religious ones. But Dumont insists that the latter encompass the former. "The encompassing" is given priority over "the encompassed." The next quotation shows his point clearly ;

> There is scarcely need to repeat that whilst the aspects called 'politico-economic' are thus considered secondary in relation to the ideology of caste, this is not the result of any prejudice but only of the necessity of giving a faithful picture of the system as it appears to us ... For the moment it is a question of a comprehensive description, one which is both intelligible and all embracing (ibid., 39).

In this way, Dumont continuously insists on the importance of purity and impurity as the primary ideology of caste society. He believes that he can penetrate beneath the apparently diverse and sometimes chaotic nature of caste society and provide us with a comprehensive view by investigating a uniform principle at the ideological level and not at the concrete level. What is at stake here is the priority of religious values against politico-economic factors such as the possession of power, territory, or wealth in Hindu society. In brief, Dumont can be said to shift his analytical focus from concrete observable phenomena to ideology in order to maintain a holistic perspective. As I have mentioned above, his holism is not just a methodological device, but should be justified by the very fact that holistic values are specific to India as opposed to Western societies. In his opinion the emphasis on the whole is deeply rooted in Hindu society and is essentially religious.[7]

Religion, on the other hand, is important for Dumont mainly in its relationship to the caste system ; other aspects of religion are not dealt with. In his argument on the priority of religion he fails to take into account any other aspect of Hinduism than the ideology of purity and pollution. For example, Hindu ideas about supernatural beings, and interaction between them and human beings, are all subordinated to the caste system, whose ideology is nevertheless "religious" in essence.[8]

For a closer look at his ideas we have to return from *Homo Hierarchicus* to his monograph, *A South Indian Subcaste,* (1986, originally published in French in 1957).[9] In this he conceptually bisects religion. One set of ideas concerns : "belief in the distinction between the pure and impure" ; the other, "belief in supernatural beings." The latter he classifies into three categories ; "vegetarian gods," to whom blood sacrifice is prohibited, "meat-eating gods," to whom it is essential, and finally "demons." Dumont considers that the only belief autonomous from social function is belief in demons, the other two being merely reflections of the caste system.

> The object of belief, which we tend to call the supernatural, is split into two here. One part is found in the supernature, so to speak, of the demons and another part—a more important one—is found in the nature of a superior caste. Here we fall back again on that well known feature, that caste mingles men and gods. And we see how easily men and things appear as divine. In the end, the true god is the Brahman (Dumont 1986 : 464).

We have already seen that he tries to explain the caste system in terms of its ideology : purity and impurity. However, when he shifts his argument to divine beings, they are explained in terms of the caste system. Dumont gives priority to society in his analysis of the Hindu world, and not to religion itself. Religion, then, is divided into two : the idea of purity and pollution, which gives a comprehensive view of Hindu society both for the Hindus and for us as well, and the rest of religious affairs, which are in turn understood in terms of society. In this way religion, except for belief in the demonic, is subordinate to, and explained in terms of, "belief in caste."

From this brief discussion, we can conclude that Dumont's opinion of Hindu religiosity is very negative in relation to the caste system, because he only finds belief in demons irreducible, whilst all other beliefs are manifestations of the caste system. Furthermore, as we have seen, he pays less attention to the concept of purity than he does to pollution, and the role of pollution is crucial in his discussion of the identification of temporary with permanent pollution. It is the latter concept which enables him to bridge the gap between the religious ideology and social reality. In the end Hinduism is reduced to the belief in the demonic, and preoccupation with pollution, both of which are troublesome and should be removed in order for Hindus to maintain an ordinary life. Put simply, for Dumont, Hinduism is a "religion of fear," an idea which is hardly tenable.

Before I point out some of the contradictions in Dumont's work on Hinduism, I would like to examine the influential work of E. B. Harper. Harper has given a more uniform and less reductionist view of the Hindu socio-religious complex than Dumont. He too, however, seems to be on the same wrong track of taking a uniform view of the caste system and religion in terms of purity-pollution ideology.

The Spells of Pure-Impure Ideology

Harper begins his article entitled "Ritual Pollution as an Integrator of Caste and Religion" (1964) with the three ritual statuses of the Havik Brahman's mundane life : pure, normal and impure. This tripartite structure of ritual status at the individual level is also found at the levels of caste and divine hierarchy. All the castes in his research area, except sectarian Lingayats, are classified roughly into three categories : Brahmans (pure), Sudras (normal) and Untouchables (impure). With regard to the divine pantheon, *devaru*s (Sanskritic gods), *devate*s (local deities), and *devva*s (spirits) are hierarchically conceptualised according to the degree of their purity. Gods are pure, deities ambiguous and spirits impure in nature.

Like Dumont, Harper sees the concept of purity and impurity penetrating the Hindu world. He does not explicitly insist that the divine world is explicable by reference to the caste system, and the caste system (permanent pollution) by reference to individual life (temporary pollution). He carefully avoids a theory of reflection like Dumont's, and proposes what we might call a "continuum theory."[10] His argument emphasises the functional parallels between the role of lower castes to higher, and that of the Brahman caste to gods. The principle is that the less pure remove pollution from the more pure, in order to maintain the Hindu socio-religious order. As the Brahmans need the assistance of lower castes to get rid of their impurity, likewise the gods need the help of the Brahmans to keep their purity.

> This society is organized around the task of caring for its gods, and a division of labor among the castes is necessary to attain this end (Harper 1964 : 196).

The relationship between society and religion in this case appears to be a reversal of Dumont's, which considers the divine world to be the reflection of the caste world. In spite of this apparent reversal, however, Harper applies Dumont's argument on the service of lower castes to Brahmans to that of priests to gods, and reaches a logical conclusion that the reason why the Brahman caste keeps its ritual status pure is to protect the ritual status of gods by removing their pollution. As a consequence, his approach has several problems in common with Dumont's. Apart from the question of the relevance of his extremely idealised picture of the Hindu socio-religious world to reality,[11] Harper also presents a negative idea of Hindu society in arguing that Hindus are organised hierarchically only for the task of removing pollution (hence the title of his article), and that the essence of god is purity, which human beings must maintain. Fundamental problems ensue from both authors' assumption that the encompassing ideology of the caste system is the idea of purity and pollution, and the assumption that through it the caste system and Hinduism are integrated.[12]

While appreciating Dumont and Harper's holistic approach to Hinduism and Hindu social order, I strongly disagree with their one-dimensional view of the socio-religious order. Next, by re-examining the work of Dumont and Harper I will suggest that there may be other dominant ideas at work in the realm of Hinduism.

Divine Power as an Alternative Key Ideology

Dumont and Pocock in their article, "Pure and Impure" (1959a), are well aware that rather than being the essential nature of the divine itself, purity has an "instrumental" value for men in approaching the divine.

> I have to become pure to approach the gods, and even if I come in contact with them, this does not mean that their nature is purity but only that purity is a condition for the contact with them to be beneficial to me (or other men or human things). We are told about purity, i. e. about the *means* of contact, not about the nature of the *object* of contact, the sacred (Dumont and Pocock 1959a : 31, emphasis authors').

The first step in overcoming the negative attitude towards Hinduism is to recognise that purity is not the essence of Hindu gods, but a preparatory condition on the human side for communication with them. To clarify this point, we shall examine the nature of human relations and of god-man relations. According to Dumont and Pocock, contact between purity and impurity endangers purity ; pollution is contagious and potent, dangerous to purity because of its contaminating nature. The more pure a person is, the more vulnerable he is to the less pure. On the other hand, when a ritually impure person comes in too close a proximity to the gods, it is he who will suffer. The gods are not defiled by him in the same way as the pure person is polluted by the impure person or object. Therefore the nature of the two contacts is reversed. The gods are immune to the human law of purity-pollution relations and, in this sense, are transcendental.

Dumont and Pocock distinguish between the sacred-profane relationship and the pure-impure relationship (ibid., 29). They contrast the nature of the purity-impurity relationship to that of the sacred-profane relationship in Polynesia, where the sacred is potent and dangerous to the profane. This is why they use the term "sacred" to describe the nature of the gods in the above quotation rather than describing them as merely "pure." The gods, being sacred, are immune to pollution. Thus, Dumont and Pocock have found two conceptual oppositions in Hinduism : sacred-profane and purity-impurity. Furthermore, by saying that the latter is restricted to the human order, they suggest that the former encompasses the latter.

> The Indian system does not consist in the substitution of purity-impurity to sacred-profane, but only in the presence, within the general framework provided by the latter opposition, of a restricted sphere governed by the former (ibid., 30).

Thus, we gain a picture of Hinduism quite different from that we have seen before. However, because of Dumont and Pocock's superficial comparison of the Hindu world to the Polynesian world, and the importance of purity and impurity in Dumont's theory of the caste system, their discovery has been—with the possible exception of Fuller (1979, see below)—misunderstood or simply ignored.[13]

Harper does not clearly mention the different nature of the man-god relationship and the human inter-relationship, and yet he admits the protective power (*śakti*) of sacred verses (*mantra*) against *devvas* (impure evil spirits).

> Adult Brahman males are seldom harmed by *devvas* (evil spirits) and also are resistant to harm from *devates* (deities), because they have strength (*śakti*) obtained from their knowledge of *mantras* (Harper 1964 : 186).

Though I have quoted only two fragments from the works of Dumont and Harper, we are arriving at a fairly firm position from which to question their conceptual framework of Hinduism, which they explicitly argue is based on the dichotomy between purity and pollution.[14]

Non-Dualistic View of Purity and Power

Although Dumont tries to maintain a comprehensive view of Hindu society by introducing the notions of the "encompassing" and the "encompassed", the dualism of ideology (purity-pollution) and secular order (empirical reality based on politico-economic factors) remains fundamental to his formulation of the theory of the caste society. A so-called "ethnosociological approach" has been used to try to overcome Dumont's dualism by introducing "power," which is not only secular but divine. As I have hinted at the importance of divine power in Hinduism in the last section, it is necessary to examine this point of view in the works of Marriott and Wadley.

> Recent ethnography tells of the same sorts of cognition among Hindus in rural areas, where the categories of gods and men are thought to be mutually continuous, uninterrupted by distinctions such as "sacred" and "profane", "spirit" and "matter." All beings are graded by "power" (*śakti* etc.), and power is understood to be synonymous with both religious virtue and effective worldly dominance (Marriott 1976 : 113).

Here, we get a clear idea of Marriott's monism (non-dualism) and of his analysis of the central role played by "*śakti*" or power. For him power is religious as well as secular, penetrating without contradiction the divine world as well as the social world. As Marriott's ethnosociology is partly dependent on his student Wadley's works on north Indian Hinduism, I shall focus my argument on her discussions to clarify my standpoint without going into ethnosociology in general, a field which concentrates on kinship and caste system.[15]

Wadley is perhaps the first modern anthropologist to focus on the concept of *śakti* and to try to analyse village Hinduism in terms of this concept. According to her, the essence of deities is *śakti*. They are defined as "power-filled" in Hindi (Wadley 1975 : 55 ; Wadley 1977 : 138), but *śakti* is omnipresent and inherent in everything. The difference between supernatural beings and natural beings is only determined by the degree of *śakti*—hence Marriott's concept of monism.

Wadley comments on the relationships between purity and power as follows :

> Rather than agreeing that purity or the principle of pure/impure is dominant in Hindu society, I contend that purity and power are two inseparable factors of any ideas of being or action in Hindu thought. Power in human affairs is always embodied and is a characteristic of the state of any being. In addition, all being is in some state of purity ... Thus Brahmans are both the most powerful beings and the most pure (among the human beings) (Wadley 1977 : 154, parenthesis mine).

There are two problems in her argument which concern us here. One is the nature of divine power, especially its relation to purity. The other is the relationship between divine power and secular power.

Starting with the first, according to Wadley, the essence of Hindu divinity is *śakti* or divine power. It is omnipresent and intrinsic. This does not necessarily mean, however, that there is no qualitative distinction between divine beings and human or other beings. Divine power is omnipresent as energy in the world, but it is not a static attribute of every natural and supernatural being. Even if he is believed to share power in common with divine beings, it is only through rituals, including austerities, that a man can gain power. Wadley herself recognises the importance of rituals for this purpose, as the following quotation suggests.

> Rituals are performed because of a recognition of the powers of another being and one's desire to receive the benefits of that power (birth of a son, curing of illness, *moksha*, etc.) or to avoid the

> malevolent effects of that power (attack by a ghost, smallpox, death etc.) (ibid., 141).

Furthermore, *śakti* itself is generated through the rituals. We should therefore pay more attention to the dynamic flow of divine power, and its nature as shown in the rituals, rather than the degree of it in various beings : it is not satisfactory to consider power as a given attribute.[16] Wadley puts little emphasis on the dynamic communication between human beings and divine power through rituals, and on their mechanism.

The other problem in Wadley's standpoint is concerned with the relationship between divine power and secular power. She considers that Hindu society is hierarchically ordered in terms of divine power. Since the degree of divine and secular power parallels the degree of purity, there is no contradiction between secular power and purity. She overcomes, or more precisely bypasses, Dumont's fundamental problem of the relationship between religious ideology and politico-economic factors by equating divine power with secular power, and then with purity. However, Wadley's account seems relevant only to a village—like the one she worked in herself—dominated by land-owning Brahmans.[17] Such an account would be hardly persuasive outside the context of a Brahman-dominated village. We might suspect that her analysis is an uncritical repetition of statements by her Brahman informants legitimating their high religious-secular status in a village hierarchy. To put it briefly, Wadley's analysis is hardly tenable in a comparative perspective.

In my opinion Dumont has not paid due attention to the religious aspect of a man of secular power, too starkly contrasting him to a man of purity. Wadley's attempt to integrate both religious and secular powers into one conceptual framework of *śakti* is insightful, but her harsh equation of divine power with secular power has proved as problematic as Dumont's separation of power from purity. Both divine and secular powers are by no means identical. To equate the two just blurs our understanding of the relationships between the religious order and the social order. Regarding this, I would like to reiterate that the relationships between divine and secular power be elicited by analysing certain Hindu rituals, because it is mainly through these rituals that secular power is deified.

The Distinctive Nature of Hinduism

It is appropriate to refer here to C. Fuller's article, "Gods, Priests and Purity" (1979), as it questions the relevance of the purity and pollution ideology for studying Hinduism.

According to Fuller, the most essential concept in the religious realm is *śakti* or divine power. In this regard, his standpoint is close to Wadley's, but he refuses straightforwardly to equate divine power with purity as Wadley does.[18] Certainly purity is important, but is not essential to Hindu divinity ; here he criticises Harper's continuum theory of religion and caste. According to Fuller, the Hindu deities are best understood as transcending the realm of purity and pollution, and they are therefore not vulnerable to pollution. The concern about purity-pollution ideas at *pūjā* or worship does not mean that the status of the deities is conceived in terms of purity in the same manner as the caste status is supposed to be. Rather it is an expression of respect to the deities, a manifestation of the devotees' inner or spiritual feelings towards the gods, who are not defiled by pollution.

> Purity and pollution are an idiom by which respect to the gods is shown (Fuller 1979 : 470).

With reference to other facts (food transaction at worship and the status of the Brahman priest), Fuller concludes that the relationship between deities and human beings do not parallel the relationship between the higher caste and the lower caste, and that Harper's continuum theory is untenable. He proposes the study of Hinduism in its own right rather than in relation to the caste system or in terms of the ideology of purity and pollution.

The Limits of the Holistic Approaches to Rituals

Finally, it should be noted that both structural-functionalism and idealism assume a harmonious whole (equilibrium system) in their analyses. For the former, every institution is integrated to reinforce social solidarity, while in the case of the latter, concepts are integrated into one encompassing ideological system. As a result, both approaches account little for the dynamism of reality, replete with social and ideological conflict, and have great difficulty in explaining social change (Bloch 1977). Rituals are said to promote social solidarity, or strengthen the harmonious ideology (cosmology, and related belief system), or reveal the basic classification system. The idealist replaces a structural-functionalist concept of social solidarity with one of the uniformity of the ideological system, and the discovery of the relationships between various basic concepts and their meanings becomes the main task of the anthropologist.

The real problem of the idealist approach is apparent in the way indigenous concepts are dealt with as being based on a harmonious system of ideas. Because of this assumption it is considered possible to discover a consistent "system" of thought. In the process of elucidating this system, which takes the form of a systematisation, less clear-cut and context-bound indigenous words are taken out of the context, and paradoxically become context-free transcendental analytical concepts. For example, Dumont's emphasis on the ideas of purity and pollution and on their "encompassing" nature are, contrary to his insistence and popular belief, not based on strict semantic analysis of these ideas, but should be considered to be the result of his structuralist systematisation under the influence of Levi-Straussian binary oppositions. As a result other ideas like "auspiciousness" and "good" are reduced to the single main dichotomy between purity and pollution.[19]

With regard to the assumption that the ideological system is harmonious, it is interesting that Fuller (1979 : 459) refers to Evans-Pritchard in order to support his view. In his opinion, the present state of anthropological study of Hinduism is not far from a structural-functionalist approach to religion in the sense that it sees the religious order as congruent with the social order, or worse as a function of it. Fuller's favourable reference to Evans-Pritchard is paradoxical, because the Dumontian theory of Hindu society and Hinduism, and more generally the principles of idealist holism are partly inspired by Evans-Pritchard (Dumont 1980 : xiv). Indian society was idealised by Dumont a long time ago. As a result, in his work, the religious order (ideas of the gods and their relationships with men) and the ideology of the caste system are inseparable from each other. For Fuller the explanation is nothing but the functionalist view of religion. Through his reference to Evans-Pritchard the intellectual closeness between the functionalist and idealist holistic views is revealed. This is because in spite of the shift from the empirical level to the ideal one, idealist holism assumes implicitly that the universe of ideas—cosmology, interrelated sets of basic categories, and ideas of the social world and so on—constitutes a harmonious whole.[20] So, when rituals can be interpreted as expressing the encompassing ideology, the idealist tends to take it as it is, in the same way as a functionalist considers the main function of ritual as integrating society, and overcoming a conflictual reality. Here the idealist approach and functionalist approach to ritual come close.

I have already discussed Harper, who sees pollution as an integrator of the otherwise divided caste society. Now I would like to show some examples, which assume that ritual and belief in gods, rather than pollution, function to integrate Hindu society into one system.

In his analysis of *pūjā* or worship, Babb comments on its integrating function as follows :

> In sharing the *jutha* (consecrated left-overs) of the deity, the group—whatever its composition—suppress manifest differences within itself by reaching beyond the world of men, and mundane relationship between men, for a point of reference against which the group as *a whole* can be defined. Whatever the normal cleavages within the group, for a moment it has become unified as one pole in hierarchical opposition to divinity (Babb 1975 : 59-60, emphasis mine).

In more general terms, David suggests the harmonious nature of the society lies in the relationship between god and man :

> All castes both share and are committed to *a single system* of exoteric symbols prescribing a hierarchical servant/master code for human conduct toward the divine (David 1977 : 219, emphasis mine).[21]

Although David is concerned with caste relations, and not class relations, the next example shows that even the class relationship is seen, by another writer, as part of an harmonious whole expressed through festivals :

> The coalescence of the cosmic and the mundane in festivals sponsored by commercially and politically ascendant groups is characteristic of much Hindu thought. The mundane can be subsumed as *one plane of the cosmic* and has its proper place as such. It is right and proper that the mundane should serve the ends of the cosmic and thus be served via festival sponsorship and participation. It is, after all, part of *the same whole*. Furthermore, this serves to redistribute the wealth of the community, as the members capable of sponsoring festivals are also obliged to do so by community sentiment. (Christian 1982 : 265-66).

As is easily seen, expressions like "a whole," "a single system," and "cosmos" are key terms in the above quotations.

My question is to what degree the world view expressed in the rituals or festivals can be said to be essential, as opposed to everyday knowledge and experience : certainly the religious view is more systematic and comprehensive (and interesting for anthropologists) than everyday life, but it does not necessarily mean that people behave implicitly following that view, or that the religious view is more fundamental than everyday knowledge and experience.

I take one more example to clarify the above point. Kinsley has recently presented a comprehensive picture of the village goddess festival (1986 : 204). According to him, the village goddess is concerned with village welfare and prosperity. But she is directly associated with disaster, especially epidemics. She is said to inflict disease as well as protect the village from them.

Kinsley points out that during the festival time the goddess intrudes into the village and possesses villagers. An ordinary time is temporarily sustained, and a chaotic situation is to dominate the village. This is also an occasion when the village is infused with divine power and subsequently revived. It is a time when the villagers have a direct access to the sacred. In extreme situations, rules observed at ordinary times are broken, and forbidden actions are permitted. Kinsley refers to Turner's concept of liminality to explain such actions (Turner 1969). Furthermore he quotes the following statement by Lannoy concerning the function of the festival.

> The festival rite utilizes the potency of disorder. It harnesses the disorder of "the other mind," possession, trance, dreams, ecstacy ; if these powers are harnessed properly, the society recovers a special potency from chaos beyond the limits of order (Lannoy 1971 : 201).

This means that the festival provides an occasion when the villagers dare to face the disorder and utilise its chaotic power to revive their lives and to create a new order. Chaos is necessary to regenerate a socio-religious order.

Such characterisation of the festival, however, lacks the analysis of its political functions, as I have already pointed out. It simply restates a structural-functionalist assumption of village solidarity in a more subtle way. It is certainly true that Turner's general argument on the ritual should be distinguished from that of previous structural-functionalist approaches. While functionalism considers society to be harmonious, Turner acknowledges social conflict in a society. But such conflicts are, according to him, overcome and social tensions redressed through rituals or a temporal realisation of what he calls "communitas." Even though the approaches outlined above all view society from differing perspectives, they share a common conception of the role of ritual. To sum up, previous works on village festivals, whether emphasising their functions or symbolic meanings, tend to ignore the real social differentiation within villages and its relationships to the festivals.

I view society in terms of politico-economic conflicts and ideological struggles rather than in terms of "mystical solidarity" (Leach 1961 : 298). Following from this, my interest in studying rituals lies in their relations to such social conflicts. In order to go beyond some of the problems in previous studies of Hinduism, it is necessary to investigate the complex relationship between the ideologies expressed through rituals and everyday social activities under the constraints of politico-economic forces. This should give some idea as to whether, or not, the rituals serve the dominant groups rather than, as Turner assumes, the community as a whole. Hindu festivals do emphasise the communal or egalitarian aspect of society, but they also serve to legitimate a political structure by symbolically converting secular power into divine power. What I find interesting is the articulation of this political function with the representation of the village as a community, which can be revealed through the analysis of ritual symbolism and cosmological meaning.

Thus, this is not to deny or exclude other dimensions of meaning. We could discern at least two dimensions of meanings in the festivals : personal or existential and cosmological. Personal meaning is clearly prominent in votive rituals performed during festivals, while cosmological meaning provides a narrative basis (myths, episodes, symbolism) on which the festivals are structured. I try to relate these dimensions to the political functions of the festivals. But it is wrong to imagine that the former are reducible to the latter or *vice versa*. To repeat, it is necessary to avoid presenting Hindu world as a single tightly bound system. Rather I hope to show how rituals work in various dimensions and, when possible, I present various interpretations of a particular event or ritual. The analysis will concentrate on two village festivals in a single community and discuss the articulation of the meanings of rituals conducted in them with their political function.

Conclusion

To sum up, a brief examination of anthropological studies on Hinduism has shown several important shifts in theoretical direction. Srinivas, although armed with the structural-functionalism of Radcliffe-Brown, failed to dispose of atomistic and diffusionist tendencies. His work was understandably welcomed by American anthropologists under Redfield's influence. Dumont managed to restore a holistic approach by shifting the focus from the concrete level to the ideological level. His identification, however, of the predominant ideology in Hindu society with religious ideas of purity-pollution created confusion in the anthropological study of Hinduism. Although Dumont's primary problem is with the relationship between religious ideology and politico-economic factors, others, whose primary interest lies in Hinduism itself, have almost totally neglected this problem. Their tendency was to present a more univocal view of society and religion, by giving the religious ideology of purity and pollution the central role in their analyses. This uncritical view was only furthered by Wadley's introduction of "power" into the explanation of the religious ideology of purity-pollution. In her view, there is no contradiction between religion and politico-economic factors, because power incorporates both religious and secular power, and goes hand in hand with purity : the purer a being is, the higher, and more powerful, it is. In this way, she has produced a univocal view of the Hindu world in its strongest form, where every being is ordered in terms of power and purity-pollution concepts. The importance of divine power and the subtle difference between power and the ideas of purity-pollution, however, has been pointed out in Dumont and Pocock's early article, in Harper's cursory reference to the power of *mantra,* and in Fuller's more comprehensive and critical discussion on the distinctive nature of Hinduism. In spite of significant differences, both structural-functionalist and idealist holism share the assumption that a society is harmonious. Even those anthropologists who recognise the conflicting social forces in a society tend to present rituals as a solution to these various conflicts. To conclude, although such arguments are not totally refutable, I suggest that Hindu festivals form a field where political relationships are continuously reiterated and partially legitimated, in relation to culturally bound meanings. It is from this point of view that my analysis of Hindu rituals and festivals begins.

Plan of the Book

This book is designed to present the relationship between religion and power by focusing on two dimensions of meaning, personal and cosmological, in Hindu rituals, and their political functions to legitimate the power structure in the village. Chapter 2 first describes the everyday activities of the villagers, especially the Karaiyars (Fisherman caste) who are dominant in the village. Then, after providing a basic knowledge of the religious activities and organisations concerning the village festivals in chapter 3, I proceed, in chapter 4 to discuss aspects related to the personal dimension of the festivals. These are : the concept of *bhakti* ; possession ; and votive rituals.

Chapter 5 is devoted to the Bhadrakālī goddess festival. Symbolically the festival shows the transformation of Kālī from a violent, epidemic-causing goddess into a benevolent, grace-offering one. The villagers make every effort to placate the goddess and propitiate her. Accordingly the village as a whole is reanimated, as are the villagers. I will endeavour to show how cosmological dimensions and personal dimensions of symbolism are articulated with the, not so apparent, political implications of the festival.

Chapter 6 starts with an analysis of *abhiṣeka* (consecration rituals), the understanding of which is a necessary step towards the analysis of the Draupadī goddess festival which follows in chapter 7. In my view, this ritual is significant in that it provides men of power with a means to convert their secular power into divine power. This process will be shown by focusing on sacrificial rituals and their symbolic meanings. In addition, I will try to substantiate the statements which I have already made about divine power, and its relation to purity.

Another festival, the Draupadī goddess festival is the topic of chapter 7. My aim is, again, not only to investigate its symbolical dimensions, but also the relationship between these and the political functions of the festival. The narrative and cosmological backdrop of this festival is an Indian epic, the *Mahābhārata*. As with Bhadrakālī, Draupadī, the heroine of the epic changes from a suffering woman into a victorious queen. People undestand the parallel of her anguish and restoration with their own experiences of affliction and recovery. Unlike the Bhadrakālī goddess festival, however, its political functions are clearly manifest in the participation of men of secular power in *abhiṣeka* rituals, conducted by the Brahman priest, during the festival.

In the concluding chapter, I draw a comparison of these two goddess festivals, and return to general themes, such as religion and power in Hindu society and an alternative interpretation of Sanskritization.

CHAPTER TWO

THE SETTING

This chapter aims to present some basic information on Cattiyur in Puttalam District, North Western Province, where the research for the present work on Hindu village festivals was conducted. The chapter consists of four main parts : the village setting, its castes, economy, and political arenas.

Village

Cattiyur is a huge fishing village by Sri Lankan standards. It is located on the narrow isthmus between the Mannur Lake and the Indian Ocean. It lies on the west coast of Sri Lanka, about seventy-five miles north of Colombo, the largest, and former capital, city of Sri Lanka (see figs. 1 and 2). Cattiyur is geographically separated from adjacent inland villages by swamps and marshes. This badly drained land lies along a canalised waterway that runs from Puttalam down to Colombo by way of lagoons, backwaters and rivers. Though Cattiyur lies in the Dry zone, it sometimes suffers from fresh water flooding, and access to it, from the outside, becomes difficult. This and other geographical conditions mean the village has remained a relatively discrete and independent, if not self-sufficient, social unit. On the other hand, Cattiyur is by no means as cut off from the external world as are those tiny villages situated deep in mountains, or those surrounded by thick jungle. Except during rain and its aftermath it is fairly easily accessible from the outside.

The bus road to Pambala links Cattiyur to the outside, including the town of Chilaw, a local centre of about twenty thousand people mainly dependent on fishing. Though it is not the district capital, Chilaw provides

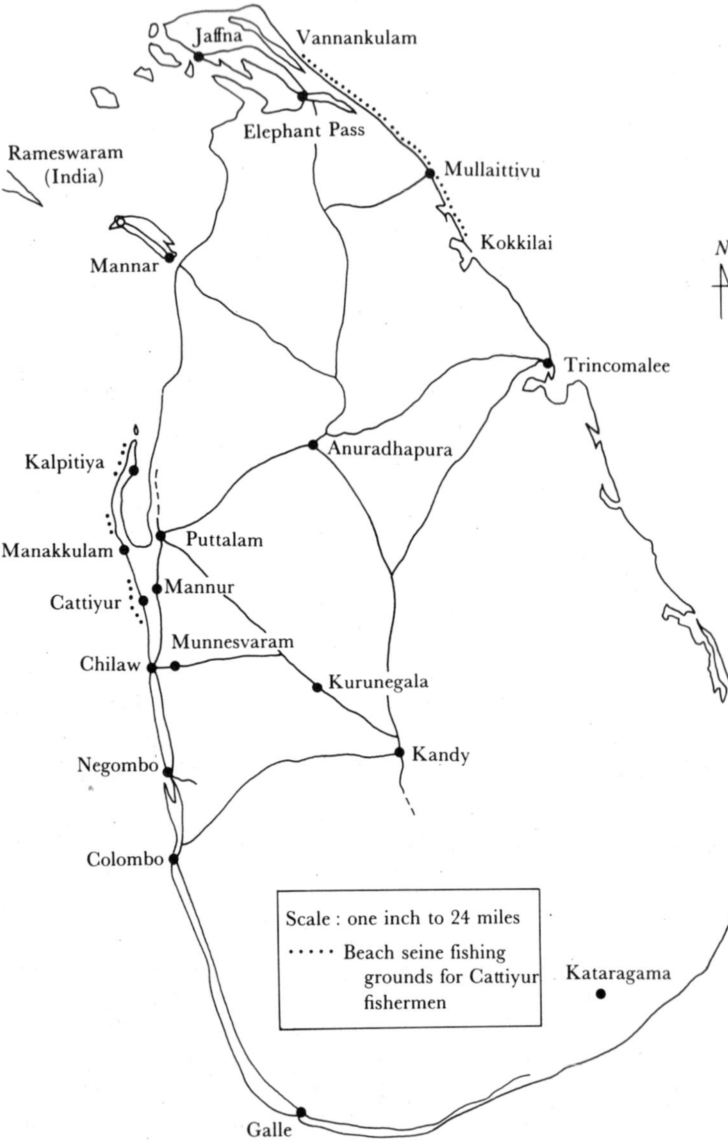

FIGURE 1. SRI LANKA

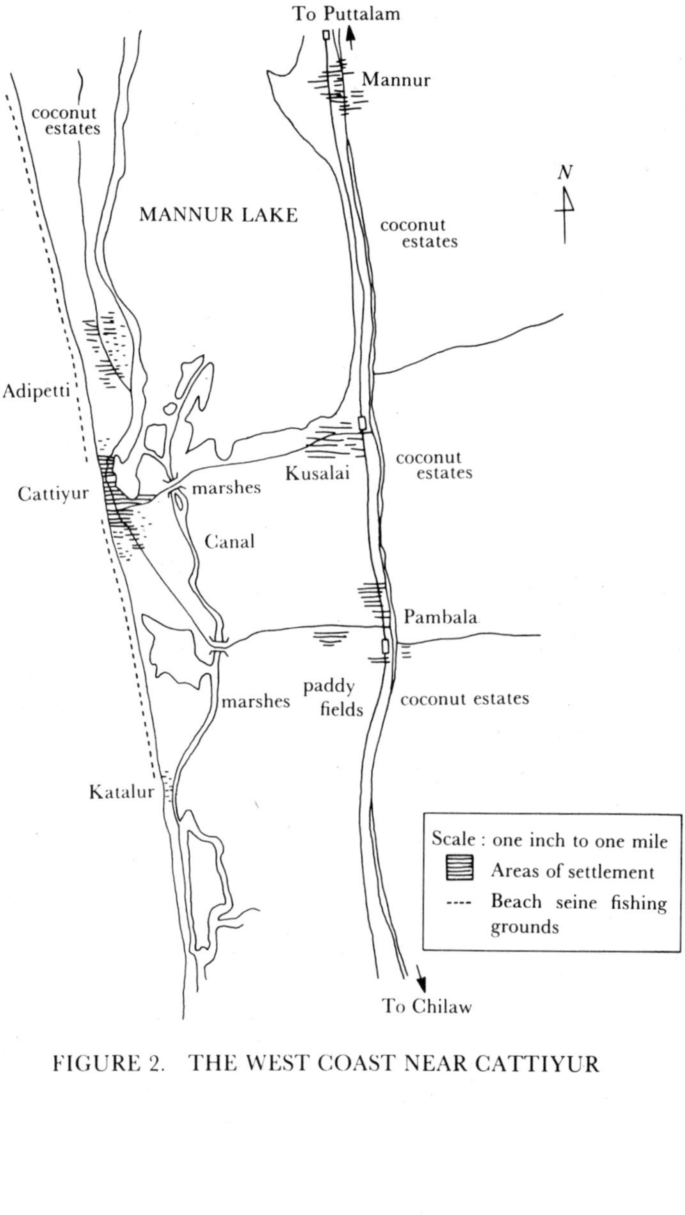

FIGURE 2. THE WEST COAST NEAR CATTIYUR

most services necessary to the villagers : a public hospital, a post office, schools, law courts, other administrative offices, pharmacies, private dispensaries, garages, book shops, photo-studios, cinema theatres and so on. From Chilaw, one can take a city bus or a private van to Negombo and Colombo, which takes three hours by bus.

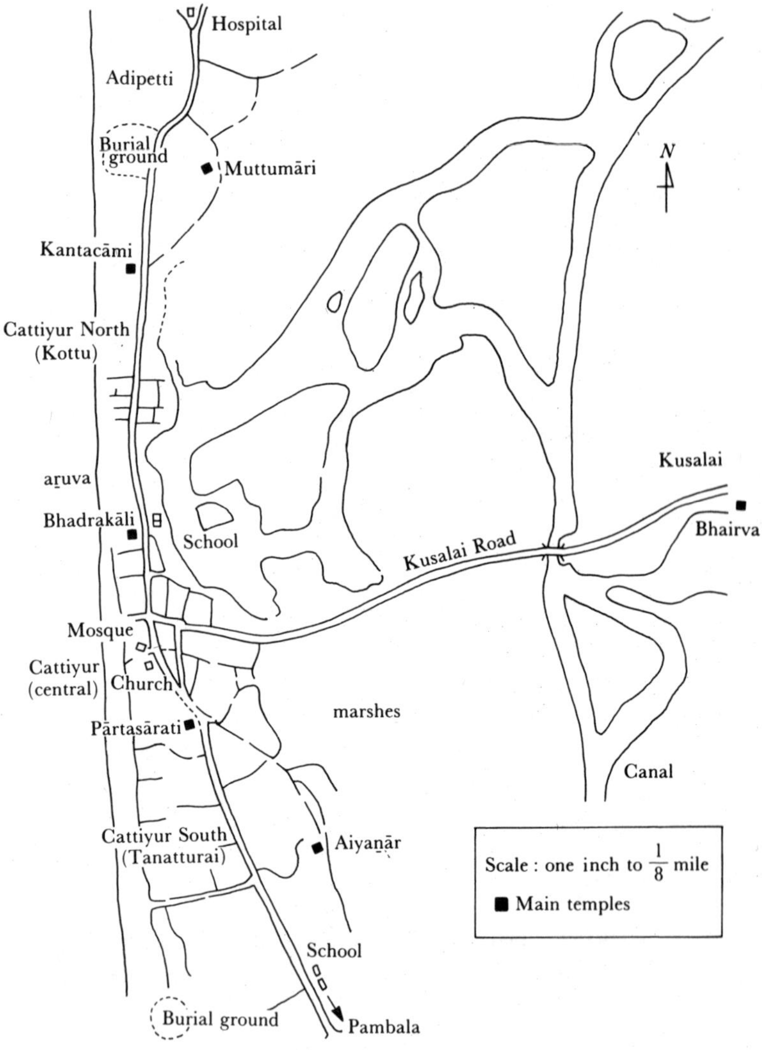

FIGURE 3. CATTIYUR

Cattiyur is divided roughly into three parts, Tanatturai, Cattiyur Central (or Cattiyur in its narrow sense), and Cattiyur North or Kottu (see fig. 3).

Arriving from Pambala, the first thing that comes into view, on the right side of the road, is a village school, then, on the other side there are some houses in a row. The area from these houses to the village library further down the road is called Tanatturai (from *taṇṇīr* or water and *tuṟai* or place or port). The name clearly suggests that this area is ill-drained and not suited for human habitation. The lower sub-caste of the Karaiyar or Fisherman caste have traditionally lived here.

Cattiyur Central covers the area from the Pārtasārati temple in the south, to the Bhadrakālī goddess temple in the north. Except for the open space in front of the Pārtasārati temple, this central area is densely populated. Most of the important buildings surround the Pārtasārati temple : the village development office (Gramodaya Mandalaya office) with the Maternity Centre, the Gramasevaka office (a government agency responsible for Cattiyur), the vegetable market, the cooperative shop, and three general shops, two textile shops, two tea shops and a barber shop.

The bus road then forks. One branch is called Post Office Road, because the village post office is located on it. The other road comes from a Catholic church and a mosque to the junction where it meets the Post Office Road. Most of the fish caught by raft fisherman and 17.5ft. fibreglass

PLATE 1. A TYPICAL FISHERMAN'S HOUSE

boat fisherman are auctioned to cycle traders at this junction. Residences along the roads are largely constructed from bricks and roofed with tiles, but behind them are numerous smaller houses made from "cadjans" (plaited coconut fronds) with only two or three rooms (see pl. 1). Many small lanes run between these houses.

Cattiyur North, or Kottu,[22] forms an independent cluster of houses along the road sandwiched between a sandbar called *aṟuva* to the south and the extensive swamps to the north and east. The sandbar is the narrowest part of the isthmus between the sea and the Mannur Lake, or, to be more precise, a branch of the canal, which leads to the Lake, and cuts Cattiyur North off from the rest of Cattiyur. The swamps, together with the coconut estate belonging to the Muttumāri goddess temple in Adipetti, prevent the residential area of Cattiyur North expanding further north, and so constitute the northern border of Cattiyur.

Moving to the north past the small Kantacāmi (Murukaṉ) temple, the Muttumāri goddess temple, a burial ground and the Adipetti hospital, broad coconut plantations with houses scattered under the trees contrast with noisy and cramped Cattiyur.

Adipetti forms an administrative unit of the Gramasevaka and the Gramodaya Mandalaya together with Cattiyur. Under the government colonisation scheme its land was allocated to Cattiyur villagers in 1958. Since then the population has increased, but most of them are closely related to the Cattiyur villagers and outsiders are few.[23]

The unique geographical and historical formation of Cattiyur cannot be understood without referring to the locally dominant caste, the Karaiyar or the Fisherman caste. In the next section I shall discuss the caste composition in Cattiyur.

Castes

Caste Ideology

The word *cāti* (Skt. *jāti*) can refer to various social categories. At one level it refers to religio-ethnic groups like Hindus (*caivarkaḷ* or Śaivites), Muslims, and Catholics. At another it refers to small kin groups, a little larger than a household. Its most prevalent meaning, however, refers to categories whose identity is based on occupation (*toḻil*).

Occupational groups, or castes, are hierarchically ordered in a vague way, but the ideas of purity and pollution are less explicit in Cattiyur than we would expect from anthropological literature (e. g.

Dumont 1980). When pressed, the villagers may admit that lower (*tāḻnta*) castes are impure (*acuttam*), while high (*uyarnta*), or good (*nalla*), castes are pure (*cuttam*). We must, however, be careful not to interpret their statements of "being lower" as an expression equivalent to that of "being more impure." Lower castes are not always impure (*acuttam*) by birth. The word *acuttam* refers to their appearance rather than their blood. Ritual pollution caused by birth or death is called *toṭakku.* As one villager said, the lower caste may not be *acuttam,* if they are tidy. I would like to emphasise this point : caste status is not expressed in terms of purity, especially blood purity in Cattiyur, nor in other places in Sri Lanka (McGilvray 1982 : 88-89 ; Phaffenberger 1982 : 56-59, 223-30).

The origin of caste is not attributed to a series of inter-marriages between the original four castes or *varṇa*s. Instead, the emphasis is placed on the role of a king at the time of the creation of the various castes, and the assignment of various services to them. In relation to this the concepts connected with service and command are more important than purity. One of the stories of the origin of caste I heard in the village refers to a Hindu king, who is said to have allocated various kinds of occupations to his subjects, who were subsequently differentiated into small occupational groups. The following story, from the Munnesvaram Śiva temple, near Chilaw, also tells us of the role of the king in relation to the creation of the castes in the region. The following is based on Somaskanta (1927 : 12-18, 35-38).

> King Kulakkottum came to Sri Lanka in 512 year of Kaliyuga. Hearing of the greatness of the Munnesvaram temple, the King went there and renewed its shrines and performed the *kumbhābhiṣeka* (the temple consecration ritual). Then for the performance of daily worship and conducting social functions, he brought various servants (*toḻumpālarkaḷ*) from Tamilnadu. The king enjoined them to perform their social functions properly and sincerely. In order to supervise the services of these people, a prince was brought from Madurai in Tamilnadu. He had a coronation and became the king of this area. Then, King Kulakkottum left for India and had a peaceful life.

Nineteen castes are listed here, and a brief account is given of each caste, detailing its function, its service (*paṇiviṭai*) to the temple and location. For example, "The Paṇṭārams were made to reside in Pantariyamulai and were ordered by the king to do such work as lighting lamps, chanting hymns, preparing holy ash." The king described to the

Brahman priests the manner of daily worship and warned them that they would fall into hell (*narakam*) if they failed to do it.

It is obvious from these stories that the role of king is crucial in accounting for the origin of caste.

Occupation orders the hierarchy which is graded in terms of a command-service relationship rather than in terms of purity. Those being served are higher than those who do the serving (*paṇiviṭaikkāraṉ*). This is the main ideology which surrounds the caste relations, at least among the Cattiyur Hindus. Whether their traditional occupation is pure or not, the Karaiyar caste is higher than the rest as it is the caste being served by, and not serving, others. The accepted superiority of the Brahman caste in the caste hierarchy clashes with the above ideology. For the Karaiyar members the Brahman caste is one of their servant castes. The priestly Paṇṭāram caste also questions the Karaiyar's claim. Even the Brahman, and the Paṇṭāram caste members, however, utilise the ideology of service for their claim to superiority : they serve deities, not men.[24] Therefore they are higher than the secular Karaiyar. Barnett contrasts the kingly model of the caste system, where the main principle is command and service, to the priestly model, where the main principle is purity and pollution (Barnett 1970). This ideology, based on the account of regal foundation, certainly serves to legitimate the overwhelming politico-economic domination of the Karaiyar caste in the village, especially net-owners, who play the role of patrons in religious affairs.

The Karaiyar

The fact that the local Hindu Karaiyar (literally it means shore-man), with its distinctive historical background, is "dominant" (Srinivas 1959) makes Cattiyur very atypical on the west coast. Statistical data below show that 87.2% of the total population of Cattiyur are Hindu and that 97.1% of these are Karaiyar (see tables 1 and 2). The same is true of the neighbor village, Ādipeṭṭi (see table 3).

There are also seven other castes integrated into village affairs through caste duties : a) the Brahman (Pirāmaṇaṉ, or Aiyar) ; b) the Paṇṭāram ; c) the Goldsmith (Taṭṭāṉ) ; d) the Washerman (Vaṇṇāṉ) ; e) the Barber (Ampaṭṭaṉ) ; f) the Paṟaiyaṉ ; g) the Cakkiliyaṉ.[25] First I introduce the Karaiyar caste, and then give brief accounts of the other castes.

In common with other, non-Hindu, Karaiyar in Sri Lanka, some Cattiyur villagers claim that they are descendants of the Kuru family (Kurukulam or a royal family of the Moon) in the *Mahābhārata* and that

TABLE 1
POPULATION : RELIGIOUS CATEGORIES IN CATTIYUR

Religion	Population	Household
Hindu	3,767(87.2%)	694(87.5%)
Karaiyar	3,658(84.7%)	667(84.1%)
Other	109(2.5%)	27(3.4%)
Muslim	372(8.6%)	67(8.4%)
Christian	182(4.2%)	32(4.0%)
Total	4,321	793

(Source : Census carried out between Nov. 1982 and Feb. 1983)

TABLE 2
POPULATION : CASTE AND HOUSEHOLD MEMBERS IN CATTIYUR

					Age			
					18+		0 ~ 17	
	Household	Total	Male	Female	Male	Female	Male	Female
Hindu								
Karaiyar	667	3,658	1,793	1,865	1,028	1,112	765	753
Brahman	1	7	4	3	3	3	1	0
Paṇṭāram	1	5	3	2	1	1	2	1
Goldsmith	8	37	16	21	7	11	9	10
Barber	4	22	12	10	6	5	6	5
Paṟaiyaṉ	2	9	3	6	1	2	2	4
Cakkiliyaṉ	3	15	7	8	3	3	4	5
Outsider	8	14	11	3	8	1	3	2
Sub total	694	3,767	1,849	1,918	1,057	1,138	792	780
Muslim								
	67	372	195	177	118	91	77	86
Catholic								
	32	182	97	85	50	44	47	41
Total	793	4,321	2,141	2,180	1,225	1,273	916	97

(Source : Census carried out between Nov. 1982 and Feb. 1983)

TABLE 3
POPULATION : CASTE AND HOUSEHOLD MEMBERS IN ADIPETTI

					Age			
					18+		0 ~ 17	
	Household	Total	Male	Female	Male	Female	Male	Female
Hindu								
Karaiyar	295	1,410	695	715	371	367	324	348
Panṭāram	3	26	13	13	9	7	4	6
Goldsmith	7	33	13	20	9	10	4	10
Washerman	4	15	7	8	5	5	2	3
Cakkiliyaṉ	1	6	3	3	1	1	2	2
Sub total	310	1,490	731	759	395	390	336	369
Catholic								
	1	5	2	3	1	3	1	0
Total	311	1,495	736	765	397	394	339	371

(Source : Census carried out between Nov. 1982 and Feb. 1983)

they are of Kṣatriya, warrior caste, origin (Raghavan 1961 : 6 ; Roberts 1982 : 26-27). The very fact that Cattiyur is one of the few villages in Sri Lanka which have Draupadī (heroine of the *Mahābhārata*) temples and which celebrate her festival, reinforces their claim.[26] On the other hand, in relation to the *Mahābhārata,* another slightly different claim is that Satyavatī, the mother of Vyāsa, the composer of the *Mahābhārata,* was brought up by the head of the fishermen. Naturally enough the story and its festival have spread among the Fisherman castes and are well maintained by them. This claim fails to relate the Fisherman castes to the royal family, thus to glorify their caste status : they were related to the *Mahābhārata* story as fishermen and not as warriors.

The Cattiyur Karaiyars are said to have emigrated from Ramesvaram in Tamilnadu, South India to Mannar, eighty miles north of Cattiyur, in the mid-seventeenth century. They moved southwards from Mannar to Puttalam and Mannur, and finally settled in Cattiyur in, probably, the early eighteenth century.[27] Though different in details, the local Karaiyars share a myth of emigration similar to that current elsewhere in Sri Lanka.[28] It is told in Cattiyur as follows :

> There was a beautiful daughter named Kamalakkanni of a fisherman family in Ramesvaram, Tamilnadu. One day a king (or a

> local chief) in the area saw her and fell in love with her. He asked her parents for permission to marry her. However, the king was notorious for his cruel behaviour and the parents were reluctant to offer Kamalakkanni to him. They consulted other villagers on this matter. It was extremely difficult for them to refuse the request of the king who was very powerful, and they finally decided to agree to the matter and fixed the date for the wedding ceremony. However, on the suggestion of their chief,[29] all the villagers (eighteen families : twelve fishermen, three fishermen of lower status, two Washermen and one Barber[30]) abandoned the village the day before the wedding day. They headed for Sri Lanka in seven large boats leaving a bitch tied to one of the auspicious poles of the ceremonial canopy under which the wedding was to be performed. Next day the king and his men came to the village in procession, and found nothing but the bitch barking under the canopy. Understanding that she was for him, the king became so angry that he made every effort to find out where the villagers had gone. Meanwhile, the fishermen and their service castes after reaching the coast of Sri Lanka, near Mannar, went southwards and finally settled down in Cattiyur. A few years later, the king discovered their whereabouts and threatened to punish them if they did not give Kamalakkanni to him. Hearing of the situation, Kamalakkanni committed suicide and was deified as a *kulateyvam* (a family deity).[31]

Whether this story is true or not, it is clear that the villagers, especially the Karaiyar caste members, maintain a strong corporate identity based on a shared history and local residence. The story helps them to distinguish themselves from other Ceylon Tamil Hindus, including the Karaiyar caste members in both northern and eastern parts of Sri Lanka, and, still more, from the Indian Tamils of the tea plantations.[32]

The story of emigration from India to Sri Lanka in the middle of the seventeenth century explains the relative isolation of the Cattiyur Karaiyars in this area. Most of the fishermen on the west coast were immigrants from India, and have converted to Catholicism, speaking Tamil at home and Sinhalese in public. Cattiyur is far from both the northern and eastern Tamil home regions, and is described as one of the largest pockets of Hindu Tamils in the South. Their relatively recent migration may have saved the Cattiyur Karaiyar from compulsory conversion to Catholicism by the Portuguese, who governed the coastal area from 1505 (Mannar was occupied in 1560) to 1658, when the Dutch, who had a more tolerant religious policy, expelled them from the island

and took over their position.

As a dominant caste, the hierarchical status of the Cattiyur Karaiyar is no doubt high, but the Goldsmiths and the Paṇṭārams are always ready to assert their superiority. The Karaiyars compare themselves to the powerful land-owning Veḷḷāḷars of the north, and call themselves "the sea (*kaṭal*)-Veḷḷāḷar". Fishing is their traditional occupation and they have no specific ritual duty, except for the role of ritual and festival patrons, as is the case with the Veḷḷāḷars.[33]

As might be expected from their historical background, the kinship networks of the Cattiyur Karaiyar hardly extend beyond the village. Even if we admit that the self-containment of social units is easily exaggerated, it is clear that Cattiyur does constitute ideologically, at least, a whole universe to the Karaiyar.

The Karaiyar are divided into two major categories, for which I use the term sub-caste, although some say that they are of different origin and do not belong to the same caste. The higher sub-caste can be subdivided into more than ten, hierarchically ordered, named *puṟattār*s or sub-groups. Certainly most net-owners and estate owners belonged to the privileged *puṟattār*s, but there were a few net-owners belonging to the lower *puṟattār*s around the turn of the century, and now one of the most powerful net-owners is from the lower sub-caste. There is, therefore, now no strict congruence between economic status and *puṟattār* or sub-caste.

The ritual duty of the members of the lower sub-caste was to carry torches in festival processions—a duty which they now refuse to perform. Until 1979 Brahman priests were not allowed to serve them at domestic rituals and they could not use auspicious ritual items. The Barber caste used only one conch-shell for processions at domestic rituals of the members of the lower sub-caste while two were used for the other members of the Karaiyar. They could also neither use white cloth on their umbrellas in ritual processions, nor gold chain for their wedding necklaces (*tāli*) which, instead, had to be of yellow-thread.

The smallest social category is called *kuṭumpam*. This term is vague, and sometimes refers to the villagers as a total group. Usually, however, *kuṭumpam* refers to the household, which is not necessarily a close kin group, and does not necessarily include a woman ; a household may be composed of one or two men. Economic and coresidential aspects are more important in the designation of household status. Most households have their own discrete premises. Even when more than one household shares a house(*vīṭu*), each will have its own kitchen, and be economically independent.

The Karaiyar members practice uxorilocal residence, and one of the daughters, probably the youngest, is expected to stay with her parents in her natal house, and inherits, sometimes with her sisters and brothers, immovable property (the house and the land on which it is built—which are all poor fishermen own). Men inherit fishing craft and gear. Beach seines are handed down only through the male line.

Non-Dominant Castes

The Brahman caste

Generally, throughout the sub-continent and Sri Lanka, Brahmans are considered the highest status caste. Some anthropologists have already pointed out, however, that, in Sri Lanka, they are weak in politico-economic terms, and few in number (e. g. Banks 1960 : 66-69). Temple priests employed by the powerful land-owning castes, particularly by the Veḷḷāḷars in Jaffna form the majority. Although the Brahmans are perceived as pure and respectable, they are considered to be a service caste.

The first Brahman priest came from Jaffna to Cattiyur in the late nineteenth century, and started working as a chief priest at the then Draupadī temple (now Pārtasārati temple or more formally Pārtasārati-Draupadī temple). Since then, several Brahman priests have stayed briefly in Cattiyur and served the villagers (see chapter 3 for more details). Kumaracami and both his sons were working as temple priests during most of my stay in Cattiyur, and I describe them as chief priests in this book. Working for two temples in Cattiyur, the Pārtasārati temple and the Aiyaṉār temple, they perform daily worship and festivals held at these temples, and, if required, they go to another two village temples which are taken care of by non-vegetarian Paṇṭāram priests. They perform domestic rites of passage : puberty rites ; wedding ceremonies ; funeral rites, and house opening rites. Villagers also often consult them about auspicious names for new born babies and auspicious dates for various domestic rites, and for new economic activities. The Cattiyur villagers do not keep horoscopes, as the Brahmans complain, but are, nonetheless, anxious to know auspicious dates and times for various activities.

By village standards the Brahmans are well-off and have a stable income. But when, in July 1983, the Hindu Temple Administrative Committee of the Karaiyar tried to tighten the religious budget, and to put the Brahman and the Paṇṭāram under stricter control, Kumaracami and his family left for Jaffna. A new Brahman was brought to the village, but he too was dismissed in March 1984, because it was found that he lacked proper knowledge of the domestic rituals. Subsequently, another Brahman was called for. These frequent changes indicate the weak and unstable status of the Brahman priest in Sri Lanka.

The Paṇṭāram caste

The traditional occupation of the Paṇṭāram caste, alternatively known as Pūcāri in the region, is said to have been making garlands for temple images. In Cattiyur the Paṇṭāram is usually regarded as a non-vegetarian priestly caste especially associated with goddess temples in the past. They rank lower than the vegetarian Brahman. Their traditional occupation of garland-making strongly suggests that they were a service caste attached to temples. Thus, the Karaiyar caste, who are the collective patrons of the village temples, look down upon the Paṇṭārams, and consider them lower than themselves. The Paṇṭārams, however, who now serve deities (rather than patrons) as priests, would deny this evaluation of their relative status.

There are four Paṇṭāram households : one in Cattiyur, three live by the Muttumāri goddess temple in Adipetti. Muttaiya, a former chief priest of both Muttumāri and Bhadrakālī goddess temples, is now seventy-five years old and has no obligation to perform temple rituals. He seldom goes out. Parandaman, who is his third son, is the chief priest at the Muttumāri temple. He performs daily worship there and special rituals at its festivals : what is more important, however, to the present work is his role as medium for the goddesses, Draupadī and Bhadrakālī, at their festivals. Besides priesthood and mediumship at village temples one member of the caste is in charge of the recitation of the *Mahābhārata* during the Draupadī goddess festival. Now Parandaman plays this role as well. Parandaman's elder brother, Cokkalingam became the Bhadrakālī temple priest for some years after his father's retirement. Then his brother-in-law, Kulantaivel succeeded to him. Parandaman's other elder brother is a priest at the Draupadī temple in Mannur (see fig. 11).

Paranḍaman's income from temple service is the same as that of the Brahman, but, as he does not usually perform domestic rites of passage, his total earnings seem to be far less. Extra-income is derived from his special role at the festivals. Parandaman and Muttaiya are sometimes consulted on health matters by the villagers. They are not shamanic figures, but do concoct magical powders and potions.

The Goldsmith caste

The status of Goldsmith in the caste hierarchy is not clear. Certainly this caste is ranked high, but it remains marginal. Some Karaiyars consider the Goldsmith to be higher than themselves, but others do not. The Goldsmiths consider themselves second only to the Brahmans. Therefore the statuses of the three castes, the Goldsmith, the Paṇṭāram and the Karaiyar are open to dispute. Unlike the Paṇṭāram caste, the Goldsmiths are not under the tight control of the Karaiyar caste,[34] and tend to be far better off than the rest of the villagers.

As part of their traditional occupation, they have a collective obligation to make a wedding necklace (*tāli*) for Draupadī and to patronise her wedding ceremony, which is held during the festival dedicated to her (see chapter 7). They are the only caste besides the Karaiyar, who act as collective patrons in the village festival, but this patronage stems from an obligation inherent in their traditional occupation, and is not financial support *per se*. It has little in common with the role of dominant caste patronage.

The Washerman caste

There are four closely related households of Washermen. They are said to have come as the village servants (*kuṭimakkaḷ*) of the Karaiyar caste. All the Washerman caste members live in Adipetti. Their ritual duty is mainly to provide white cloths on the occasions of village festivals and rites of passage.

The Barber caste

The Barbers perform several caste obligations on ritual occasions, especially at funerals. During the mourning period of thirty days, when the Brahman priests are reluctant to participate because of serious death pollution, it is members of this caste who conduct most funerary rituals. They blow conch-shells at the funeral, wedding, and puberty-rite processions. A hair cutting service for children is also provided at the hair-cutting ceremony. Like the Washerman, they are said to have come as a service caste with the Karaiyar from India to Sri Lanka.

There are two Barbers who are called village barbers (*ūr* Ampaṭṭaṉ). In the past they cut hair free on Fridays, when beach seine operations were off. Apart from the ritual services on the occasions of rites of passage, this was their duty (*kaṭamai*), but in return they could obtain fish from any beach seine for performing it. Now they receive a few rupees for cutting hair on Fridays, and they retain the right (*urimai*) to obtain fish. They own no barbershop, but visit the villagers' houses for cutting hair. The village barbers live in shabby huts at a minimum standard of life.

The Paṟaiyaṉ caste

The village Paṟaiyaṉ adults, one male and two females, are all street sweepers working for the Gramodaya Mandalaya office (see below), for which they receive three hundred and fifty rupees per month. They are all from the outside. They have a caste obligation to act as messengers for village meetings.

The Cakkiliyaṉ caste

Lowest in the caste hierarchy, the four men and one woman of the Cakkiliyaṉ caste are employed as night soil collectors by the Gramodaya Mandalaya office and receive three hundred and fifty or four hundred rupees per month. Their only ritual obligation is digging graves.[35]

Both the Paṟaiyaṉ scavengers and the Cakkiliyaṉs are manual workers with stable incomes, even if their status is low. Some of their children work in beach seine fishing like other lower castes.

Economic Activities

This section provides the background needed to understand economic activities and social stratifications based on the distribution of wealth. In Hinduism wealth and religious commitment are closely related. Firstly, expression of one's religiosity seems different between the rich and the poor, and secondly, net-owners as a group play an important role as patrons in village festivals. It is important, too, that politico-economic conflicts, for example, caused by the rise of new beach seine owners, or by the introduction of mechanised fibreglass boats, have resulted in changes in the membership of the festival patrons. I shall describe the patronage system and its changes in the next chapter.

Beach Seine Fishing

Among the 945 adult male (from 18 to 65 years old) Karaiyar caste members 794 (84.0%) are engaged in fishing and related occupations. 550 (78.5%) out of 794 are dependent on beach seine operations, but only 73 (9.2%) are net-owners (see table 4). An overwhelming majority of the villagers and their households are, thus, dependent on beach seine operations.

Seasonal patterns

In Cattiyur there are two types of fishing activity, according to ecology : there is fishing in the lagoon and the canal to the east ; coastal fishing is practised in the sea, which is confined to within a few miles from the seashore.

The coastal fishing is further divided according to technique : 1) beach seine fishing, 2) *teppam* (raft) fishing, and 3) 17.5 ft. fibreglass boat fishing.[36] The beach seine fishing can be further divided according to the craft used to set the net : 1) *pātai* (a flat bottom boat), 2) *vaḷḷam* (a dugout canoe), and 3) *kaṭṭumaram* (a large raft with an outboard engine).

With the relatively low rate of mechanization of fishing craft, climatic conditions, especially seasonal monsoons, still seriously constrain fishing activities in Cattiyur. The west coast on which Cattiyur is situated

TABLE 4
OCCUPATIONAL DISTRIBUTION
ADULT MALE KARAIYAR CASTE MEMBERS IN CATTIYUR
(Jan. 1983)

Fishing		
Beach seine	Beach seine owner *pātai, vaḷḷam*	60
	Kaṭṭumaram owner	13
	Accountant, etc.	18
	Indebted labourer	340*
	Non-indebted labourer	192**
Non-beach seine	Fibreglass boat owner	38
	Fibreglass boat crew	23
	Raft fishing	59
	Brackish water fishing	27
	Fish trader, etc.	24
Sub total		794
Non-fishing		
Estate owner & farmer		11
Shopkeeper		16
Shop assistant		2
Teacher and other white collar		27
Unemployed		95
Total		945

*In the off-season, of 340 indebted labourers, 303 migrate to the east coast as wage labourers, 18 as non-indebted labourers, and 13 work in the lagoon at Cattiyur.

**In the off-season, 130 out of the 192 non-indebted fishermen become wage labourers on the east coast, 24 remain as the non-indebted labourers, and 17 work in the lagoon at Cattiyur.

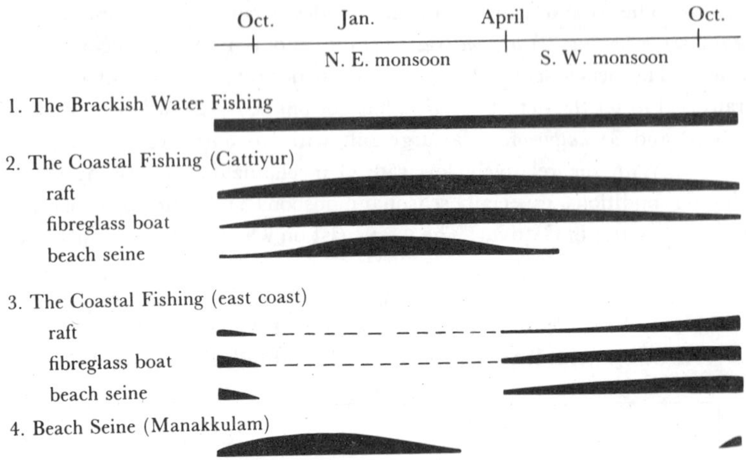

FIGURE 4. SEASONAL FISHING PATTERNS

PLATE 2. BEACH SEINE FISHING

is subject to the south-west monsoon during the period between mid-April and mid-October.[37] Fishing activities, especially beach seine operations, are seriously disrupted during this period (I shall call it the "off-season"). By contrast the sea is generally calm on the west coast from mid-October to mid-April (see fig. 4).[38] There are fishing camps around Manakkulam twenty miles north of Cattiyur, where Cattiyur beach seines (using *vaḷḷam* and *kaṭṭumaram*) operate (see fig. 1). As the Manakkulam coast is affected by the south-west monsoon, these coasts can only be fished during the season between late September to early February. This period largely parallels the fishing season in the vicinity of Cattiyur. During the off-season, many fishermen migrate to fishing camps on the east coast around Mullaittivu between February and April.

Raft fishermen and mechanised fibreglass boat fishermen are less affected by the monsoon and can go to sea during the south-west monsoon season. Most of the fibreglass boat fishermen and some raft fishermen, however, go to the east coast with their families.

By contrast brackish water fishing is little affected by the seasonal monsoon. Those who are engaged in such fishing can stay in Cattiyur and continue fishing all the year.

Operation

Beach seine fishing is a simple method of fishing. Every morning fishermen gather at the fishing ground, and wait for shoals of fish to come to the shore. When they spot a shoal, they launch a boat loaded with the seine net. A few minutes later a boy jumps into the sea from the boat, taking back one end of the hauling rope to the beach. The fishermen on the beach hold it. In the mean time the boat returns to the beach, after curving around to enclose the shoal. Then fishermen pull in the net (pl. 2). In Cattiyur they usually haul nets once a day, an operation that takes four hours.

Fishing grounds

Beach seine operation requires an unimpeded sandy beach free of submerged reefs and rocks. From Colombo to Chilaw the beach is largely fringed with rocks, which makes it difficult to launch seine boats, but this belt of rocks moves away from the coast several miles south of Cattiyur and is not present along the Cattiyur beach.

There are a total of thirty fishing grounds (*pāṭu*) used by local net owners around Cattiyur. These have been allocated to owners by the Fishery Department at Puttalam on the recommendation of the Gramasevaka. Licenses have to be renewed each year, but this is a formal procedure, in so far as the licensee does not change. A new net-owner has to donate seven thousand rupees to the Hindu Temple Administrative Committee as an entry fee to the Cattiyur fishing grounds. This means that the fishing grounds are actually under the control of the Committee.

There is one beach seine owner who has the rights to four fishing grounds and five who have two each, and sixteen others who have one each. There are six beach seine units which are jointly owned by more than one household. Except for two of these partnerships, the share holders are brothers in each case.

Kaṭṭumaram (raft) beach seine owners have no fishing grounds in Cattiyur, but some of them fish after the *pātai* groups have finished. If the catch is good the *kaṭṭumaram* owner must give a portion of it to the license holder of the fishing ground.

Fishing grounds on both Manakkulam and the east coasts from Kokkilai to the south to Vannankulam to the north are leased from the local Fishery Department. Fishing groups set up camps at these fishing grounds. They are located in deserted areas far away from residential sites (especially north of Mullaittivu), and the fishermen spend six to eight months there.

Beach seine owners

A beach seine owner is called a *cammāṭṭi*, and is more of a trader (*mutalāḷi*) than a fisherman. He owns the means of production (beach seines, craft,

TABLE 5
BEACH SEINE OWNERS (CATTIYUR AND ADIPETTI) : LOCATION AND TYPE

	Types	Units
A	Cattiyur net-owner	
A_1	Cattiyur coast only	11
A_2	Cattiyur and east coast	17
B	East coast net-owner	
B_1	East coast only	27
B_2	Manakkulam coast only	2
B_3	East coast and Manakkulam	12
C	*kaṭṭumaram* net-owner	
C_1	East coast only	12
C_2	Manakkulam coast only	2
C_3	East coast and Manakkulam	2

entitlement to fishing grounds and so on) and rights to market fish.

Net-owners in Cattiyur fall into four groupings according to the place where they operate, and the craft they use. As I have already shown, the place and the kind of craft used are co-related. Thus the following four categories are apparent: 1) the "Cattiyur" net-owners, who operate in Cattiyur with *pātai*-boats ; 2) "the east coast" owners, who operate on the east coast with *vaḷḷam* ; 3) the "Manakkulam" owners, who operate in Manakkulam with *vaḷḷam* ; and 4) the *kaṭṭumaram* owners, (named from the type of net they use), who operate mainly on the east coast and in Manakkulam (see table 5 for a detailed classification of net-owners and their numbers). Though these are not exclusive categories, none of the Cattiyur beach seine owners has fishing grounds on the Manakkulam coast, because the fishing season there largely overlaps with Cattiyur's. Most of the Manakkulam beach seine owners have grounds on the east coast as well, but not all the east coast net-owners have grounds on the Manakkulam or on the Cattiyur coast. Again, not all the Cattiyur beach seine owners have a fishing ground on the east coast. Those who have only one fishing ground on either west or east coast have to stop operations for a few months, or even for half a year. They may remain idle or help their close kin who carry out beach seine fishing.

There were fifteen Cattiyur beach seine groups operating in 1903.[39] According to the villagers, the number increased to nineteen by 1955 and had reached twenty-five in 1965. The first east coast net-owner from Cattiyur was a Muslim villager, who had worked for a net-owner from Jaffna as a foreman and later gained a fishing ground around 1959.[40] Gradually other villagers followed his example, but it was not until recently that the net-owners operating on the east coast became the majority among the village net-owners. Cattiyur fishermen started migration to the east coast as wage labourers for Jaffna beach seines in the 1950's. The operations at Manakkulam started in 1955.

Beach seine labourers

There are two kinds of beach seine labourers in Cattiyur : debtor (*tōṇikkāraṉ*) and non-debtor (*iḻuppukkāraṉ*). The former receives an interest-free loan as an advance from a beach seine owner, and then works for him until he returns the loan. He and the others who work the net are entitled to two thirds of the total catch, but as debtors they have to sell their portion to the net-owner. The non-debtor does not receive an advance, and does not need to sell his share of fish to the net-owner. If he is not satisfied with his share, he can quit the beach seine and join a new one. Therefore the net-owners try to keep more indebted fishermen than

Oct. to Feb./April	Feb./April to Oct
Cattiyur	East Coast
1) debtors	→ wage labourers
2) non-debtors	→ wage labourers
Manakkulam	East Coast
1) wage labourers	→ wage labourers

FIGURE 5. SEASONAL EMPLOYMENT PATTERNS

non-debtors in order to ensure stable operations.

On the other hand, most fishermen in the camps on the east coast, and on the Manakkulam coast are wage labourers (see fig. 5). Like non-debtors, they can change net-owners, but they receive a monthly salary (*campaḷam*) and not a share (*paṅku*) in the catch.

The contract period for the debtors is from 15th October to 14th April. Outside this contract period they can work for different net owners, whether on the west or east coast. The actual seasonal patterns of individuals may be more complex than the basic patterns, outlined above.

Share system

The shares for non-debtors and for women working in the yard, and for debtors' meals are first deducted from the total catch. One third of the rest goes to the net-owner, while the rest goes to the debtors. The latter, however, must sell their share to the net-owner at a fixed, usually cheaper, price than that offered by Cattiyur traders, to whom the non-debtors usually sell their share.

To take an example, when the total catch is 1,800 pounds, the overall scheme of income distribution in the Cattiyur beach seine organisation is shown in fig. 6.

total catch	......	1,800 lbs.		
to 20 women*	......	200 lbs.	→ local traders	
to 10 non-debtors*	......	300 lbs.	→ local traders	
for debtors' meals	......	100 lbs.		
to a net-owner	......	400 lbs.	(one third)	→ Colombo market
to 30 debtors	......	800 lbs.	(two thirds)	→ Colombo market

*There is no clear fixed rate for women and non-debtors ; it depends on various factors (the number and percentage of the non-indebted labours per unit, the day's catch, the kind of fish given etc.), and is a source of dispute. According to the villagers, the share rate for the non-indebted fishermen is often higher than that for the indebted fishermen.

FIGURE 6. AN EXAMPLE OF SHARE DISTRIBUTION

The whole of the 1,200 pounds is bought by the net-owner. He might, for example, buy them at Rs. 2.00 per pound, and then sell at Rs. 4.00 in Colombo through the contracted commission agent. His gross profit would be Rs. 3,200.00, while the fishermen as a group would get Rs. 1,600.00, a sum to be split amongst 30 fishermen. Boat crew members, however, receive half a share more than the haulers. Ten percent commission fees for Colombo agents and other overheads (ice, transport etc.) must be deducted from the owner's profit, and selling prices at Colombo fluctuate daily. But the net-owner can alter his buying price accordingly, and this is generally less than half the selling price. Labourers have little information about fish prices in Colombo and have to assess the fairness of the rate they receive from the going rate of other net-owners, though the latter's generosity in this respect is as questionable as their own employer's.

In the rest of this section, I give brief accounts of raft and mechanised fibreglass boat fishing, and non-fishing occupations.

PLATE 3. RAFT FISHING

Other Coastal Fishing

Raft fishing

The *teppam* is a raft made of four roughly shaped logs which are held together by coir ropes and pegs (pl. 3). Its length is about twelve feet and the width ranges from four to one and half feet. It is a traditional craft along the east and the north west coasts. It is paddled or has a mast and boom for sailing. The raft fishermen usually use nylon drift gill nets with floats and weights. These nets effectively make walls of netting that cross the path of moving fish.

Fibreglass boat fishing

A seventeen and half feet fibreglass boat (*yantirappaṭaku* or an engine boat) with a thirteen or fifteen horse power outboard engine is a relatively new mechanized craft, introduced to Sri Lanka in the early 1960's and to Cattiyur in 1970. Mechanization rates have been lower in this area than in the rest of Sri Lanka.[41] Even so, fibreglass boats have—especially among young fishermen[42]—become very popular in the past few years, since import restrictions were liberalised.[43] Significantly, unlike beach seine labour, the fibreglass boat fishing gives fishermen a sense of independence. Although its initial costs are high, fibreglass boat fishing is more profitable and easier to operate than raft fishing.

The fibreglass boat fishermen use gill nets identical to those used

TABLE 6

COMPARISON OF INCOME BETWEEN CATEGORIES OF FISHING OCCUPATION (Nov. to Dec. 1982) (Rupees)

Fisherman		(1)Monthly Income	(2)Daily Income (per fishing day)	(2)x100/165
Raft fisherman		998.0	41.7	25.3
Fibreglass boat fisherman		1558.2	71.4	43.3
Beach seine	owner	3537.5	165.5	100.0
	labour	387.8	18.1	11.0

Note : It should be noted that November and December are the best months for raft fishermen and fibreglass fishermen, and the average monthly income through the year should be lower than the above figures.

by the raft fishermen. However they carry more nets, and go farther afield than the raft fishermen. The fibreglass boat fishermen can fish on the Cattiyur coast all the year, but most of them migrate to the east coast with their boats and women in January, when the prawn season starts there. Prawns are the most profitable source of income for the fibreglass boat fishermen. This is the main reason why the fishermen migrate to the east coast as early as January. My data shows that fibreglass boat fishermen earn far more than raft fishermen (see table 6). This kind of boat requires two full-time crewmen. After deducting the costs of fuel, two thirds of the fish go to the two crewmen and one third to the owner. When one of the crewmen is the owner, he receives two thirds.[44]

Non-Fishing Occupations

There are three occupational groups which used to be, and in some cases still are, important as sources of finance for fishermen. None of them are dependent on fishing. They are : 1) estate owners ; 2) shopkeepers ; and 3)

TABLE 7
LAND TENURE IN CATTIYUR

Land owned in acres	Estate owner	Net-owner	Farmer	Other	Total
Up to 2	0	14	2	15	31
2 to 4	0	3	1	2	6
4 to 6	0	3	0	1	4
6 to 8	0	0	0	0	0
8 to 10	0	1	1	0	2
10 to 15	1	2	0	0	3
15 to 20	1	1	0	0	2
20 to 30	1	0	0	0	1
30 to 40	0	0	0	0	0
40 to 50	6	0	0	0	6
Total no. of owners	9	24	4	18	55

salaried men, that is, teachers and other white collar office workers (working for the post office, banks, courts and so on).

Big estate owners

The villagers consider the estate owners to be very rich, and envy their life style; the latter may have a monthly income of about two or three thousand rupees without actually working for it. They say coconuts fall down and turn into cash at night while the owners are sleeping. As table 7 shows, net-owners and some other villagers have coconut gardens around Cattiyur or around fishing camps on the east coast. Their land tenure is, however, not as substantial as these big estate owners.

In Cattiyur there are nine big closely related estate-owning households, which belong to the most affluent sector in the village. Two forefathers originally bought large coconut estates and their descendants (both male and female), whom I call estate owners, have inherited them and continue to live on them.

Here I introduce the case of S. P. (Sivanathan Pillai). He is the wealthiest villager in Cattiyur, married to the daughter of a teacher of Cattiyur. He is related to the village headman's household ; his late elder brother was a doctor and studied in London. S. P.'s family moved out of Cattiyur to Chilaw in 1970. S. P. was the chairman of the now defunct Cattiyur Village Council from 1958 to 1970. His economic interests include extensive business activities outside Cattiyur as well as the family plantations. He has also become involved in beach seine fishing as a fish trader. He financed four ill-managed beach seine units, finally taking over their control between 1958 and 1968. He now manages the operation of these beach seines in Cattiyur. It was not uncommon for estate owners to be beach seine owners in the past. Now S. P. is, however, the only beach seine owner among the estate owners.

As the chairman of the Village Council, S. P. had close connections with local politics, as presumably did other estate owners. Their influence in village affairs, however, in both the economic and political fields, ceased—or at least declined—in the 70's. When the UNP (the United National Party) was defeated by the pro-socialist SLFP (the Sri Lanka Freedom Party) in the 1970 general election, S. P., a UNP supporter, left the post of Village Council chairman and moved out to Chilaw. P. K. S., a net-owner and the then President of the Cattiyur SLFP branch, took over the chairmanship.

In 1972 the United Front Government, dominated by the SFLP, introduced a Land Reform Law that limited the maximum private ownership of estates to fifty acres. As a result, the estate landowners lost a large part of their wealth. Another factor which reduced S. P.'s power is that, in 1978, electoral boundaries were redrawn and Cattiyur was moved from Chilaw electoral constituency to Puttalam constituency. As a result his connections with the local Chilaw MP of the UNP became less important for Cattiyur politics.

Generally speaking, in spite of their economic power, the Cattiyur estate owners have become marginalised and separated from the rest of the village over the past ten years. Their estates are outside the village and have little economic influence over it. One of the traditional roles of the estate owners is money lending, and they are sometimes called Ceṭṭiyār (a traditional money lender caste in India). But, as traders from the outside, especially from Colombo, expand their influence, the Cattiyur estate owner's role of local financier is becoming less important. Coconut estates require only a small labour force and no villagers work for them.

Shopkeepers

In contrast to the closed kin groups of the Cattiyur estate owners, the other two non-fishing occupational groups maintain fairly close kin and economic relationships with fishermen.

There are twenty general shops of substantial size. Shopkeepers are sometimes would-be beach seine owners. Given the entrepreneurial nature of beach seine ownership, this is not surprising.

Teachers and office workers

Education, and secondly political connections, are the main qualifications for an office job. The children of the rich beach seine owners, the estate owners and the shopkeepers tend to have stronger aspirations for education, and higher educational attainments, than other villagers (see fig. 7 for an example of the close relationships between net-owners, teachers and shopkeepers). The income from white collar jobs is not as high as the net-owners get, but is more stable and, above all, the work is more respectable. Nowadays, however, it is extremely difficult for Tamil youths to find such jobs, due to the policies of successive governments.

Unemployed youths with higher education are very keen on local politics, mainly because it is indispensable to have the recommendation of a local MP in order to get a job in the government sector. Their irritation with the village elders is reflected in village politics. I shall return to the role of the youths in village politics in the next section.

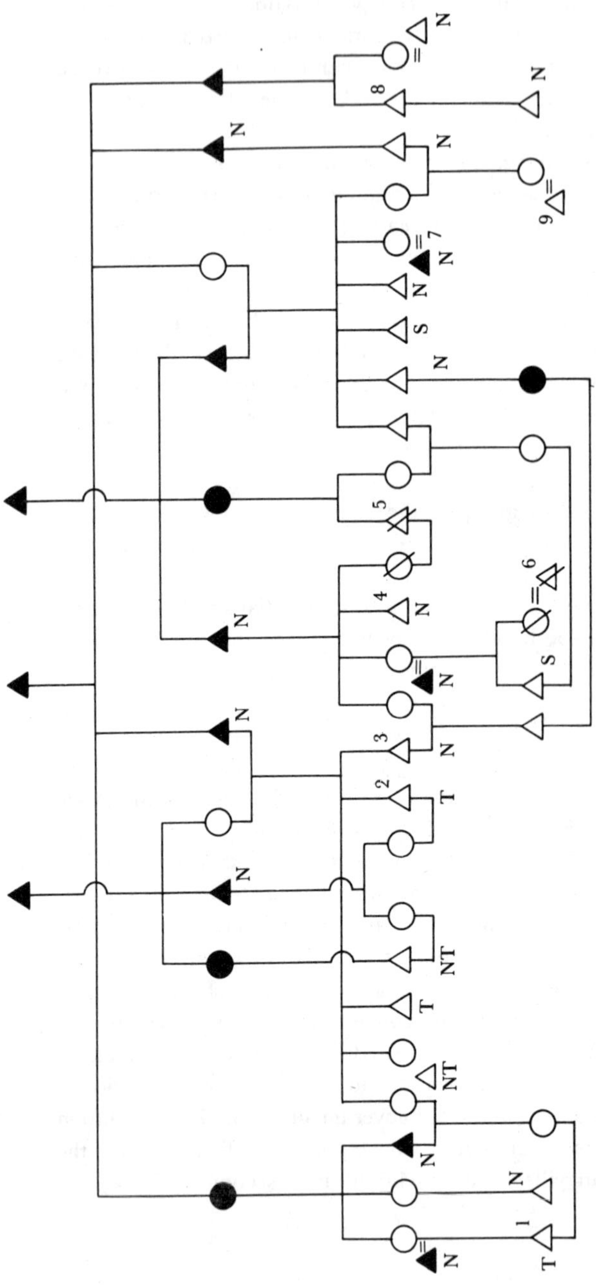

N=Net-owner
T=Teacher
S=Shopkeeper

1 = One of the four graduates of Cattiyur
2 = Principal of a primary school
3 = N. M. M. (powerful net-owner)
4 = Former Village Council Chairman (SFLP)
5 = A wealthy coconut estate owner and trader
6 = Former secretary of the UNP local branch
7 = An important elder
8 = The partner of the medium for the *Mahābhārata* recitation
9 = President of the former UNP local branch

FIGURE 7. SOME OF THE KINSHIP RELATIONS

Local Politics

In the past the village was politically dominated by the higher status kin groups—probably until the 1930's. The village headman, however, was still selected from this group up to the abolition of the post of village headman and the setting up of the Village Council. As I have already described, one of the wealthy estate owners—Sivanathan Pillai (S. P.)—became the Village Council Chairman in 1958 and remained in power for the following twelve years. With S. P.'s eclipse, and that of the estate owners in general under the SLFP government, the beach seine owners became more active in local politics than before, although their activities were more or less confined within the village.

Now the educated youth and some east coast net-owners are also vying for political power. Their influence is still small, but their aspirations make for uncertainty in village affairs.

There are three focal points in present-day Cattiyur politics : 1) national party branches, especially the Cattiyur branch of the United National Party (UNP), which is the present ruling party ; 2) the Gramodaya Mandalaya ; 3) the Hindu Temple Administrative Committee.

Party Politics

When I went to Cattiyur, it was already five years since the 1977 general election, in which the UNP defeated the pro-socialist SLFP and gained an overwhelming majority in the Parliament. Its ruling position was successfully consolidated by the Presidential election of October 1982 and the referendum in December which extended the Parliament for another six years without election. During my stay in Cattiyur in 1982-83, political activities were therefore almost exclusively centred on the UNP branch, and those who supported SLFP and the pro-separatist Tamil United Liberation Front (TULF) in the 1977 general election were not as active as before. A preliminary census showed that the majority of villagers said that they supported the UNP.[45]

The main function of the Cattiyur UNP branch is to keep a regular contact with the local MP of Puttalam District and to work as the sole political intermediary between the village and national level political mainline. As the MP has tremendous influence on local administration as well, it is vital for the villagers to have intimate contacts with him.

To be more specific, the main aim of the branch besides the provision of general social welfare is to recommend young villagers to the

MP, and get them some office work in the public sector, or to introduce new jobs to the village. Therefore it is little wonder that the young men, who had been discontented with the leadership of older UNP branch members, set up a new branch in spring 1983 and eventually gained the local MP's recognition. For the village youths, party politics at the national level was of little significance. What they wanted were strong connections with the local MP, who would, they hoped, provide jobs. They were opportunistic, and would have set up a branch of a different party if the ruling party had not been the UNP. Unlike the Tamil youths in Jaffna, they still maintain some confidence that some of their expectations will be met by the government.

The Gramodaya Mandalaya

The Gramasevaka (G. S.) is an appointed government officer in charge of a village or several villages, and works under the Assistant Government Agent. In other villages the appointee may be politically important. The Cattiyur Gramasevaka, on the other hand, is an outsider who, although he has been working in both Cattiyur and Adipetti for twenty years, keeps a tactful distance from the villagers, and avoids getting too involved in village politics.

More important to the villagers is the Gramodaya Mandalaya, which is a village-level government body for development under the Ministry of Planning, and is different from local government Village Council. The latter has ceased to function, and it has been superseded by the Gramodaya Mandalaya. The Gramodaya Mandalaya consists of sixteen rural development societies from both Cattiyur and Adipetti. Their functions are to improve living conditions and promote rural industries (coir factory, sewing, "cadjan" making and so on). Member groups include the Cattiyur School Association, the Fishermen's Association, the Hindu Temple Administrative Committee and others, all of which are eligible for aid from the Government through the Gramodaya Mandalaya. The chairman of the Gramodaya Mandalaya is effectively the representative of the village, since the village headmanship was abolished and was replaced by the Gramasevaka in the 1960's. The chairman can be expected to play an important role in local politics both inside and outside the village.

In the case of Cattiyur, however, the Gramodaya Mandalaya did not work as had been expected. This is because there was serious antagonism between the local MP and a chairman, called Sodynathan, who had been the president of the UNP branch and a grandson of the former village headman, and thus was considered an apt representative for the village. The latter resigned his post and another villager, Kantaiya, took it over in early 1982. The new chairman had been an active member of the Cattiyur UNP branch and gained favour with the MP. Most villagers, however, did not recognise him as their representative. The former incumbent again assumed the chair and was accepted by the MP in November 1982. The antagonism remained.

The Hindu Temple Administrative Committee

While the previous two political and administrative bodies are important in relation to the patronage of the local MP, the rural development societies attached to the Gramodaya Mandalaya are more concerned with internal village affairs, but most of them could not function practically due to the shortage of money. The only important society was the Cattiyur Hindu Temple Administrative Committee.

The Hindu Temple Administrative Committee has rich financial resources.[46] It is usually the Hindu Temple Administrative Committee which calls village meetings, where both religious and political issues are discussed in public. Prior to 1980, the Committee members were beach seine owners, their close relatives, or friends. But, like the UNP branch, the Committee was taken over by relatively young villagers in the election of 1982.

The new Hindu Temple Administrative Committee members are all young : under thirty-five. Only two are net-owners : one is an east coast net-owner, and the other a share-holder of one of the old and ill-managed beach seines in Cattiyur. Two of the members are fibreglass boat owners ; one works as an assistant to one of them. Two work in local government offices. One is a textile shopkeeper and another works at this textile shop. The last member has no fixed job. They are young rebels, who, along with other young men, later created a new Cattiyur UNP branch and replaced the old one. Their actions were supported by other young villagers. They are not as rich as the net-owners, but are very active in local politics. They represent a new generation of villagers, who are liberal, educated and relatively free of the net-owners. The committee members should be changed every year by election, but there was no agreement as to the 1983-4 members among the villagers. As a result the young committee members continued to work for the next year. After I left the village, the net-owners' domination in the Committee was resumed in 1984, presumably because the villagers felt a need to show strong solidarity in the face of increasing troubles with non-Hindu people from the area.

Conclusion

To sum up, Cattiyur forms a relatively self-contained social universe for the Cattiyur Karaiyar caste. They are dominant and effectively control the key politico-economic and religious niches in the village. Most of the other castes are conceptually, at least, their servants. The higher sub-caste of the Karaiyar caste is in turn divided into several sub-groups. Though their group boundaries are not as clear as they used to be, the sub-castes are still kept apart, and the lower one suffers socio-religious discrimination. Endogamous tendencies at various levels along with the cross-cousin marriage rule, create and maintain close kinship ties within the caste.

What appears from this account is a fairly conventional image of the Hindu society based on territory, kinship and caste affiliations. On the other hand, Cattiyur is not a self-sufficient village with a subsistence economy. Rather, in spite of the strong force of primordial and localised kinship relationships, the force of the market economy plays a far greater role in the present village life than in other societies with a similar standard of life.

The overwhelming majority of Cattiyur villagers are engaged in fishing activities, directly through production or indirectly through trading. Most fishermen are dependent on the beach seine operations, however, and the beach seines are still attractive objects of investment for enterprising villagers. Unlike land owners in agrarian societies, the net-owners are not substantially wealthy and certainly some beach seine owners are not particularly well off. A rich net-owner may also owe large sums to Colombo commission agents, and a humble raft fisherman may stand on firmer ground. The number of the villagers who take jobs other than beach seine fishing, such as fibreglass boat fishing and white collar jobs, is increasing. Consequently, the beach seine owners are becoming less and less powerful in the village. There does remain, however, crucial economic and social differences between beach seine owners and the rest of the fishermen. Large amounts of money pass through the former's hands, and they usually have a number of villagers under their influence. What is important is the fact that in spite of the ups and downs of individual net-owners, and the decline of their position in general, as the class which controls the main local means of production they still dominate the village economy. At any rate those who can mobilise large sums of capital and labour can still stage and control expensive religious rituals. It is safe to conclude that the socio-economic status of the net-owners is still high, and that the beach seine owners as a whole are dominant in the village. This class distinction is, I think, of the utmost importance to the understanding of religious life in Cattiyur, which is analysed in the following chapters. I should note that in spite of the gradual expansion of the political and economic activities of the villagers, their religious activities remain relatively free from outside, especially dominant Buddhist influences. Political elements in the village festivals are still mainly concerned with parochial affairs rather than national level politics.

CHAPTER THREE

DEITIES, THEIR TEMPLES AND RITUALS

This chapter is intended to provide readers with basic knowledge of religious affairs in the village in order to better understand the following chapters. The topics discussed here are the basic classification of Hindu supernatural beings, their temples, specialists, daily rituals and annual festivals, and finally the patronage system that support the festivals.

Supernatural Beings

In this section I present an overview of the ideas of the supernatural beings held by the villagers. A more concrete description of each deity housed in the village temples will be given in the following chapters.

Supernatural beings in Cattiyur are roughly classified into three groups : *pēy* (*picācu* and *āvi*), *tēvatai* and *teyvam.*

Pēy (*picācu*) and *tēvatai* are more or less the same in their negative nature, and the category of *tēvatai* includes some *pēy*. *Pēy* or *picācu* is a collective term for evil spirits. They live everywhere, but particularly in the "forest" or wilderness (*kāṭu*) and burial grounds. There is no semi-permanent temple for evil spirits. They are considered to be cunning, but not particularly powerful.

Close to *pēy* are *āvi* (the souls of the dead). *Āvi* may also attack and possess people. If somebody dies an accidental death, villagers are alarmed as it is likely to cause his *āvi* to wander in this world, so a special ritual similar to exorcism is held by the exorcist (*aṇṇāvi*) at the end of the six-month mourning period.[47] Here is a case of dangerous *āvi*, reported in the village :

When a man committed suicide about five years ago, the residential area around his house was sealed off by sinking four wooden stakes, which had some sacred verses inscribed on them, at the four corners of the area. This was done on the last day of the mourning period, and was intended to prevent his *āvi* from returning home and to ward off other evil forces. On the last day of the mourning period when his soul was released through a hole in the roof to the outside, a pregnant woman happened to pass by his house and was possessed by him. Consequently, she died during childbirth.

Tēvatai is a generic term which includes several demonic spirits such as Cuṭalaimāṭaṉ, Turkkai, Kalyāṇavairavaṉ, and Karumpaṟaiyaṉ. Cuṭalaimātaṉ is a demonic being that resides at cremation grounds (*cuṭalai*) and is identified with Śiva. Turkkai (from Durgā) is said to be Kālī, or the soul of a dead widow. Kalyāṇavairavaṉ is a lower form of Bhairava (Vairavaṉ in Tamil), sometimes considered as a fierce manifestation of Śiva. The other three are said to be *pēy* who live on cremation grounds. Though there is no absolute distinction between *tēvatai* and *pēy*, the former is often sent by someone—notably by an exorcist himself—for the purpose of sorcery. *Tēvatai* is said to possess a person only for some specific reason, while a *pēy* does so at random and at anytime. This distinction, however, is not always accepted.

Teyvam (*cāmi* or *kaṭavuḷ*) is a broad and general term for what we might call deities, gods or goddesses. *Teyvam* can be further divided into sub-categories, according to gender, dietary rules, and locality. There are, on the one hand, benevolent and vegetarian male deities like Śiva, Viṣṇu, Kṛṣṇa, their sons, such as Gaṇeśa, Murukaṉ or Aiyaṉār, and their consorts like Pārvatī and Lakṣmī. They are not expected to possess their devotees, still less to cause them affliction.

On the other hand, there are also fierce and non-vegetarian male deities such as Bhairava and Vīrabhadra, and their female counterparts, the goddesses Kālī, Māri or Muttumāri, and Pēcci. They are ambivalent in nature. For example, Māri who protects villagers from smallpox may also cause smallpox if she is offended. The smallpox patient is believed to be possessed by her. However, her propensity for possession is ambiguous, because she is a deity and not an evil spirit. The underlying reasoning is that the goddess can protect the village from smallpox, because she herself has control over it. The same logic applies to the relationship between a deity and an evil spirit. Kālī or Bhairava, who have the power to dispel an evil spirit's attack, are thought to share the nature of the evil spirit. The image of Vīrabhadra, the deity who guards a temple at its entrance, is half-demonic (cf. Dumont 1986 : 407-10).

At first sight, then, it looks as though we might systematically classify deities into several fundamental and hierarchically ordered categories on the basis of a single criterion, such as purity, vegetarianism, or power. The problem, however, is that several deities, notably Śiva, would cut across such divisions. For example, Śiva is at one and the same time benevolent and transcendental, fierce (in a form of Bhairava and Vīrabhadra) and demonic (in a form of Cuṭalaimāṭaṉ). By the same token Mohinī, a female form of Viṣṇu, is considered to be a beautiful enticing demoness. The ambiguity or the "fluidity" of the divine identities, as Uma Shankari puts it (1980 : 166), is inherent in the nature of certain supernatural beings. Furthermore, even when they are called by the same name, the characters of the supernatural beings vary according to context, such as the type of rituals and the social background of the worshippers. Kālī, or more exactly Bhadrakālī, assumes different characteristics even as the festival proceeds (see chapter 5). Bhairava is more ferocious and demonic when housed in a forest (*kāṭu*) shrine than in a village goddess temple. Muttumāri in Adipetti is benevolent, but fierce in the bush near Katalur. Mohinī is feared as demonic by ordinary villagers, while she is a tutelary deity to exorcists who perform love-magic. These cases reflect the relativity of the nature of particular beings. Actually some villagers were obviously embarrassed when I asked which was the most powerful goddess in the village, since such a question does not specify a context. A general question like mine did not make sense to the villagers.

The criticism made above does not mean that the relationships among the supernaturals are totally fortuitous. There are two significant principles which relate the main deities to each other. One is incarnation or *avatāra* (Tam. *avatāram* or *amcam*) or manifestation (*rūpa,* Tam. *uruvam*), and the other kinship, or to be more precise, familial relationship (Ryan 1980 : 71-73).

According to the first principle, every fierce deity—such as Bhairava, Vīrabhadra and Māṭaṉ—is a fierce manifestation of Śiva. In the same way every female deity is a manifestation of Śakti (goddess). Minor female deities like Nācci or Kaṉṉi are said to be incarnations of Kālī.

According to the second principle, an effort is made to connect them into a kinship network. Thus, female deities, especially those who are considered to be dangerous, are reckoned as Śiva and Śakti's daughters—sisters to each other—rather than as Śiva's consorts or incarnations of Śakti. Male counterparts are represented as their husbands. Bhadrakālī is the wife of Vīrabhadra, and both appear together on the gate of the Muttumāri goddess temple. On the other hand, these male deities are considered to be sons of Śiva-Śakti. My informants were quite inconsistent here. Some say that Rākkuruci in Mannur village is a daughter of Śiva, but others say that she is another manifestation of Kālī. When the contradiction is pointed out, they quickly return to first principles : every deity is the same and all the deities are one.[48] It should be remembered that the villagers' idea of supernatural beings are context-bound, and general remarks concerning identification tend to be inconsistent.

To sum up, no attempt to draw a coherent picture of a stable, consistent, fixed hierarchy of Hindu deities would seem possible, even if we restrict our study to a single community. Ideal types based on several characteristics—vegetarian, non-vegetarian and so forth—are roughly discernible, but some supernatural beings belong to more than one type, and these types are not mutually exclusive. What is essential for the study of village festivals for village goddesses such as Bhadrakālī, and to a lesser extent Draupadī, is an understanding of the ambiguity underlying the manifestation of Hindu supernatural beings, and the relationship of the character of manifestation to the socio-cultural context, rather than the presentation of a neat overview of the Hindu pantheon.

Temples

I pointed out in passing in the previous section that one of the main distinctions between deities and evil spirits is that the latter lack temples. Although not every important deity has a temple in the village, the existence of temples is certainly a significant clue in understanding the idea of the supernaturals held by the villagers.

Cattiyur has four village temples (*ūrkkōyil*). They are Bhadrakālī, Pārtasārati (pl. 4), Muttumāri, and Kantacāmi (pl. 5) temples. The first three are quite large (50~60 ft. in length and 30~60 ft. in width) and have several small shrines inside the building, while the last, built recently, is very small. They are all under the control of the Cattiyur Hindu Temple Administrative Committee and financially supported by the Karaiyar. The Bhadrakālī temple has two shrines for Gaṇeśa, Śiva's first son, one for Pēcci goddess, and another for Bhairava, in addition to Bhadrakālī in sanctum sanctorum (see fig. 8 and chapter 5). The Pārtasārati temple now contains three shrines for Gaṇeśa, Murukaṉ (the second son of Śiva) and Cantāṉa Kōpālaṉ (Viṣṇu's incarnate) and has images of Pārtasārati (Kṛṣṇa) and his consorts, and Draupadī (a heroine of the *Mahābhārata*) in the inner room (see fig. 9 and chapter 7). As we shall see later, this temple was originally built for Draupadī, but was restored fo Kṛṣṇa, who is a

PLATE 4. THE PĀRTASĀRATI TEMPLE

PLATE 5. THE KANTACĀMI TEMPLE

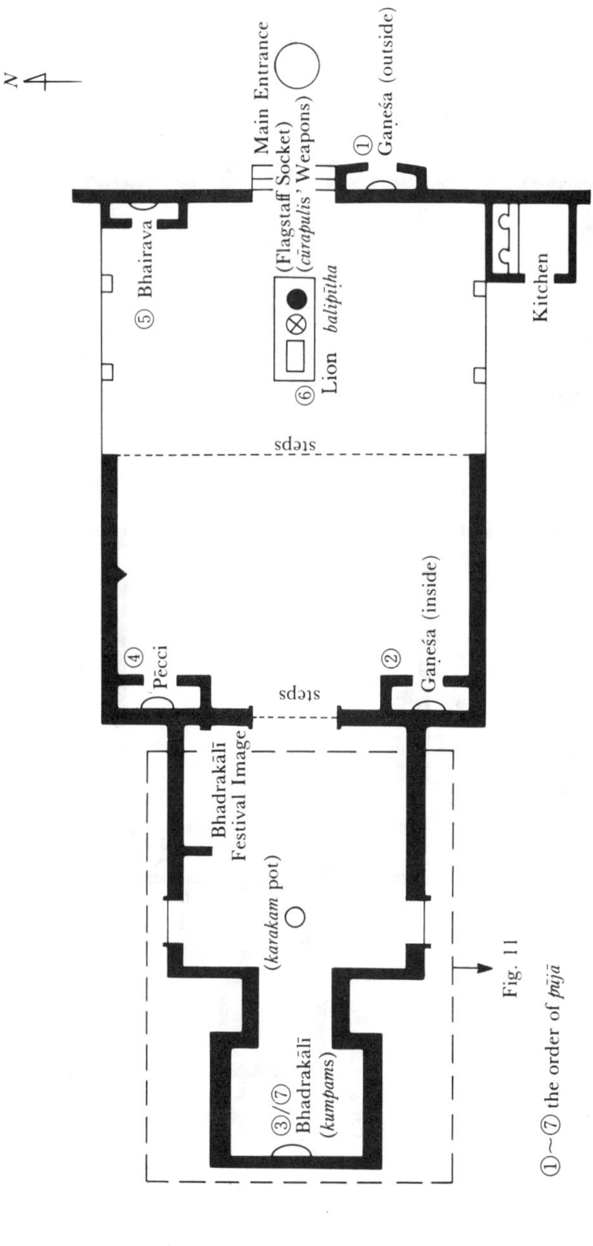

FIGURE 8. PLAN OF THE BHADRAKĀLĪ GODDESS TEMPLE (not to scale)

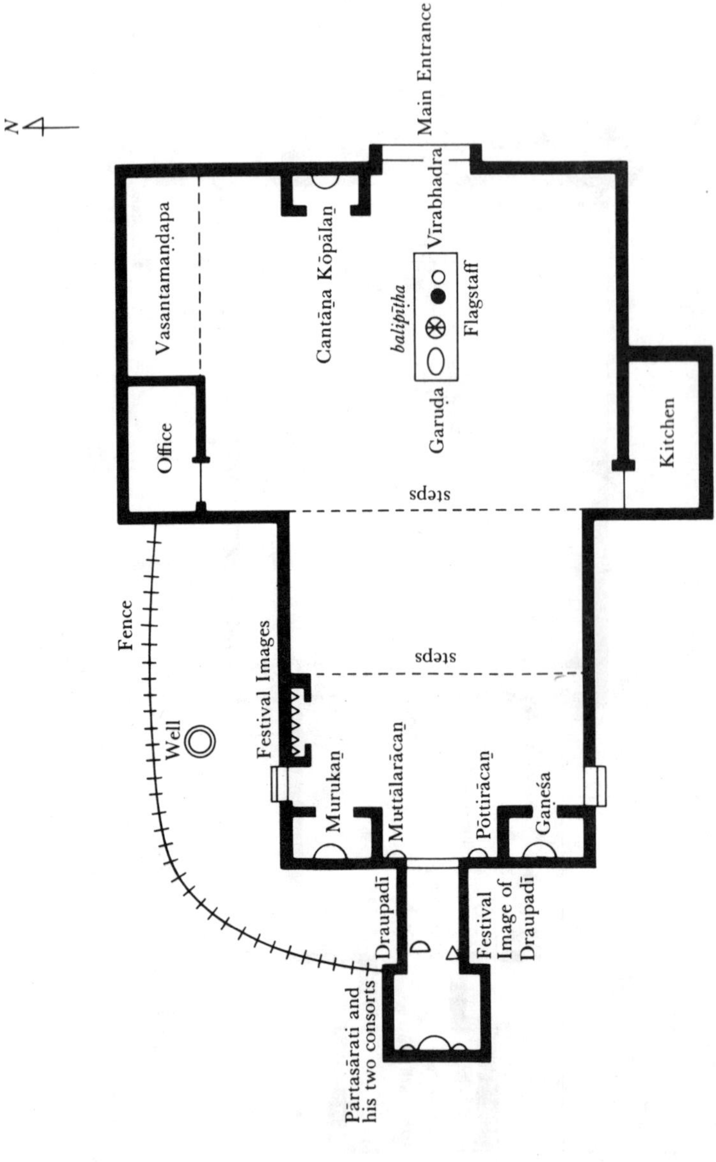

FIGURE 9. PLAN OF THE PĀRTASĀRATI TEMPLE (not to scale)

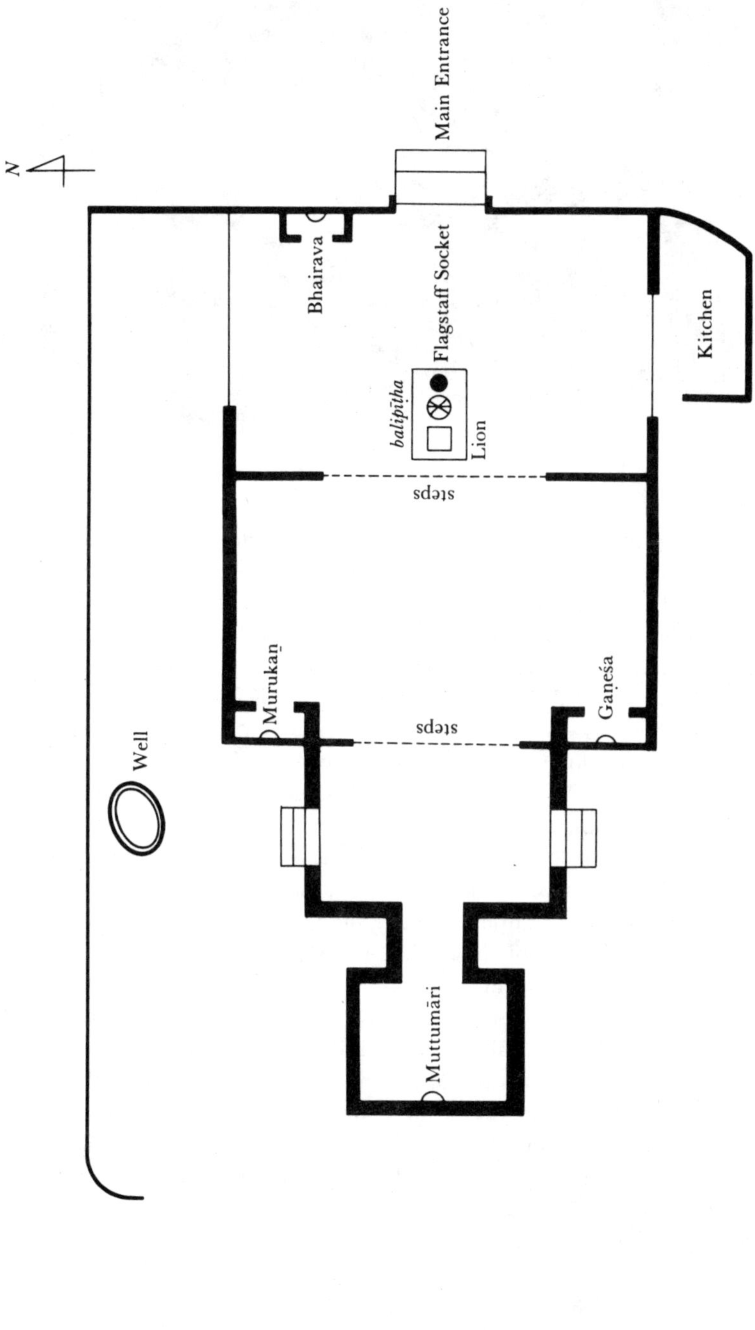

FIGURE 10. PLAN OF THE MUTTUMĀRI GODDESS TEMPLE (not to scale)

PLATE 6. THE KAṈṈI GODDESS TEMPLE

tutelary god in the *Mahābhārata*. The Muttumāri goddess temple has three shrines for Gaṇeśa, Murukaṉ, and Bhairava (see fig. 10).

The village also has several private temples. Aiyaṉār, Kaṉṉi (pl. 6), Māri, and Gaṇeśa temples, for example, are looked after by their owners. All the private temples, except for Aiyaṉār (60 ft. in length and 25 ft. in width), are small. They have, like the village Kantacāmi temple, only one room. The Aiyaṉār temple was built in 1925 by a rich estate owner and had two shrines for Gaṇeśa and Murukaṉ with nine planetary deities (Navagraha) near the entrance. Aiyaṉār has two consorts : Pūraṇāmbikā and Puṣpakalāmbikā.

Although located outside the village, and not owned by any villager, there are several temples that are closely related to the village religious affairs : to start from the south, the Śiva temple in Munnesvaram, the Kaṉṉi goddess temple in Timilai, the Muttumāri goddess temple in Katalur, the Bhairava temple in Kusalai, the Draupadī goddess temple and the Rākkuruci goddess temple in Mannur, the Muṉicāmi temple in Punaiyur, and the Vaṭakāḷi (northern Kālī) goddess temple in Vatarur. Except for the Muttumāri and Muṉicāmi temples, these temples all have some shrines inside or around the main buildings. In this regard the Munnesvaram Śiva temple is fairly large, with many shrines for the deities related to Śiva inside the temple. This temple is one of the most famous temples in Sri Lanka, and is known well throughout the island. It attracts not only Hindus, but also Buddhists and Christians. It is the most important pilgrimage centre in this region. The Kaṉṉi and Draupadī temples are a little smaller than the village temples, but have similar structures with shrines. The Rākkuruci, Bhairava and Vaṭakāḷi temples are fairly small, but also contain the shrines of minor deities supplementary to the main deities.

These temples could be classified into several categories according to the caste of the attached priest, and the kind of ritual performed (see table 8). More detailed descriptions about specialists and rituals will follow in later sections.

TABLE 8
TEMPLES : SIZE AND OTHER DETAILS

○=hold
×=not hold

Name of Deity	Size	Caste of the Priest	Festival	Daily Worship	Votive Ritual
Śiva (Munnesvaram)	large	Brahman	○	○	○
Pārtasārati (Cattiyur)*	middle	Brahman	○	○	○
Aiyaṉār (Cattiyur)	middle	Brahman	○	○	○
Bhadrakālī (Cattiyur)*	middle	Paṇṭāram	○	○	○
Muttumāri (Adipetti)*	middle	Paṇṭāram	○	○	○
Draupadī (Mannur)	middle	Paṇṭāram	○	○	○
Kaṉṉi (Timilai)	middle	Pantāram	○	○	○
Bhairava (Kusalai)	small	Paṇṭāram**	×	×	○
Rākkuruci (Mannur)	small	Paṇṭāram**	×	×	○
Vaṭakāḷi (Vatarur)	small	no priest	×	×	○
Gaṇeśa (Cattiyur)	small	Karaiyar***	×	○	○
Muttumāri (Cattiyur)	small	Karaiyar***	×	×****	○
Kantacāmi (Cattiyur)*	small	no priest	×	×	○
Kaṉṉi (Adipetti)	small	Karaiyar***	×	×****	○
Muttumāri (Katalur)	tree	no priest	×	×	○
Muṉicāmi (Punaiyur)	tree	no priest	×	×	○

*Village temples under the Hindu Temple Administrative Committee.
**Priests of other temples who come only for votive rituals.
***Caretakers rather than priests.
****Only Tuesday and Friday.

As for the village temples there is a clear division of labour with regard to the chief priests serving at these temples. The Pārtasārati and the Aiyaṉār temples are served daily by the village Brahman priests, while the Bhadrakālī and Muttumāri village temples are served daily by non-vegetarian priests of the Paṇṭāram. As is often the case in Hindu society, such division of labour reflects the nature of the deities : there is no blood sacrifice at the Pārtasārati and Aiyaṉār temples, while the

Bhadrakālī and Muttumāri goddess temples have blood sacrifices on festive occasions.

Kantacāmi temple has no regular worship, and no priest serves it. Except for a minor festival which involves other village temples in the month of Tai (January-February), it has no annual festival, while other village temples and the Aiyaṉār temple not only have daily worship, but also fairly large annual festivals. Other private temples have regular worship (usually on Tuesday and Friday) conducted by their Karaiyar caretakers, but no annual festival. They are places for votive rituals.

The Munnesvaram Śiva temple has elaborate daily worship and annual festivals. What makes this temple special to the Cattiyur villagers is the fact that they are traditionally patrons of its great summer festival. Like the village goddess temples, the Kaṉṉi (Virgin) goddess temple of Timilai and the Draupadī goddess temple at Mannur are served daily by non-vegetarian priests and hold annual festivals in summer. The Rākkuruci and Bhairava temples have no regular worship or festival. They are mainly temples for votive rituals (*neṟṟikkōyil*), and when votaries visit them, priests of nearby temples conduct rites for them. Muttumāri goddess, Muṉicāmi and Vaṭakāḷi temples have no regular worship or festival. When the villagers visit them for votive rites, one of the elders takes the role of priest. But these deities are considered to be very strong and fierce. This is especially the case of Muttumāri at Katalur. Her small "temple" at the foot of a big Bo-tree without a permanent structure is said to be located in *kāṭu* or forest, and called *kāṭṭukkōyil*.

The following sections are mainly restricted to the village temples under the control of the Hindu Temple Administrative Committee and aim to give more detailed knowledge about the ritual specialists, the rites they conduct, local festivals and their patrons.

Religious Specialists

The village temples, except for Kantacāmi, have professional or full-time priests of either Brahman or Paṇṭāram caste. Their historical background will be examined in this section. First, however, I will introduce another religious specialist, the exorcist (*aṇṇāvi*), who has no place in the village temple festivals, but is, nonetheless, important in the village religious affairs.

Exorcists

There are five exorcists in the village. All but one come from the Karaiyar caste and work at fishing. The exception is a full-time exorcist from Batticaloa, on the east coast, and now living in Adipetti. Their main role is to perform rituals at home to cure patients suffering from demonic possession or black magic. They also prepare magical amulets for success in fishing and business. They are often requested to provide love-magic.

Those who suffer from affliction by evil spirits usually consult local exorcists. These specialists do not utilise trance techniques, rather their knowledge of *mantra* is used to control the possessing being. In other parts of Sri Lanka and Tamilnadu they are, therefore, called *mantiravāti*. They are invited to the patient's home for the exorcist ritual (*kaḻippu* or removal), which varies from the tying of a *kāppu* cord to a blood sacrifice. A typical ritual of the more complex type consists of four parts : setting up the ritual pot (*kumpam*) of a tutelary deity, usually Bhadrakālī or Bhairava ;

PLATE 7. EXORCIST AT WORK

divination ; dispelling evil forces from the house ; and finally the tying of a *kāppu* cord string for protection (see chapter 6 on the *kāppu* cord). The style of divination varies between exorcists. One technique, for example, uses black oil (*mai*) contained in a dead baby's skull (pl. 7).[49] Other techniques include dropping silver sheets, or using a thread with nine knots representing nine female deities (Skt. *navaśakti*). Divination at a healing ritual is absolutely crucial, since it is essential to identify the possessing being. In the next set of rituals the exorcist offers various items to the tutelary deity, and buries five stakes engraved with magical words, at the four corners of the homestead and at the entrance. All the offerings are carried away from the house and burned near the lagoon. When a blood sacrifice is offered, the victim is waved around the head of the patient three times, and beheaded. Its corpse is simply thrown away. The exorcist may also use a whip to drive out an evil spirit. On his return to the house the exorcist ties a *kāppu* cord around the wrist of each family member. Alternatively, he may prepare a special cylindrical casket (*tāyittu*) in which a sheet of copper engraved with a magical diagram is contained, and which is worn as a necklace-like amulet. This amulet protects its wearer.[50]

What is important about an exorcist is that he does not go into a trance or use minor oracles for his rituals. His power derives from his acquired knowledge of magical spells. As a result exorcism and other magical skills are open to anybody irrespective of caste or ethnicity. At the beginning of my stay there was a Sinhala exorcist living in the village who counted rich villagers among his clients. The exorcist deals with negative force with the help of some ambiguous deities such as Bhadrakālī, Bhairava or Mohinī. His ritual does not concern the village as a whole, but is of a personal nature, affecting only a patient and his family. The relationship between him and a client is temporary in principle, and he does not try to establish permanent relationships of a long-term nature with clients.

The Brahman

As for priests, there are two kinds, from different castes, the Brahman priest and the Paṇṭāram priest. I have already given a brief account of these castes in chapter 2. In this section I will give more detailed data about the historical background of Brahman priests first, and then Paṇṭāram priests.

The first Brahman called Ramacami is said to have come from Jaffna to Cattiyur in the mid-1890's. When he visited Munnesvaram during the festival of Śiva temple, he met some villagers from Cattiyur and was asked to serve the Draupadī temple (the present Pārtasārati temple). He served there for a few months and returned to Jaffna. The villagers thereafter invited other Brahman priests from Jaffna.

First, Aiyatinai came to Cattiyur and stayed for two years. Then, Vaittisvara and his two brothers became the priests of the Draupadī temple. One of them, Pancatcaram, was the father of Kumaracami, the chief priest of the Pārtasārati temple during most of the period of my stay in Cattiyur. However, these brothers all left for Jaffna in 1905, after a brief stay in Cattiyur. From that year to 1937 four unrelated Brahman priests from various places had stayed in Cattiyur. In 1937, Kumaracami came from Jaffna to Cattiyur with his father-in-law. Even after the father-in-law's return a few years later, Kumaracami remained and had two sons. Kumaracami stayed in Cattiyur for forty seven years, from 1937 to 1983, and was deeply involved in village affairs. In the summer of 1983, however, there was some trouble concerning money between him and the Hindu Temple Administrative Committee. Following this, Kumaracami and his family left the village and a new Brahman was brought in.

The Paṇṭāram

As for the Paṇṭāram caste, one of their ancestors came to settle down in Cattiyur. He used to be a priest of the Draupadī temple before Ramacami. In the 1890's when Ramacami came, Cokkalingam of the Paṇṭāram caste played the role of medium during the festival (see fig. 11). He was a priest of both Muttumāri and Bhadrakālī temples. He retired in 1915 and Citamparam his elder son succeeded to him. But Citamparam died young and Cokkalingam resumed the priesthood for the following eighteen years. His younger son Muttaiya subsequently became the priest of the two goddess temples in 1934.

On the occasion of his third son, Parandaman's marriage in 1974, Muttaiya retired and Parandaman assumed the role of medium during the festivals of Draupadī and Bhadrakālī, and became the full-time priest of the Muttumāri goddess temple,[51] while Muttaiya's elder son, Cokkalingam, who is a part-time worker at the village post office, became the priest of the Bhadrakālī goddess temple. However, in spring 1983 after some trouble between Cokkalingam and the Hindu Temple Administrative Committee, his sister's husband Kulantaivel took over his position. Muttaiya's second son, Citamparam, is the full-time priest and medium at the Draupadī goddess temple in Mannur.

In other places a medium is called *kāppukkāraṉ*, or sacred cord-wearer, because he wears a sacred cord (*kāppu*) on his wrist during

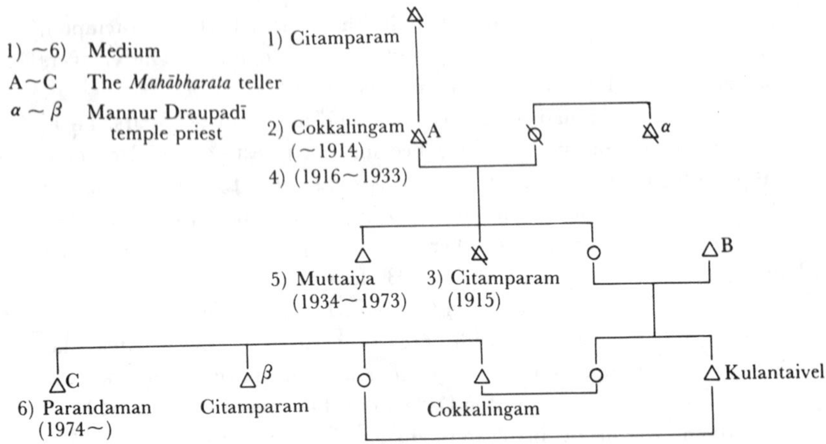

FIGURE 11
FAMILY HISTORY OF THE PAṆṬĀRAM CASTE IN CATTIYUR

the festival and goes into trance (cf. Diehl 1956 : 252 n.3 ; Frasca 1990 : 136-37 ; Moffatt 1979 : 252). In Cattiyur, on the other hand, the medium is simply called *cāmi* or *aiyar*. These terms are usually used for a priestly figure in general, and using these terms for the medium is related to the fact that mediums in Cattiyur are also priests.

To sum up, the medium, who uses possession as an essential means for communicating with the divine, is a member of the Paṇṭāram caste, a non-vegetarian, priestly caste without knowledge of Sanskrit. The Brahman performs elaborate rituals with incantations in Sanskrit. Such a division of labour seems common elsewhere (Dumont and Pocock 1959b). But, there are points which are unique to Cattiyur. For example, the medium is himself a priest. His caste is not vegetarian, yet he does not belong to a lower caste. They claim that their status is second only to the Brahman. As temple priests, or mediums, they perform public or communal rituals, but at home they are often consulted by the villagers. Both Brahman and Paṇṭāram are concerned with worldly affairs and personal matters. On the other hand, the exorcist reminds us, in opposition to the priest, of a shaman. His status is acquired and caste-free in principle, and his activities are always concerned with personal matters. His fame depends on his own ability. Exorcists implicitly, or explicitly, compete with each other. On the other hand, possession or trance has no place in their rituals.

Worship

In this section I present daily religious activities at the main village temples. Holding daily worship means that the temple has a full-time priest and is financially stable. As we shall see, worship which aims at the prosperity of a community, is essential to the village temples. As I have pointed out, not all temples have daily worship and some are visited only for votive rituals. I shall discuss them in the next chapter.

To take an example from the Bhadrakālī temple, the Paṇṭāram priest performs *pūjā* or worship to each idol of the temple in turn in a clockwise direction twice every day : once (*uccikālappūcai*) at 11 : 00 a. m. and once (*cāyaraṭcaippūcai*) at 8 : 00 p. m . He starts by worshipping Gaṇeśa at the shrine outside the temple gate (see fig. 8) and then proceeds to the Gaṇeśa shrine inside the temple, followed by the stone image of Bhadrakālī in the sanctum sanctorum, then the Pēcci goddess outside it, Bhairava in the small shrine under the temple bell tower, Kālī's mount (*vāhana,* Tam. *vākaṉam*),—the lion—and the *balipītha* (Tam. *palipīṭam*) or sacrificial altar. Both the vehicle and the altar are on the three foot high plinth. The priest offers one rice ball on the latter. Then the priest enters the sanctum sanctorum once more and conducts *pañcāratti* (Tam.), waving clockwise seven flaming camphor tablets on a special lamp stand several times before the image. He concludes the whole sequence of worship by clapping his hands and placing his palms pressed together at his chest for a few seconds to bid a farewell to Bhadrakālī.

The priest repeats the following acts in front of each idol except for the mount of Bhadrakālī, which receives only camphor : he 1) offers some water and flower petals, 2) burns incense, 3) lights an oil lamp, 4) burns a block of camphor, 5) consecrates public offerings, called *naivedya* (Tam. *naivēttiyam*), by sprinkling water and petals over them, and finally, 6) performs *pañcāratti* with the seven flames of camphor. These activities are to entertain each god or goddess. During the *pañcāratti* devotees enthusiastically put the palms of their hands tightly together and raise them over their heads.

To offer further explanation, *naivedya* is an offering at "public worship" whose purpose is to increase the prosperity of the world or cosmos (Fuller 1979 : 461). The items offered vary according to the temple, occasion, and deity. In the case of the Cattiyur village temples, the *naivedya* consists of rice balls (Tam. *pali uruṇṭai*) mixed with jaggery, which are cooked in the temple kitchen (*yāgaśālā,* Tam. *yākacālai*) by a temple servant.

Pañcāratti is considered as a climax of the worship and is considered to be a special type of *āratti*. *Āratti* is a very common ritual act. It consists of waving a light, usually in order to show respect to deities, or in order to protect them against the evil eye. In the case of *pañcāratti*, the fire of the *āratti* can be considered as a medium carrying the divine power from the idol to the worshippers.

Prasāda (Tam. *piracātam*), or consecrated offerings, are distributed among the worshippers after the final worship in the sanctum sanctorum. The priest first passes around among the devotees the fire of the *pañcāratti*, which remains after the last worship of the main idol. They place their hands over the fire, and move them towards their faces, touching them lightly over their bodies from the eyes down to the chest—as if they were absorbing the divine power from the fire into his body. Then sacred ash, sandal paste and vermilion powder are passed around the congregation. They take these items one by one and make a *poṭṭu* mark (a sign of Śaivites) on their foreheads. Finally, the priest distributes rice balls. *Prasāda*, which includes fire, sacred ash and other non-edibles, is considered to contain divine power and religious merit accrues to those who eat it. I shall elaborate on the meaning of *prasāda* again in chapter 6.

From the above account we can understand that temples which have regular worship by the priest are not just places to pray or to have an auspicious sight (Skt. *darśana*) of a god, but are places full of divine power that a devotee can tap, and take home in the form of *prasāda* that can be shared with family members.

It should be noted that there are some variations in the form of worship, although their aims are more or less identical, and the form of temple worship described above is considered to be an abbreviated one. A complete form of worship starts with the invitation of a deity. An example of this type of worship will be presented in chapter 6.

Annual Festivals

In this section I briefly explain the main annual festivals celebrated by the villagers. In order to give a more general framework they include not only temple festivals, but also domestic festivals. Explanations of the festival all come from villagers' accounts.[52]

The Tamil year is divided into twelve solar months, lasting from twenty-nine to thirty-two days ; it is based on the position of the sun in the ecliptical zone.[53] The year begins with the month of Cittirai, which corresponds to April-May (see table 9).

In the month of Cittirai there are two festivals.

TABLE 9
ANNUAL CYCLE OF FESTIVALS

Month		Name
Cittirai	(Apr. — May)	1. Tamil New Year's Day 2. Cittirai Cevvāy
Vaikāci	(May — June)	
Āṉi	(June—July)	(Timilai Kaṉṉi goddess festival) (Mannur Draupadī goddess festival)
Āṭi	(July—Aug.)	1. Draupadī goddess festival 2. Āṭi Cevvāy
Āvaṇi	(Aug.—Sep.)	(Munnesvaram Śiva festival)
Puraṭṭāci	(Sep.—Oct.)	1. Bhadrakālī goddess festival (Vēḷvi) 2. Navarātri 3. Maheśvara Pūjā
Aippaci	(Oct.—Nov.)	Dīpāvalī
Kārttikai	(Nov.—Dec.)	Tirukkārttikai
Mārkaḻi	(Dec.—Jan.)	Tiruppāvai
Tai	(Jan.—Feb.)	Tai Poṅkal
Māci	(Feb.—Mar.)	1. Mācimakam 2. Mahāśivarātri
Paṅkuṉi	(Mar.—Apr.)	Paṅkuṉi Uccavam

1) Tamil New Year's Day (*varuṭappiṟappu*). The villagers take an early morning bath, dress in new clothes, and visit the village temples. There is no special ritual, only a minor *abhiṣeka* or consecration ritual at the temples.

2) Cittirai Cevvāy (Cittirai Tuesday). This is celebrated in three open spaces in Cattiyur on Tuesday. Young women dance a *kummi* dance throughout the night to devotional songs of the Māri goddess. This dance is intended to increase the women's fertility under the protection of the goddess Māri. Parandaman, or chief priest of the Muttumāri goddess temple, is invited to perform worship at the two places, but his presence is not essential.

There are no festivals in the month of Vaikāci (May—June).

No festivals are held in Cattiyur in the month of Āṉi (June—July), but the villagers go to the Mannur Draupadī goddess temple to observe or participate in a firewalking ceremony. Some of the village votaries, mostly women wishing for children, visit the Kaṉṉi goddess temple festival in Timilai.

In the month of Āṯi (July—August) major Hindu festivals are held throughout Sri Lanka. Some of the villagers visit these festivals, among which the festival at Kataragama is the most popular.

1) Āṭi Tiruvilā, the festival at the Pārtasārati temple (here called the Draupadī goddess festival). This is the most important festival in Cattiyur ; it is held for twenty days, the famous Indian epic, *Mahābhārata*, is recited and some of its famous scenes are enacted by the villagers. The climax of the festival is firewalking ceremony. This festival is analysed in full detail in chapter 7. The fishermen return from fishing camps on this occasion.

2) Āṭi Cevvāy (Āṭi Tuesday). This is a domestic fertility rite, performed secretly by women on three consecutive Tuesdays of the month.

No festivals are held in Cattiyur in the month of Āvaṇi (August—September), but the Cattiyur fishermen come back from fishing camps again and stay in Munnesvaram village in order to attend the last few days of the Munnesvaram Śiva temple festival. This festival starts a few days after the firewalking ceremony for Draupadī at the Cattiyur Pārtasārati temple.

There are three festivals in the month of Puraṭṭāci (September—October).

1) Vēḷvi (blood sacrifice). This festival is held for ten days at the Bhadrakālī temple. As the name suggests, the climax of the festival is the blood sacrifice of a goat to the goddess. This festival is analysed in detail in chapter 5.

2) Navarātri (nine nights). This festival is celebrated for nine days by Hindus all over India for three manifestations of Śakti (a goddess) ; Durgā, Lakṣmī and Sarasvatī. In Cattiyur, this festival is celebrated at the Muttumāri goddess temple. On the ninth day, Sarasvatī *pūjā* (worship of the goddess Sarasvatī) is conducted by the village Brahman priests at two locations. In 1982 these were held in a village hall near the Pārtasārati temple and at a net-owner's house in Kottu.

On the tenth day, early morning, another Sarasvatī *pūjā* is conducted by school teachers at school, and preschool children receive their first lesson in the Tamil alphabet. This day is traditionally considered to be good for the first day of learning and other activities.

In the afternoon a movable image of the goddess is taken out from the Muttumāri goddess temple to the seashore, and its chief priest enacts Śakti's victory over the buffalo-demon, Mahiṣāsura.

3) Maheśvara (another name of Murukaṉ) Pūjā. This is held for Murukaṉ in front of his shrine at the Muttumāri goddess temple to mark

the beginning of the fishing season. Murukaṉ, on this occasion, is considered as the king of the sea, and net-owners' wives prepare a large quantity of *poṅkal* or sweet milk rice gruel for him.

Puraṭṭāci is also the month when preparatory activities for the fishing season start, and a series of the rituals which mark each stage of these activities are performed by net-owners and their employees. They include a blood sacrifice and offerings to *pātai*-boats and visits to several small temples around the village.

In the month of Aippaci (October—November), Dīpāvalī is celebrated to commemorate the victory by Kṛṣṇa over the demon Naraka. This festival is very popular throughout India. There is no special ritual at the temples or in the home. The Hindu Temple Administrative Committee organises a sports meeting. The villagers like to buy new clothes on this occasion.

In the month of Kārttikai (November—December), a festival called Tirukkārttikai is celebrated among the Tamil Hindus. Although this is a festival for Śiva, it is held at the Pārtasārati temple. A bonfire is prepared in front of the temple. This bonfire symbolises Śiva's *liṅga* of fire. According to one villager, this festival is based on a story of a dispute between Brahmā and Viṣṇu about their greatness. They asked Śiva to decide who was the greater. Śiva took the form of the fire *liṅga*, and asked Viṣṇu and Brahmā to reach its ends, but they failed and thus came to recognise Siva's greatness.

Mārkaḻi (December—January) is an inauspicious month and so no marriage ceremonies are held. To gain the protection of Gaṇeśa, women prepare a *kōlam* or ritual painting in front of the house every morning. Every night, two old men go around the village in the dead of night singing devotional hymns.

There is a ten-day festival called Tiruppāvai at the Pārtasārati temple during the month of Mārkaḻi. During this festival, devotional hymns to Tiruppāvai composed by a Vaiṣṇava devotee, Āṇṭāḷ, are recited at the temple.

Ancestors, especially recently deceased relatives, are worshipped at home and at burial grounds on the last day of the month.

Tai Poṅkal is held on the first day of Tai (January—February) to celebrate the renewal of the sun or year. *Poṅkal* or rice gruel is cooked at dawn in front of the house. The next day, cow owners may offer *poṅkal* to their animals, a rite known as Māṭṭuppoṅkal (from *māṭu*, or cow).

In addition to Tai Poṅkal and Māṭṭuppoṅkal, which are very popular among the Tamils, there is an offering of *poṅkal* at temples in Cattiyur. *Poṅkal* is cooked in front of the four village temples and the

Aiyaṉār temple on consecutive Tuesdays and Fridays after the first of Tai. Blood sacrifice is also offered at the Muttumāri and Bhadrakālī temples. This temple *poṅkal* seems peculiar to Cattiyur. *Poṅkal* is a very important ritual, and I shall analyse it further in chapter 5.

In the month of Māci (February—March), there are two festivals.

(1) Mācimakam festival is held for ten days. Sins are expiated by bathing in the sea. The movable image of the goddess Muttumāri is taken out to the seashore on the tenth day and is used as the object of worship. Other goddesses in general are also celebrated on this occasion.

(2) Mahāśivarātri (great Śiva's night). The village temples are open through the night, and the villagers observe a vigil in order to gain blessings from Śiva. Some villagers visit the Munnesvaram Śiva temple.

In the month of Paṅkuṉi (March—April) Paṅkuṉi Uccavam is held at the Aiyaṉār temple to celebrate Śiva's wedding. This is, they say, because Aiyaṉār is the son of Śiva.

From the above description it is clear that the villagers celebrate several festivals well-known, both inside and outside the Tamil world. They include Navarātri, Dīpāvalī, Tirukkārttikai, Tiruppāvai, Tai Poṅkal, Mācimakam, Mahāśivarātri, and Paṅkuṉi Uccavam. There are, however, some less well-known occasions like Cittirai Cevvāy or Āṭi Cevvāy observed mainly by women. Maheśvara Pūjā and other fishing rituals are, I suppose, very specific to the fishermen. The most important festival is that of Draupadī, and the second that of Bhadrakālī. They are unique, but can be classified as village goddess festivals which are said to be found in every village in Tamilnadu and elsewhere.

Of the temple observances, the Draupadī goddess festival, Bhadrakālī goddess festival, Navarātri, Maheśvara Pūjā, Tirukkārttikai, Tiruppāvai, Paṅkuṉi and Mācimakam stand out in importance. Tirukkārttikai and Tiruppāvai are related to Viṣṇu, and held at the Pārtasārati temple, while Navarātri, MaheśvaraPūjā, and Mācimakam are held at the Muttumāri goddess temple. Paṅkuṉi Uccavam is held at the Aiyaṉār temple.

The festivals should be held every year to celebrate the deities, so financial backing is indispensable. In the next section I will describe in detail the patronage system for the annual festivals.

The Patronage System

A patron, called *upayakkaraṉ* in Tamil, plays a significant role at main rituals. He meets the expense of the rite and gains merit (*puṇya*, Tam. *puṇṇiyam*). The number of patrons varies according to the occasion and scale. The word *upayam* means a gift or endowment, but in the context of the present study it usually means the ritual which an *upayakkāraṉ* patronises, or more often the day when such a ritual (or a set of rituals) is conducted. There are two kinds of patrons for the festivals. One is caste-based, the other class-based.

All the adult male members of the Karaiyar contribute annual fees of twenty-five rupees to the Hindu Temple Administrative Committee. This distinguishes the Karaiyar from other castes in the village. They provide financial support, while some castes render traditional service and others have no role during the festivals. The Karaiyars are collectively the patron of the village festivals, and their representatives are the Hindu Temple Administrative Committee members. Such a role corresponds to the fact that they are dominant in the village. Furthermore, this sharp division between castes according to the patronage and service corresponds to the way castes are conceptualised by the villagers. As I have already pointed out, service is of far greater importance to the ideology of caste in Cattiyur than are purity and pollution.

The other type of patronage is not based on caste, but on economic conditions. In principle all net-owners pay about three hundred and fifty rupees to support the six annual festivals. These are the festivals for Draupadī and Bhadrakālī, Navarātri, Tirukkārttikai, Tiruppāvai, and Mācimakam. The principle of recruitment in this type more or less reflects the economic changes in the village. Earlier the villagers had contributed to the festival as a whole without any clear distinctions between net-owners and other villagers (though the former were likely to pay more than the latter). But in 1950, when the Draupadī goddess temple was transformed into the present Pārtasārati temple, it was formally decided that the main village festival expenses should be met by the net-owners then operating in Cattiyur. In the same year, due to this establishment of a stable financial source, the Navarātri festival started at the Muttumāri goddess temple, which was also collectively sponsored by the village net-owners.

According to Alexander (1982 : 210), beach seine fishing became far more lucrative in the 1940's than it had been before. This was because of wartime food shortages and the improvement of communications with Colombo ; rising prices must have helped the net-owners to accumulate wealth and to differentiate themselves from the rest of the villagers.

In the mean time the number of net-owners had increased as a result of access to new fishing grounds taken on lease on the east coast, and the new east-coast net-owners (about ten in number) were accepted as patrons of the festival in 1973. In the same year another festival (Tiruppāvai), which is performed in honour of Viṣṇu and his devotee, Āṇṭāḷ, started at the Pārtasārati temple. This festival was also supported by the net-owners collectively. So, up to a point, economic expansion and the elaboration of the village festivals went hand in hand.

Furthermore, two Colombo merchants were accepted as regular *upayakkāraṉs* at the village meeting in 1979. The villagers were reluctant at first, but finally decided to modify the regulation of the patronage system for the village festival. These merchants were of Indian origin, and were not villagers, and their occupations had nothing to do with either Cattiyur or fishing. Their motivation appears to have been purely religious, and this could be considered as a typical case of *bhakti,* or devotionalism, backed by wealth (see chapter 4).

Though fibreglass boat fishermen are not accepted as *upayakkāraṉs* collectively in the festival, one of them became an *upayakkāraṉ* in 1982. This was achieved with the support of his younger brother, who is the clerk at the Cattiyur Gramodaya Mandalaya office, the secretary of the Hindu Temple Administrative Committee, and one of the most active members in local politics. I do not know if he is a regular patron, but it reflects an emerging tendency that the patronage system is becoming more and more open to those other than the beach seine net-owners.

In addition, among the net-owners, there is a new class of people. For example, there are two net-owners of the lower sub-caste of the Karaiyar. This is perplexing to some villagers, because the lower sub-caste used to be servants (torch-bearers) rather than patrons of the festival. In relation to this, the rapid increase in the number of the beach seine net-owners has diminished the prestige of being a festival patron. Thus some wealthy and aspiring net-owners are seeking more distinctive ways to make financial contributions.

We have seen that the change in the nature of the Pārtasārati temple and the establishment of a new patronage system occurred in the same year, 1950. This is not, I believe, accidental. As I shall argue later, the Brahmanical rituals and the patronage system based on secular power are closely related.

Conclusion

This chapter has been concerned with the background of religious life in Cattiyur, which is necessary for the following discussion about temple rituals and village festivals. I have shown that there are various supernatural beings acknowledged by the villagers, and that they are roughly classified by their nature. These categories are, however, not fixed, but dependent on context. The main clues to understanding the villagers' idea of supernatural beings lie in the arrangement of the types of religious specialists, rites performed and the conduct of annual festivals. They were discussed in order, and finally the village patronage system was described.

CHAPTER FOUR

DEVOTION, POSSESSION AND VOTIVE RITUALS

The intention behind this chapter is to help the reader understand the personal, or existential, dimension of Hindu religious life. First, the concept of *bhakti,* or devotion, is analysed in concrete settings, with a brief general introduction to devotionalism in India. Next, possession as an experience of one's devotion and one's deity's response to it is discussed. Finally votive rituals, especially ecstatic ones, are described and their symbolism analysed. Most Hindus participate in village festivals by performing votive rituals. These rites are also an expression of an individual's devotion to a celebrated deity. The final section is therefore directly related to the following chapters about village festivals.

Devotion

Bhakti,[54] or devotion, is one of the three paths to salvation in Hindu doctrine. The others are the paths of ritual observance and of knowledge (Singer 1972 : 137). Devotionalism requires love of, and total devotion to, one's personal deity. Divine grace reciprocates the devotee's dedication.

According to Dumont, this is a revolutionary doctrine "since it transcends both caste and renunciation, and opens an easy road to salvation for all without distinction" (Dumont 1970b : 55). Here Dumont finds some synthesis between the religion of society and the religion of renunciation. Through the love of one's personal deity, a devotee can become "a free individual" (ibid., 56).

Although the *bhakti* had already been proclaimed as the primary path to salvation in the *Bhagavad Gītā* of the *Mahābhārata,* it was not until the seventh or eighth century that more emotional and ecstatic *bhakti* came to the fore in South India—later in North India (Brockington 1981 : 130-72). Certainly it is not impossible to find an emphasis on egalitarian values and some anti-caste feelings in the *bhakti* literature,[55] but it is generally thought that practitioners of *bhakti* were, on the whole, not seriously committed to an anti-caste, anti-materialist, and socially radical ethic, but were content to leave the caste system intact.[56]

In order to understand the concept of *bhakti,* and the extent to which it can be mobilised to provide criticism of materialistic secular power, I shall give some examples of the way in which *bhakti* is used for a different, almost opposite purpose.

First I present three examples of the way *bhakti* is used in the potent criticism of materialism.

1) The first example is a fishing ritual called Maheśvara Pūjā in honour of Murukaṉ, performed in order to ensure good catches during the new fishing season. Here, Murukaṉ is believed to be the king of the sea. The ritual is held at the Murukaṉ shrine in the Muttumāri goddess temple in October, when the fishing season starts in Cattiyur. On that day, the Cattiyur net-owners who have fishing grounds in Cattiyur prepare large quantities of *poṅkal* (rice gruel). They are the *upayakkāraṉs* or patrons of this ritual, which is intended to increase their prosperity, and their names are recited by the temple priest at the end of the ritual. After the *poṅkal* is prepared and offered to the deities in the temple, a small portion of it is taken to the sea, and Murukaṉ is also worshipped from the beach. In this ritual, however, the *poṅkal* is actually offered to Murukaṉ by an ordinary labourer, and not by a representative of the net-owners. The labourer has a *kāppu* cord for consecration tied by the priest to mark his special status, and he receives the first *prasāda* (consecrated leftovers). He is selected on the basis of several criteria : he should be a non-drinker, non-violent, and pious in nature. Thus in this case the value of devotion and piety is given more emphasis than obviously economic factors such as net-ownership, in spite of the fact this festival is explicitly supported by the net-owners.

2) The second example is provided by a remark by a Cattiyur villager that the Munnesvaram Śiva temple festival is "a joke". This, in spite of the fact that its affairs are conducted on a far greater scale and in a far more elaborate fashion than are any Cattiyur festivals. The problem, as another villager put it, is that it has no *bhakti,* but is driven by greed for money—implication being that the Brahman priests of the temple merely pursue their economic interests through the festival.

3) In the village festivals a handful of devotees (*pattār* or *aṭiyār*)[57] are more active than any net-owning *upayakkāraṉ*. They attend every ritual function, and help the priest and the medium all day long. The musicians

and temple workers of the Karaiyar caste are also called *pattār*.[58]

The concept of *bhakti* is, however, easily exploited for the justification of a given secular status, and for material prosperity as well. Given the importance of wealth in Hindu religious doctrine, devotionalism is not necessarily contradictory to material prosperity in this world (Singer 1972 : 353). Uma Shankari points out that *bhakti* justifies donation and sponsorship :

> It (sponsorship of temple rituals) is also a concrete expression of devotion, the chief and substantial donors in fact come to enjoy a great deal of prestige in the temple, for the *bhakti* system would require that a wealthy devotee readily surrender his wealth to his chosen deity, as a true devotee places whatever he has in the service of God. (Uma Shankari 1984 : 177)

For example I saw M. S. T., one of the most active net-owners, at the Pārtasārati temple every evening. He is a typical self-made man, whose father was a poor prawn fisherman. He drove a tractor in the village procession, pulling the festival image of Pārtasārati and his two consorts, around the village every day during the Draupadī goddess festival.

Another already established net-owner, N. M. M., is also well known for his commitment to religious affairs, and can be heard singing devotional hymns toward the end of regular worship (*pañcappāṭṭu*) and on important occasions such as Tiruppāvai for Viṣṇu in the month of Mārkaḻi.[59]

It would make little sense to hold that these net-owners are only pretending to be sincere devotees to disguise their economic activities.

To take one more example, the Mannur Draupadī goddess temple is smaller, and its festival is less spectacular than the Cattiyur counterpart. The present state of the Mannur temple is scornfully blamed by the Cattiyur villagers on the Mannur residents' lack of devotion. This contemptuous attitude implicitly refers to their lack of generous financial aid to the temple.

There is, however, a case where an interpretation based on *bhakti* has been used to excuse inadequate donation. In the 1982 Bhadrakālī goddess festival, the medium was ferociously possessed by the Bhadrakālī, who demanded the immediate completion of the temple restoration as the villagers originally had planned. The medium possessed by the goddess tried to bite his own arm and could not properly perform rituals. Most of the villagers interpreted this incident—one called it *narapali* or human sacrifice—as a manifestation of Bhadrakālī's wrath ; indeed Kālī gave this explanation through the medium's mouth. But a few distrusted the medium's possession and suggested that it was not authentic. They felt that Bhadrakālī would have understood the hardship they faced in restoring the temple, and would appreciate their sincere devotion to her. They excused themselves by referring to their poverty, not their lack of devotion. For them the delay was just a material matter, and not a spiritual one. This interpretation, though held by the minority, illustrates another dimension in the villagers' understanding of the transaction between deities and men in terms of devotion. Devotees and their gods are beyond mundane reciprocal relationships : the deity, at least in this case, should expect transcendental spirituality (devotion) from the devotee and not material contributions.

To sum up, *bhakti* serves to reinforce the Cattiyur villager's pride in two opposite ways : the lavish expenditure on religious affairs is proof of sincere devotion as well as a materialist display. Both rich and poor refer to it for various purposes. The form of the ritual expression of *bhakti*, however, differs between classes. Possession during the festival is a typical expression of devotion by the poor. It almost only occurs among ordinary fishermen and rarely among net-owners or the educated men. The latter use offerings or other means to express their devotion.

Possession

Dumont refers to the possible connection between possession and emotional devotionalism :

> It remains that both possession, a functional feature of folk religion, and *bhakti*, a characteristic of many sects, rest upon a common psychological condition, and that *bhakti* takes up in more or less sublimated form an aspect of common religion ignored by Brahmanic orthodoxy. (Dumont 1970b : 57)

In other words Dumont recognises some *bhakti* elements in popular Hinduism, and his observation is in line with the general view of *bhakti* as a path to salvation for the masses.

Bhakti is used as an equivalent to *aruḷ* (divine grace) or *śakti* (divine power) in Cattiyur. For example, the statement "*bhakti* has come to him (*avarukku patti vantatu*)" means that he has been possessed by a deity. It is the devotional and ecstatic aspect of the Cattiyur Draupadī goddess festival that annually attracts several thousand devotees from elsewhere who come at this time to an otherwise unknown fishing village. In the following sections first I shall delineate indigenous categories of possession in order to understand the devotional elements in ecstatic rituals.

Types of Possession

Two types of spirit possession are generally distinguished in Hinduism (Babb 1975 : 233 ; Dumont and Pocock 1959b : 56 ; Harper 1964 : 189). One is possession by a deity (divine possession), and the other is possession by an evil spirit (demonic possession). Divine possession is found in festivals and shamanic seances, when the devotees and specialists such as mediums and diviners are supposed to be in a pure state. Human beings are not, however, always able to reach the state of purity necessary for such divine contact, since they continually suffer from both minor and serious pollution. While they are polluted, people are not allowed access to the deities. This means that an impure person cannot get divine protection. He or she is excluded from the protective circle of deities. This helpless situation is often expressed in terms of fear of attack by evil spirits. As serious pollution is caused by life crises, this idea is best seen in rites of passage. According to reasoning similar to that suggested by the interpretation of ambivalent nature of the deity in control of smallpox, cases of possession may be ambiguous. Obviously, the ambiguous nature of possession depends on the nature of the possessing agent. Three kinds of possession can be found in Cattiyur : *ca<u>nn</u>atam, c̄ami āṭutal* and *pēy piṭittal.*

Ca<u>nn</u>atam (divine possession)

The word *ca<u>nn</u>atam* or *uru* covers a wide range of types of possession, ranging from the experience of the divine by the non-vegetarian medium of the Paṇṭāram caste to the more ecstatic possession experienced by devotees. This section is mainly concerned with the former case. The chief priest of the Muttumāri temple, Parandaman, is divinely possessed on only two occasions : at the Bhadrakālī and the Draupadī goddess festivals. Even on these occasions, he rarely goes into the frenzied state typical of possession, hopping around or shouting aloud with his body trembling. His experience seems well under control. This mediumship is hereditary : his father and grandfather have previously played the role of medium to Bhadrakālī and Draupadī in their festivals. Personal experience and devotion to divine beings, however, are also seen as important prerequisites to the ability to experience *ca<u>nn</u>atam.* Here I introduce Parandaman's experience of his first firewalking.

According to Parandaman, when he concentrates on the goddess in front of her image, her power (*śakti*) or grace (*aruḷ*) enters him because of his personal devotion to her. Hence *caṉṉatam* is also known in Tamil as *pattinaṭaṉam* or dancing (*naṭaṉam*) of devotion (*patti*). In this sense devotion underlies divine possession. Parandaman told me how he first received the *aruḷ* (grace) :

> Parandaman had succeeded to his father's role as the medium of the Draupadī goddess at the time of her festival. During this period he is supposed to be the goddess herself, and remains in her temple for the eighteen days of the festival. On the last day he leads about a thousand devotees in firewalking, which is the climax of the festival. It is he who first walks on the burning embers. Though he accepted his father's role just after he got married, that first year he was totally unconvinced of his ability to walk on the fire uninjured. Surprisingly he had never earlier taken part in the firewalking as a devotee. Overwhelmed by fear, he broke a taboo and came back home from the temple to meet his father on the day before the firewalking and pleaded with him to lead the firewalking in his stead. His father refused, and the medium returned to the temple in distress. That night he had a dream, in which he was at the edge of the ditch of burning embers, but was too frightened to tread the fire. Then across the fire he saw a beautiful girl in a yellow robe. She spoke to him kindly, "Why do you fear, my son ?" and led him to the other side of the firewalking pit. The devotees followed him and tried to seize his cane. The medium shouted to them desperately, "You mustn't do that !" With this shouting he was awakened. Thinking that he had completed his task, he asked a temple assistant who was sleeping beside him whether the firewalking had been successful. Seeing that the medium had had a dream, the assistant gently encouraged him, saying, "Do not worry, *cāmi,* you've received Draupadī's grace." From this the medium found the courage (*tempu*) to fulfill his role.

This story, although not exactly an example of possession, clearly shows the precondition for *caṉṉatam,* because he must be in *caṉṉatam* when walking on fire : it is not necessarily caused by an hereditary ability, but selectively by the benevolence of a deity in reaction to one's humble devotion. The divine nature of the possessing agent is beyond question.

In spite of its personal nature and the emphasis on devotion, the ability to achieve *caṉṉatam* is considered as something exclusive to Parandaman and his family (the Paṇṭāram caste), thus it is institutionalised. The Draupadī goddess festival was postponed in 1983, because

Parandaman was polluted after his wife's miscarriage. The villagers discussed whether to postpone the festival or use a substitute for him. The point frequently made by those who wanted to postpone the festival was that only Parandaman had *mantra śakti* (Tam. *mantira catti*), power which originates from the knowledge of *mantra*. Without *mantra śakti* divine power, they thought, would remain dangerous and could not be controlled. The difference between the type of *caṉṉatam* represented by religious specialists like the medium, and the type which is characteristic of ordinary devotees, depends on the possession of *mantra śakti,* which makes the former's *caṉṉatam* more calm. *Mantra śakti* is a necessary, though not a sufficient condition for controlling possession. The ordinary devotee, who has no knowledge of *mantra,* may fall into *caṉṉatam* during worship through the concentration of consciousness on the deity, but such a trance is rarely controlled.

Kumaracami, the Brahman priest in charge of the Draupadī goddess temple, claimed that he could experience *cannaṭam* during his worship of Draupadī, though he admitted that his was momentary, very weak and sporadic. When I asked him why he did not take over the medium's role of Draupadī when the medium was impure, he simply replied that it was not the custom (*vaḷakkam illai*). The other Brahman, who later came to live in Cattiyur, said that he had no *mantra śakti* suitable for Draupadī. In this case, then, power (here *mantra śakti*) and purity (associated with vegetarianism, or the caste ranks of officiants) are not correlated. Nor is divine possession (as far as modest *caṉṉatam* is concerned) explicitly denounced as a custom of the lower castes.[60] Violent possession may be called *caṉṉatam,* too, but the term in these cases is restricted to divine possession experienced at the temples, or during the festivals. In this respect *caṉṉatam,* whether it be controlled or violent, is different from *cāmi āṭutal.*

Pēy piṭittal (demonic possession)

People, who feel fear (*payam*), are liable to be caught by *pēy*s, resulting in demonic possession : *pēy piṭittal* (being caught by an evil spirit) or *pēy aṭittal* (being hit or attacked by an evil spirit). Their possession is inauspicious and troublesome. It is impure, above all, in the sense that demonic possession makes the possessed misbehave : they eat raw fish or dance naked, for example. *Caṉṉatam* provides the medium with power, while demonic possession makes its victims mad and drives them to impure activities.

Caṉṉatam is experienced at rituals in temples, especially by the medium in established village temples (centre), while demonic possession happens to passers-by in deserted places called *kāṭu*. But demonic possession does not necessarily manifest itself in trance, and any kind of misfortune may be attributed to *pēy* (cf. Moffatt 1979 : 241).

Cāmi āṭutal (divine dancing)

In contrast to these two types of possession, *cāmi āṭutal* is rather ambiguous. As I have said, *caṉṉatam* is the condition of controlled or modest trance which occurs on religious occasions after basic purificatory rituals such as bathing. *Cāmi āṭutal* by contrast denotes a sudden and violent trance caused by deities, especially fierce ones, though ordinary devotees may fall into a violent form of trance that is also called *caṉṉatam*. *Cāmi āṭutal* does not always require purificatory rituals, nor does it always occur in temples. The literal meaning of *cāmi āṭutal* is a dance by a deity (*cāmi* means a deity). It is by definition divine possession. What distinguishes it from demonic possession is, however, very subtle. Both make the possessed dance fiercely and shout aloud. In terms of the outward behaviour of the possessed there is little to indicate the kind of possession involved.

To sum up, *caṉṉatam* covers a wide range of possession from momentary bliss to violent trance, but the identity of the possessing agent is beyond question, and the occasion is always a religious one. On the other hand, *cāmi āṭutal* is ambiguous in nature. It appears very similar to demonic possession, and occurs in non-religious contexts ; the possessing agent is a fierce deity whose nature is hardly distinguishiable from a demonic being (see fig. 12).

Types		*Caṉṉatam*	*Cāmi āṭutal*	*Pēy piṭittal*
Possessed person	(priest)	medium	devotee	patient
Possessing agent		god or goddess ←——→		evil spirit
Effect		grace or divine power ←——→		illness
State of purity	pure ←——→			polluted

FIGURE 12. TYPES OF POSSESSION

Ambiguity of the Possessing Agents

In this section I shall now present three examples in order to illuminate the importance of contextual elements, when assessing the identity of the possessing agent.

Mannur, a village across the lagoon, has a Draupadī goddess

temple. Firewalking is held there during the festival dedicated to her. It is normally only male devotees who walk the fire. But, in the 1982 festival, I saw a woman suddenly rush into the fire walking pit in a fit. Her way was blocked by several men, but she resisted them so ferociously that they could not quickly quiet her.

I later asked some of the villagers about the incident. Some told me that she had gone into *cāmi āṭutal,* possessed by Draupadī, as it was the goddess' festival time. One informant said that a *pēy* had caught her, for as a rule women were not allowed to take part in the firewalking. According to him, Draupadī is a benevolent goddess who bestows grace only on devotees. That woman, as she had broken the festival rule, was not considered to be a devotee worthy of receiving divine grace in the form of possession.

The next example shows that different interpretations of possession depend on the relationship of the interpreter to the victim.

When I visited one family whose daughter, I had heard, was suffering from serious possession, her father told me that she had been possessed by Bhadrakālī when she was watching the *karakam* procession and *kummi* dance in front of the temple on the final day of the festival (see chapter 5). At that point Kālī's power is believed to be particularly strong. On this account her possession had nothing to do with an evil spirit.

Later on I asked the exorcist whom the family had consulted. His view was that she had been possessed by an evil spirit called Cuṭalaimāṭan̲ because of her misbehaviour. She had gone to collect firewood near the burial ground (*cettayiṭam* or place of the dead) in a skirt that was stained with menstrual blood. The Cuṭalaimāṭan̲ called her, and she took fright. The interpretation provided by the exorcist is, I think, typical in that he demonstrated his ability to detect some secret fault on the part of the possessed, rather than allocating blame elsewhere as the possessed's family had expected. A further characteristic of exorcist's divination is revealed by the next example.

In this case a girl called Selvi was held to be simultaneously possessed by several supernatural beings.

> Selvi's father, Kantaiya has a fishing ground on lease at Manakkulam on the west coast (north of Cattiyur), but had stopped operations for a few years, as he found it unprofitable and had some difficulty in labour management. When I was staying in the village he was working for a wealthy net-owner. He was an active member of the local UNP (the ruling political party in Sri Lanka) branch, and became the representative of the Cattiyur Gramodaya

Mandalaya in March, 1982 in the aftermath of a dispute the local MP had had with the presiding representative, Sodynathan (see chapter 2). But Kantaiya was dismissed in November of the same year, and Sodynathan was re-elected because Kantaiya was unpopular among the villagers, and was considered as a puppet of the local MP. Unlike Sodynathan, whose father's father was a traditional village chief, and whose father was a retired officer of the Fishery Department, Kantaiya came from an ordinary family. His family was not well off, in spite of his close connection with the local MP.

Cinnanti aged twenty-one, was the third son of a wealthy lagoon fishing family. His eldest brother, who had married out, and lived with his wife's parents, was one of the most promising of the younger, entrepreneurial, net-owners. He had two fishing grounds at Manakkulam and on the east coast, and a lorry for transporting fish. Cinnanti fell in love with Selvi, Kantaiya's eldest daughter aged seventeen. But Cinnanti's family did not agree to his marrying her, mainly because of Kantaiya's eccentric behaviour, which embarrassed many villagers, and his family background. Kantaiya and his wife, however, thought that this marriage would halt their social and financial decline, and conspired in their daughter's elopement with Cinnanti, which took place on 4 January 1982, just after Cinnanti's brothers and kinsmen had migrated to the east coast. The couple stayed in the district capital, Puttalam, for a while, but their hiding place was soon discovered and they had to return to the village. Elopement is not uncommon in Cattiyur, but some people vociferously accused Kantaiya and his wife of collusion in the elopement. But, now that Cinnanti and Selvi had lived together, even though for a short time, Cinnanti's family could not keep refusing their marriage. Registration eventually took place on 31 January, and Cinnanti moved into Kantaiya's house to stay with Selvi, but no proper wedding ceremony was held.

Selvi suddenly started dancing at midnight on 16 March, and an exorcist was sent for. But he failed to calm her down, and she insisted that she stay in the Muttumāri goddess temple. When I went to see her at the temple, she was living in one of the rooms attached to the temple. These rooms are kept for those who are suffering from chicken pox or other diseases believed to be caused and healed by Muttumāri.

When daily worship started, Selvi dashed into the temple building and started shouting. A villager told me that she had been pregnant

> for three months. In trance she was considered to be the Muttumāri goddess herself and was consulted by some villagers who were present. They addressed her as *amman̲* or *ammāḷ* (mother) and she called them *kuñci* (child) in turn. She called a temple priest "*aṭē*," a term of address usually used for boys, and her father "*nī*" ("*nīṅkaḷ*" is usually used for parents). She even told her father to leave her alone, as he was impure (*acuttapākapum*) from drinking all the time. Selvi (or more precisely Muttumāri on her behalf) complained of the misery she had suffered as a result of the elopement: she had not liked her husband at all but was persuaded by her "elder brother" (mother's elder sister's son). She had no proper wedding ceremony, and no *tāli* (wedding necklace, the sign of auspiciousness of married woman). What is worse, she was now pregnant. She then started hitting her abdomen, shouting that she would kill her baby. Her mother quickly stopped her. When the worship was over, she calmed down and returned to the room in the temple precinct.
>
> A few days later, Selvi did not stop screaming even when the temple worship had been completed. The priest therefore recited *mantras* and tied a sacred cord around her neck. She then became completely quiet and left the temple the next morning. She has not suffered since then, and gave birth, just before I left Sri Lanka, in November 1983.

This case would be a good example for a functionalist analysis of possession (e. g. Harper 1963) : a young helpless woman in distress (elopement, pregnancy, no wedding ceremony, and the tense relationships of her father with other villagers) expresses her opinions in public with no hesitation, and scolds those who had brought about her miserable situation, especially her father and husband. Such an act is inconceivable in ordinary life. But my concern here is with the nature of possession and the local interpretation of it, rather than with an explanation which only makes sense to us.

The villagers' opinions on the identity of the possessing agent(s) varied. One told me that Muttumāri, Bhadrakālī and Māṭan̲ were possessing Selvi, another villager enumerated eight deities (including Muttumāri and Bhadrakālī) and two evil spirits. Later on one of the village exorcists told me that it was a *tēvatai*, called Turkkai, who had been responsible for the possession.

Next I shall give their opinions as to the cause of Selvi's possession.

The first goes as follows. The sixteenth of March was the last day of the long temple consecration ritual (*mahākumbhābhiṣeka*) held for the newly renovated Bhadrakālī goddess temple, and a special consecration ritual (*śaṅkhābhiṣeka*) was conducted (see chapter 6). One of the villagers suggested that when Selvi had passed by the temple, she was affected by Bhadrakālī's power, which had been aroused by the *abhiṣeka,* and subsequently attracted the attention of Bhadrakālī's retinue (Tam. *paṭai*), Māṭaṉ and Muttumāri.

The second one refers to a Muttumāri goddess festival (Mācimakam), which had ended on 26 February with her ritual pot (a pot for her temporary abode during the festival) being thrown away in the sea. According to an old woman, immediately after the pot was discarded in the sea, Selvi happened to be passing the temple on her way back from bathing. Dancing back from the sea to her temple, the Muttumāri goddess had hit upon her. Now other deities and evil spirits were also possessing her.

An exorcist's interpretation is more reflective, and touches on a deeper level in the understanding of the causes of possession. He suggested that Selvi had taken some abortive medicines and had had some problems with occasional bleeding, which had attracted Turkkai.

The first two interpretations are interesting because they show a common ambivalent feeling (*payapatti* or "fear and devotion") towards goddesses like Muttumāri and Bhadrakālī, who are liable to possess a young girl if they are "aroused" on special occasions, even though not offended. The other examples of ambiguous possession, by Draupadī (case 1) and Bhadrakālī (case 2) also reveal the same idea that these village goddesses are dangerous during their festivals.

If these interpretations are straightforward, the exorcist's interpretation is intended to reveal unknown facts, which most people would be reluctant to admit. The identification of the possessing agent and of the cause of the possession is part of exorcism, and is crucial for the exorcist's reputation. By carefully choosing Turkkai, an inferior form of Kālī (see chapter 3), as the possessing being, he also indirectly accepted the ambiguity of the goddess, though he did not neglect to point out that it was pollution (blood) which had attracted her, thus pointing a finger at Selvi and her family for their immoral intention to abort her child.

In this section I started with the concept of *bhakti,* then proceeded to various types of possession, and finally the ambiguous nature of the possessing agent. The last point is certainly related to my argument concerning Hindu supernatural beings in the last chapter. I would like to emphasise again the flexibility in the interpretation of ambiguous possession, the recognition of the ambiguous nature of deities in order to underwrite my standpoint that the village festivals are meaningful only if we understand the ambivalent nature of the deities. Next I argue that during votive rituals, *bhakti,* in the form of possession, is frequently recognised

Votive Rituals

If a person is suffering from demonic possession or other troubles, one of his or her close relatives or family members makes a vow to a particular deity, and after the recovery the victim performs a votive ritual in thanksgiving. Votive rituals provide a path through which most of the Hindus participate in village festivals. There are few anthropological analyses of the votive rituals, and of their relationships to the festivals. This section provides basic data of the votive rituals and their symbolism, which is directly concerned with what I call the existential, or personal, dimension of Hindu festivals.

Vows

The two Tamil words, *viratam* and *neṟṟi,* are usually translated as a vow, but they differ in application in some respects. *Viratam* is mainly intended to gain a divine boon (*varam*) by observing an austere ritual, particularly observing vigils or fasts (*nōṉpu*). It is usually performed individually for personal gain, but on certain occasions it may be conducted as part of an annual festival.[61]

The *neṟṟi* ritual (*neṟṟikkaṭaṉ, kaṭaṉ* or debt) is performed in fulfillment of an initial vow to carry it out ; it is a rite of thanksgiving (repaying one's debt to a god). When someone suffers a misfortune, such as a serious illness, accident, business failure, or demonic possession, a family member, or close relative makes a vow (*neṟṟi*) to a particular deity. The patient as a *neṟṟikkāraṉ,* or a votary, performs a particular ritual to "pay off the debt" (*neṟṟikkaṭaṉ kaḻittal*) to the deity, when he recovers. The thanksgiving may be repeated annually, perhaps even by children after the decease of the person previously granted divine aid ; or it may be repeated for just for a few years (the period may be part of the initial vow) to maintain the deity's compassion.[62]

Votive rites should be performed as promised at the outset, and I did not come across any case in which a votary failed or neglected to perform a votive rite. Nevertheless, villagers do not place much emphasis on concepts of divine punishment or curse (*kaṭavuḷ capam, cakuṉam*), or of the deity's displeasure (*teyvakkuṟai*). If he fails to perform a votive rite, the votary runs the risk of losing divine protection and facing a more dangerous situation, but the relationship between votary and deity is not conceived as existing on a strictly reciprocal basis. Indeed, the deity's generosity is considered as positive evidence that he is not involved in the mundane transactions which dominate human relationships. But this is not always the case and the point is subtle.

Villagers take vows for various reasons. Here I present basic data on the reasons votaries were engaging in certain popular votive rites during the Draupadī goddess festival. The rites concerned are *pāṟkāvaṭi* for men, *pāṟcempu* for women.[63] They are of an ecstatic nature, but are not considered especially difficult to perform (see below). Correspondingly, the reasons given for their performance are not especially serious. Votaries are not always forthcoming about the reasons for making vows, especially when they involve serious matters, so the data should be treated with caution. Table 10 does give a general picture of the reasons for making vows, but it

TABLE 10
REASONS FOR MAKING VOWS

Reason	Male	Female	Age				Total
			18+		0~17		
			Male	Female	Male	Female	
Health (not specified)	24	32	13	14	11	18	56
Accident	7	1	6	1	1	0	8
Disease (general)	9	4	7	0	2	4	13
Chicken pox	4	3	4	1	0	2	7
Operation	3	3	3	2	0	1	6
Grief, Anxiety	2	0	1	0	1	0	2
Fertility*	2	1	0	0	2	1	3
Pilgrimage**	2	1	0	0	2	1	3
Labour Pain	0	8	0	8	0	0	8
Litigation	0	2	0	2	0	0	2
Other	3	0	3	0	0	0	3
Unknown	2	3	2	3	0	0	5
Total	58	58	39	31	19	27	116

*Two wanted a male child, and one a child of either sex.

**These pilgrimages were undertaken because wishes for children were realised.

is not exhaustive. Other reasons could be added to it, such as anxiety over examinations, employment, fishing, safety during a long journey or seasonal migration, marriage and other life crises.

Kinds of Votive Rituals

As with place and form, the occasion for votive rites varies. They sometimes take place over ten years after the original vow was made. I received information about the extent to which the rites were continued from 104 out of the 116 votaries at the Draupadī goddess festival. Their original vows had been made about 3.8 years earlier on average, ranging from 4 months to 16 years, though many votaries may have already performed rites several times by the time I interviewed them.

Although small-scale rites are conducted on Tuesdays and Fridays, both of which are sacred to the Hindus, most votive rites are performed during the festivals at village or pilgrimage temples. Thus, it is sometimes difficult to distinguish votive (individual and voluntary) rites from non-votive (obligatory) rites in the festivals. For example, a minor ritual of offering called *arcanā* (Tam. *aruccaṉai* or more commonly *celavu* or expenses) is a personal rite, but those who make an offering at the festival rarely have a clear reason for it.

Vows are made on behalf of the afflicted by their senior relatives, especially by the mother and mother's brother. I call such a person a vow-maker as distinguished from a votary. As table 11 clearly shows, the mother is the main vow-maker who makes a vow on behalf of her child.

Vows to a deity may be a promise to cook *poṅkal* (rice gruel) or to build a temple. The kind of observance promised depends, to some extent, on the deity concerned, and might be one of the following : an *arcanā* offering ; an offering of some coin (*paṇam ceytal*) ; an offering of *poṅkal* on Tuesday and Friday ; an offering in the shape of parts of the human body made from silver sheet (*neṟṟicāmaṉ*) ; a hair offering ; the action of rolling around the temple building ; the action of carrying two milk pots under a decorated pole (*pāṟkāvaṭi*), carrying a milk pot on the head (*pāṟcempu*), or carrying a burning pan (*akkiṉiccaṭṭi*) with both hands, sometimes with skewers pierced through one's cheeks, lips and tongue (*vēṟkāvaṭi*) or with hooks in the flesh of the back (*tōḷikkāvaṭi*) ; firewalking (*tīmiti*) ; and the performance of other rituals, such as *abhiṣeka,* feasting (*kuḷirttal*), offering a wedding necklace (*tāli*) to the goddess, and so on. As we will see later, other popular vows include one to play the role of a mystical being such as *cūrapuli* (a guardian of Bhadrakālī) in her annual festival, or as epic heroes in the Draupadī goddess festival. These actors

TABLE 11
VOW-MAKERS

Vow-maker*	Number(%)
M	68(58.6%)
MB	12(10.3%)
MM	3(2.6%)
MF	3(2.6%)
F	2(1.7%)
WF	2(1.7%)
eZ	2(1.7%)
HZ	1(0.9%)
M, F, MB	1(0.9%)
Unknown	22(19.0%)
Total	116

Source : Census conducted at the Draupadi goddess festival in 1982.

* F = father ; M = mother ; B = brother ; eZ = elder sister ; H = husband ; W = wife. MB should be read as mother's brother.

frequently experience possession by the epic heroes, especially when there is an act of killing (see chapter 7).

Generally speaking, the more serious the ailment and the more difficult it is to put right, the greater is the scale of a votive rite. But the scale of the rite also depends on the economic condition of the votary. The rich tend to perform more expensive rites than do the poor for the same cause. The rich villager may visit pilgrimage temples or even travel to India. The poor must be satisfied with merely worshipping at the village temple ; or, if the matter is very serious, resort to ecstatic rituals involving self-mutilation.

Symbolism of the Votive Ritual

Votive rituals are full of sacrificial symbolism. Consider a simple example. A man rolls around the temple, fully outstretched, holding a coconut and sprigs of margosa leaves over his head. After he has completed a round of the temple, he smashes the coconut on a round stone in front of the temple. The rolling is interpreted to be equivalent to a period of *dīkṣā* (liminal period of Vedic sacrifice) ; the coconut is sacrificed as a substitute for himself. The coconut contains milk symbolising votary's evil aspect. When it is broken into pieces, the milk is flown out, and he becomes purified (see below for details). In the following pages I shall give more detailed interpretations of *pāṟkāvaṭi* and *arcanā*.

One of the most popular ecstatic votive rites in Tamil culture is the *pāṟkāvaṭi* (*pāl* or milk, *kāvu* or pole, *āṭi* or dancing). This rite reveals the rich symbolism of ecstatic votive rituals. The *kāvaṭi* is a three foot long pole, shaped as an arch, and decorated with peacock feathers, limes, and streamers of paper. In the case of the *pāṟkāvaṭi*, two pots containing milk mixed with turmeric are tied to the pole (pl. 8). This is exclusive to men. The female counterpart is *pāṟcempu*, that is the carrying of *pāl* (milk) in a *cempu* (metal pot), covered with margosa leaves, on the head.

It is observed especially during the Draupadī goddess festival in Cattiyur. Votaries take a bath in the early morning at sea and gather at the

PLATE 8. *PĀṞKĀVAṬI*

Muttumāri goddess temple, where, with the help of family members, they decorate the *kāvaṭi* and perform worship. When worship to Murukaṉ starts at the temple, some of the votaries carry their *kāvaṭi* and begin shaking in a trance. They then go out and walk to the Pārtasārati temple, where they receive sacred ash from the medium and collapse (see chapter 7 for a more detailed description).

The *pāṟkāvaṭi* is primarily a votive rite for Murukaṉ, Śiva's second son, as explained in the following myth from the Palani Murukaṉ temple.

> Agastya (a sage, who went to Mt. Kailāsa to worship Śiva) was given two hills, Śivagiri and Śaktigiri, as sites of worship, with permission to take them south. One day he met the demon Iṭumpaṉ, who had survived the slaughter, by Murukaṉ, of the hosts of Cūr. Since all the other demons had reached heaven by virtue of having been killed by Murukaṉ, Iṭumpaṉ spent his time performing their *śrāddha* (funeral) rites. Seeing he was of good nature, Agastya sent him to bring the hills. When Iṭumpaṉ arrived at the hills, a *kāvaṭi* (the shoulder pole) appeared, and the eight serpents which support the world took the form of ropes so he could tie the hills to support. In this way he lifted the mountains and carried them southwards until he reached Āviṉaṉkuṭi (Paḻani). Suddenly he felt faint ; he put the hills down and rested, but when he tried to lift them again he could not move them.
>
> Puzzled and sorrowful, he climbed one of the hills, and there he noticed a child under a *kurā* tree. "Go away," he said to the child, and added that he was a murderous demon. "This is my home," said the child ; "pick it up if you can !" "You may be small in size, but you tell big lies," cried Iṭumpaṉ as he leapt at the boy. But the child was Murukaṉ, playing his games, he killed Iṭumpaṉ at a stroke. When Iṭumpaṉ's wife Iṭumpi heard of her husband's death, she prayed to Murukaṉ, who revived him. Agastya came to worship Murukaṉ at the spot, and he ordered the demon to serve Murukaṉ there for his salvation. (Shulman 1980 : 48-49 ; cf. Ayyar 1920 : 156-59 ; Babb 1976 : 6 ; Clothey 1978 : 119).

According to Clothey, the story goes on as follows :

> Iṭampaṉ (*sic*) was restored to life and to the service of the youth, who, it proved, was Murukaṉ himself. Iṭampaṉ asked to stand ever at the god's portal and requested that whoever should offer vows to

> Murukaṉ bearing a *kāvaṭi* should be specially blessed. Both requests were granted (Clothey 1978 : 119).

> (As a result) All devotees who bring the *kāvaṭi* and worship atop the hill (of Palani) are believed to be re-enacting the worship of Iṭampaṉ whose hostility and malevolence and simple-mindedness were reportedly taken from him in that act of worship (Clothey 1983 : 39, parentheses mine).

The demon was killed by Murukaṉ, but later revived and became Murukaṉ's devotee and the guardian at his temple in Palani. Votaries who carry *kāvaṭi* poles, therefore, reenact the experience of the demonic devotee, Iṭumpaṉ ; that is, the process of a votary becoming a humble devotee through death, or through getting rid of his evil aspect.

Kāvaṭi is typically decorated with peacock feathers, the peacock being Murukaṉ's vehicle. Its relation to Murukaṉ is described in a myth from the Tiruchendur Murukaṉ temple.

> Murukaṉ and his hosts are said to have come here (Tiruchendur in Tamilnadu) in pursuit of Sūrapadma (*sic*), by then deprived of much of his army. Seeing the battle go against him, Sūrapadma entered the ocean where he became a vast, fiery red mango tree spreading expansively underwater. With his *vēl* (lance) Murukaṉ split the tree which therewith turned into a peacock and a cock (Clothey 1978 : 121-22, parentheses mine).

> Murukaṉ tamed them both by his benevolence. He then mounted the peacock and rode on it around the world. The god adopted the cock as the emblem on his banner (ibid., 83).

Thus, when a votary carries a *kāvaṭi* decorated with peacock feathers, he becomes a peacock, Murukaṉ's vehicle. The votary again enacts a process of transformation : the demon becomes a humble devotee of Murukaṉ. A small, lance-shaped skewer is sometimes pierced through the votary's flesh, harking back to Murukaṉ's demonic enemies who were killed by his mighty lance.

In the transformations of both Iṭumpaṉ and Śūrapadma the symbolism of sacrifice is evident. The sacrificial victim is described as the god's vehicle or mount. Becoming a vehicle is a typical expression of submission to a deity (ibid., 41). Possession, sacrifice, and becoming a vehicle or a guardian for the god all involve the transformation through total surrender of self to a divine being.

Votive rituals which entail neither possession, nor self-torture, also express self-sacrifice in its broader sense. Next I shall analyse the symbolism of *arcanā* offerings.

During worship, the priest takes private offerings, called *arcanā,* and consecrates them after the *naivedya* (public offerings). By contrast to *naivedya, arcanā* is offered for private thanksgiving. It usually consists of a coconut, a bunch of ripe bananas, on which five lighted joss-sticks stand, ten to twenty betel leaves and areca nuts (*tāmbūla,* Tam. *tāmpūlam*), some money, and other items necessary for rituals : incense powder and cakes of camphor. They are placed on a plate. After reciting the offerer's name, and waving a camphor flame, the priest consecrates the *arcanā* by sprinkling water and flower petals over it. He then breaks the coconut into two, and returns one of the halves (*kāḷañci*) to the plate. He also removes some of the ripe bananas, betel leaves, areca nuts, and all of the other ritual items. In exchange, he puts some sacred ash on the plate. When the worship is over, the priest returns what remains of the *arcanā* (the half-coconut, the rest of the bananas, betel leaves and areca nuts) along with the sacred ash to the offerer as *prasāda,* consecrated leftovers.

Generally speaking, these offerings are considered as substitutes, and are "destroyed" as sacrificial victims in the stead of the offerer. Among these offerings coconuts seem significant. Elaborate explanations about the halving of a coconut were given to me by the priest and the villagers. Whether the coconut is halved or smashed into pieces, the act is called *tēṅkāyppali* (*tēṅkāy* or coconut, *pali* or sacrifice). Coconut sacrifice is a standard ritual act, which is explained by the myth that Śiva used a coconut as a substitute for his own self-sacrifice. The coconut has three spots which are associated with Śiva's three eyes. Elsewhere they are said to be the eyes and mouth of a man, or the coconut is simply described as a human head (Gray 1979 : 93 ; Oppert 1893 : 461 ; Uma Shankari 1980 : 342-43). A coconut sacrifice thus directly suggests human sacrifice.

When the coconut is bisected, its milk flows out, and its white inside flesh can be seen. The former symolises *mummalam* meaning three evils, fetters to spiritual liberation, or, particularly, union with Śiva, in the South Indian Śaivite tradition. They are *āṇavamalam, kāṉmikamalam* and *māyaimalam,* or arrogance, vanity and lust respectively. By contrast the white flesh is the pure and innocent nature of the soul. The offerer destroys his own evil aspects and attains a purer ritual status through the coconut sacrifice, which is a symbolic self-sacrifice.[64]

To sum up, votive rituals exhibit both worldly and transcendental dimensions. Motivations for votive rituals are directed towards the worldly gains, but the underlying ideas and symbolism are more profound and concerned with the self-negation and otherworldly salvation. As the myths of Murukaṉ clearly show, it is not difficult to recognise *bhakti* elements, especially in ecstatic votive rituals.

Conclusion

In this chapter I considered several topics, more or less related to the personal dimension of the religious life: the concept of *bhakti*; types of possession; and votive rituals.

The festivals do not remain external to each participant. They are subjectified in some way; they become of deep personal concern to the participants. Villagers are not forced to perform various, often bizarre, rituals in the festivals: they have personal reasons for their involvement. We would fail to grasp the nature of the festivals in their totality if we did not pay more attention to the dimension of personal commitment. This does not mean that we should reduce the festivals, which are above all social phenomena, to personal motivation. Rather it means that we must see social and individual dimensions as being interrelated through various kinds of rituals, particularly those concerning religious vows. In my view, personal rituals expressing one's *bhakti* are not independent of the greater framework of festivals, and should be placed in the context of village festivals. Without the personal dimension of votive rituals the festivals would amount to mere compulsory rites and performances of passing concern to the participants. Conversely, without the collective dimension represented in the festival as a whole, personal affliction would not be dealt with, and the afflicted would remain isolated from the rest of the society. Votive rites serve to re-integrate the afflicted into the ideal world constructed in the festival. Only when we analyse votive rituals in relation to the festivals, can we reach a firm understanding of their meanings. In the following chapters structure of village festivals will be examined.

CHAPTER FIVE

ENTERTAINING THE EPIDEMIC GODDESS

This chapter is devoted to a detailed description and symbolic analysis of a village festival for Bhadrakālī, in which ecstatic rituals are predominant. This festival is, in my view, a typical non-Brahmanical festival. First, basic data on the temple, the deities present there, and those involved in the festival are given, then each of the festival rituals is described and interpreted. Finally, I analyse the festival in terms of a transformation of the goddess, from an ambivalent and dangerous one, to a benevolent one, and argue how such a cosmological transformation may be meaningful to each participant, and how it is articulated with the political dimension of the village.

I shall give a brief overview of the festival here, before going into a detailed description. On the first day, a medium, who is possessed by Bhadrakālī during the festival, makes three ritual pots. One of them, the *karakam* pot, is paraded around the village. On the third, fifth, and seventh days of the festival the medium goes into mild trance and starts going around the village with the pot on his head. This procession is interpreted as the intrusion of an epidemic. On the tenth day a goat is sacrificed in front of the Bhadrakālī goddess temple. With this sacrifice Bhadrakālī is propitiated and her violent and feverish character is transformed into a benevolent one. Then the ritual pots made on the first day are discarded. Finally Bhadrakālī's festival image is taken out for a village procession. It symbolises a triumphant occasion after the epidemic has disappeared.

Introduction to the Bhadrakālī Goddess Festival

The Origin and Development of the Temple

Here I would like to give a story of the origin of the Bhadrakālī temple. It is said that an outbreak of cholera (*petinōy*) occurred in Cattiyur in 1850, which was so serious that villagers thought they might have to abandon the village for good. One day an old man called Kottakkilavan was possessed by Bhadrakālī. Bhadrakālī told the villagers through Kottakkilavan's mouth to stay, but they were doubtful about the possessing deity's identity, as an evil spirit, pretending to be a deity, is often said to possess a villager. Sensing their scepticism, the possessed man asked the villagers to fetch some sea water. They did so, and the water suddenly blazed up in front of them like an oil lamp. It kept burning for ten days. The villagers, astonished at the strength of Bhadrakālī's power, decided to stay on in the village and asked her what they should do. Bhadrakālī ordered them to make a small hut and to worship her in the form of a ritual pot with bunches of margosa (*vēmpu, Azadirachta indica*) leaves, in which she would reside. Then the cholera would be dispelled. To the villagers' further surprise, the margosa leaves bloomed : the burning water and the blooming margosa are believed to have been caused by divine grace or power and both are described as miraculous (*putumaiyāka*). They provided strong evidence of Bhadrakālī's presence, which eventually dispelled the fierce disease and saved the whole village.[65]

This story tells us the ambivalent nature of Bhadrakālī, which is by no means unique to her. She has a close relationship to fever and tends to possess somebody. The story does not tell clearly, but, the disease could be considered to be caused by Bhadrakālī, and be an expression of her anger toward the villagers. Worshipping and entertaining her is an important means of calming her down and consequently dispelling the fever.

The original clay temple was rebuilt in 1853 and enlarged with bricks and stone in 1878. The ritual pot was replaced by a stone image sculpted in India in 1891. The temple underwent a series of repairs for twelve years from 1918 to 1929. When I arrived in the field, the second largest restoration was under way. A temporary hut was built on the northern side of the temple in 1980, where the images of Bhadrakālī, Gaṇeśa, and her lion-mount were stored, and where worship was conducted every Tuesday and Friday. The restoration was completed in January 1983, when the temple consecration ritual was conducted by a group of Jaffna Brahman priests.

The Sacred Topography of the Temple

The location of the Bhadrakālī temple on the seaward side of the main road is significant. The temple stands at the southern edge of the narrowest point of the isthmus between the sea and Mannur Lake (lagoon) on which the village is located (see fig. 3). This point is called *aṟuva*. In Tamil *aṟu* means "cut off". For when there is heavy rain, this point is breached, as happened in 1981 and 1984. The real name of the village Cattiyur derives from a Tamil word meaning "to break."

Less than a quarter of a mile long, the *aṟuva* presents a rather mysterious scene : a beautiful and quiet view of the lagoon on the one hand, and a high sand bar with the tips of waves visible over it on the other. The villagers feel insecure when passing by this deserted place at night.

In the 1981 flood a man drowned at the *aṟuva*, and his death was said to have been a human sacrifice (*narapali*) to Bhadrakālī, bringing the end of the flood. In this sense the *aṟuva* is closely related to death, and the temple stands at the entrance to the watery underworld or the world of death. It should be recalled that the origin myth of the temple itself is related to death. This death, however, is not so much concerned with the end of, but rather, with the beginning of life, that is, sacrificial death.

More generally, several temple myths in Tamilnadu suggest that the temples survive cosmic flood (Shulman 1980 : 75 ; cf. Good 1985 : 152-53). After the flood appears the new world and era. The location of the Bhadrakālī temple may also have such cosmological connotations : it is immune to the flood or breach at the *aṟuva*. In other words, the temple transcends the cosmic cycle of life and death. It is a source of new life. The temple is a place where death and rebirth stand side by side, and where death transforms itself into life. It is not difficult to understand why the central ritual of the festival at the temple of the Bhadrakālī goddess is blood sacrifice. Sacrifice is a ritual means to obtain new life.

Divine Beings

Here I will discuss in more detail Bhadrakālī and some of the other deities present in the Bhadrakālī temple and their relationships with each other.

Bhadrakālī is a particularly ferocious form of Kālī goddess, although *bhadra* in Sanskrit literally means "auspicious," and the beautiful sculptures at the gate tower represent her mounted on a lion, fighting against demons.[66]

Bhadrakālī is one of the main female deities in the Hindu

pantheon, and is often considered to be Śiva's consort. More generally she is a form of Śakti (the female principle). In Cattiyur, Bhadrakālī is the second daughter of Śiva and Śakti (here Pārvatī), the eldest being the goddess Māri. Bhadrakālī was born from the third eye of Śiva, to help Subrahmaṇya (Murukaṉ), as his chief warrior, in the fight against a monstrous demon called Tāraka.

As the local legend of the Cattiyur Bhadrakālī temple suggests, Bhadrakālī came to save the villagers from the cholera. She is a guardian of the village (*ūrkkāval*). In this sense, Bhadrakālī is the village goddess. But two other goddesses in Cattiyur, Draupadī and Muttumāri, are no less important from the villagers' point of view.[67]

Bhadrakālī is an ambivalent goddess. First, I describe her positive aspects. She is a so-called Mother Goddess (*ammaṉ*) to whom the villagers are children (*kuñci*). She is also the goddess of fishing, and the fishermen work under her protection while they are at sea. Indeed they say they sometimes come across her walking on the sea. She is also worshipped in the form of a *pātai*-boat. A cock is sacrificed, and sari and necklace are offered to the boat at the beginning of the fishing season. In the same way that a village goddess in an agrarian society is closely related to the fertility of land, the goddess of this fishing community is responsible for the fertility of the sea.

On the other hand, Bhadrakālī is generally reputed to be the most powerful and dangerous goddess among the village deities. Pregnant women avoid passing her temple at night, especially on Friday night, when Bhadrakālī is more active than usual. This is because the pregnant women are vulnerable to the divine power. Though she herself is not in any sense evil, she has a close relationship with fierce deities such as Bhairava, Vīrabhadra or Māṭaṉ. It is a common belief that if a person passes by the Bhadrakālī temple after having eaten meat curry, they will be captured by Bhadrakālī's retinue or by Bhadrakālī herself. Sudden possession by Bhadrakālī or other goddesses is called *cāmi āṭutal* and is distinguished from demonic possession by evil spirits. If enraged, however, Bhadrakālī is ready to dispatch evil spirits to catch villagers.

Bhadrakālī is the main deity presiding over exorcism rituals, which starts with the setting up of a *kumpam* (ritual pot) representing Bhadrakālī. This suggests that she has close relationships with evil forces, because generally speaking, those who have similar but stronger power can control and dispel the evil spirits.[68] As has been seen in the account of the origin of her temple, she is ambiguously involved with epidemic disease. Like Muttumāri, she herself is said to suffer from epidemics, but sends it to the villagers when angered.

Gaṇeśa is the elephant headed first son of Śiva. He should be the first object of worship whenever a ritual is performed. He removes obstacles, but he is also jealous. Gaṇeśa is a deity of boundaries and a gatekeeper. The temple has two Gaṇeśa shrines inside. The one outside marks the sacred space of the temple, and the one inside marks off the sacredness of the sanctum sanctorum and the adjacent room from the rest of the temple.

Bhairava is a popular gatekeeper whose mount is a dog. He is said to be a fierce manifestation of Śiva. He is identical to Kataṉ or Māṭaṉ, the guardian deity of the cremation ground, or even to Vīrabhadra, who is again a fierce manifestation of Śiva or the general of his army. Bhairava is also found as the replacement for Bhadrakālī as the main deity in exorcism rituals.

Pēcci also has a shrine inside the Bhadrakālī temple. I was unable to glean much information about her. She too is said to be a daughter of Śiva and Śakti, and a younger sister of Bhadrakālī. Pēcci is ferocious, but plays a role in women's fertility, as is often the case with minor female deities. Some informants told me that they would bring their first children to her shrine in the Bhadrakālī temple. Although I have never seen this done in Cattiyur, this is a common act at other small shrines of female deities.

Main Participants

During my stay in the village the priest of the Bhadrakālī goddess temple was Muttaiya's first son, Cokkalingam, who was then succeeded by Kulantaivel, Cokkalingam's younger sister's husband, in spring 1983. During the festival, however, Parandaman plays a primary role as an incarnation of Bhadrakālī. He also serves as priest in the course of the festival. Mediumship and priesthood are not clearly differentiated at the Bhadrakālī goddess festival.

There are two attendants, or guards, of Bhadrakālī, who go into trance more dramatically than Bhadrakālī's medium. They are both called *cūrapuli* (it literally means "heroic tiger"). They follow the medium during the festival. One is possessed by Kataṉ and the other by Bhairava, but these gods are identical and the distinction is of little significance. They hold a sword (*vāḷ*) and a trident (*śūla,* Tam. *cūlāyutam*) as their respective weapons (*āyudha,* Tam. *āyutam*), which are covered with margosa leaves. The two *cūrapuli*s wear margosa leaves around their waists, and smear their upper bodies with sacred ash, sandalwood paste and red powder. These serve as precautions against the heat of divine power generated through violent possession. From the following descriptions it will be clearer that playing a role of *cūrapuli* is a kind of votive ritual.

In 1982 there was only one *cūrapuli* at the festival. He was a twenty-eight-year-old lagoon fisherman, and a temporary beach seine labourer, named Kaliyappan. His father had suffered from a serious disease about twelve years earlier, his father's elder sister vowed to Bhadrakālī, on the sick man's behalf, that he would perform the role of *cūrapuli* for ten years if he recovered. When he became better, he fulfilled his elder sister's vow for the seven years from 1975 to 1981. But then he stopped, and passed on the role to his first son, Kaliyappan. In 1983, however, neither Kaliyappan nor his father took part in the festival because of the pollution caused by a relative's death, and two other fishermen took over the role of *cūrapuli*.

One of these was Kataresan, a twenty-five-year-old beach seine labourer, who had been possessed before and was known to be capable of being caught by Bhadrakālī or other deities. His story goes as follows :

> On a Tuesday in January 1982, Kataresan ate mutton curry with savory rice in his relative's house. He had to leave for a fishing camp on the east coast early next morning. He cycled to Adipetti at midnight to fetch some new clothes for the migration. When passing by the Bhadrakālī temple, he heard some music inside the building. He felt fear, but managed to run away from the place and reached his relative's house, where he started dancing in front of several paintings of Hindu deities. His mother told me that he had not noticed that some unknown deities collectively called *kulateyvam*[69] had called him on his way to Adipetti. He was sent back to his house in Cattiyur, where he was staying with his parents. He again started dancing at home, and an exorcist was sent for. He put ash on Kataresan's forehead and calmed him down. But next morning, Kataresan again danced so violently that another exorcist was called. Suddenly the possessing being revealed itself as Bhadrakālī, complaining to the villagers that she had to live on the sea while her temple was under construction, and asking them to complete it promptly.[70] Kataresan's mother vowed that when the temple restoration was complete, he would play the role of *cūrapuli*.

The other *cūrapuli* of 1983, named Kattirkaman, only became possessed at festival time. He is a raft fisherman and a petty fish trader, but is very devotional, visiting various religious centres. His family had suffered several setbacks and he himself had an accident at sea in 1982.

Kattirkaman took part in the festival as a result of vow-making.

Various other people are involved in the festival. A Washerman provides white cloths for the canopy ceiling, for covering offerings and so on. Three Sinhala drummers from Munnesvaram and a musician group of the Karaiyar called *pacanayār* (literally those who sing *bhajana* or devotional songs) play the drums and cymbals (*tāram*). There are also two village temple assistants (*kōyil vēlaikkāraṉ*) of the Karaiyar caste. They do much of the rough labouring work : carrying water, digging holes for setting up poles and so forth. Being a village temple, the Bhadrakālī temple is controlled by the Cattiyur Hindu Temple Administrative Committee, the president of which plays the crucial role of the *ūr upayakkāraṉ* or village patron of the festival. It is, however, the net-owners who meet most of the expenses of the festival.

Description and Analysis of the Festival

The following description is based on my observations of the Bhadrakālī goddess festival from 7 to 16 September in 1983. The festival was held for ten days in the month of *Āvaṇi* (August-September), the season when Bhadrakālī originally manifests herself to the Cattiyur villagers and saved the village from the epidemic disease. I shall describe and interpret each ritual of the festival in turn, and then give an analysis of the overall structure of the festival (see table 12).

The first day has the setting-up of ritual pots at about 8 : 00 p. m., followed by worship.

The medium leaves the temple for the central point of the *aṟuva*, carrying a two foot long cane (*pirampu*) and an empty brass pot. The two *cūrapulis* follow him carrying a sword and a trident, together with a band of the Karaiyar caste musicians and temple assistants. At the centre of the *aṟuva*, the medium indicates three points with the cane, where the temple assistants should dig holes. Water soon seeps into them, and they eventually join into one big hole. The joining of these holes stands for the confluence of the three sacred rivers in India : Gaṅgā, Yamunā and Sarasvatī. The medium then purifies the pot with incense, puts a one rupee coin into it and uses a ladle to scoop water up from the hole three times. One of the assistants fills the pot with the water. The medium then pours some consecrated temple water into the pot, and places margosa leaves in it. He continues to purify the pot and the two weapons with incense.

They return to the temple, but again go out to the seashore, leaving the *karakam*, the cane and two weapons behind. This time the

TABLE 12
THE BHADRAKĀLĪ GODDESS FESTIVAL SCHEDULE

Date	Time (approximate)	Ritual
1	19 : 30	setting up *karkam* and *kumpam* (pots)
	21 : 00	worship
2	11 : 00	worship
	19 : 30	worship
3	9 : 00	*karakam* procession and worship
	19 : 30	worship
4	11 : 00	worship
	19 : 30	worship
5	10 : 00	*karakam* procession and worship
	19 : 30	worship
6	11 : 00	worship
	19 : 30	worship
7	10 : 00	*karakam* procession and worship
	19 : 30	worship
8	9 : 00	votive *akkiṉiccaṭṭi* (fire pan) and worship
	20 : 00	*karakam* procession (*kummi* dance) and worship
9	9 : 00	*akkiṉiccaṭṭi* procession
	10 : 00	*karakam* procession and worship
	19 : 30	worship
	23 : 00	blood sacrifice
10	9 : 00	guarding the village
	9 : 30	rice gruel (*poṅkal*) cooking and *arcanā* offering
	10 : 30	pouring hot turmeric water
	11 : 00	blood sacrifice
	11 : 30	cock impalement
	12 : 00	worship
	16 : 30	discarding *karakam* and *kumpam* pots in the sea
	17 : 00	giving medicine
	18 : 30	village procession
	23 : 00	Bhairava worship

medium takes two earthen pots and fills them with sea water. One is called *māvilai* (mango leaves) *kumpam* or pot ; the other *vēppilai* (margosa leaves) *kumpam,* referring back to the burning water and blooming margosa of the original legend. These two pots are kept in the sanctum sanctorum until the festival is over. The *karakam* is placed at the entrance of the sanctum sanctorum, and *cūrapulis*' weapons are left standing in the flagstaff socket.[71]

After the setting up of the ritual pots, the medium starts by worshipping Gaṇeśa at the shrine outside the temple gate. He then proceeds to the Gaṇeśa shrine inside the temple, going on to the stone image of Bhadrakālī in the sanctum sanctorum, then Pēcci goddess outside it, Bhairava, Kālī's vehicle—the lion—and the *balipīṭha* (Tam. *palipīṭam*) or sacrificial altar. The medium offers one rice ball on the *balipīṭha.* He enters the sanctum sanctorum once more and conducts *pañcāratti,* waving clockwise seven flames of camphor. The rite ends at 11 : 30 p.m.

The pot has various symbolic meanings, but what seems essential is that it symbolises a womb or a female body. The pot full of water suggests the very idea of fertile womb. Following this interpretation, the water of the pot can be considered amniotic fluid while the margosa leaves in it are symbol of the vital power rising from it. The pot is thus a more suitable symbol for a goddess than a god, although pots can represent gods, too.

In this case, both *karakam* and *kumpams* can be conceived of as temporary abodes for Bhadrakālī. They say that during the festival Bhadrakālī grows up in the pots. Her divine energy, which was so strong that it kept sea water burning for ten days and caused the margosa branches to blossom in the original story, increases in these pots. Furthermore, according to one villager, mango leaves represent Śiva, while margosa leaves represent Śakti (Śiva's consort). This explanation fits in with the remarks that Bhadrakālī is a daughter of Śiva and Śakti.

Next I would like to consider the relationships among these pots, weapons and images. The placing of the *kumpams*, *karakam* and weapons inside the temple indicates a hierarchy of values. The temple constitutes a sacred space distinct from the village. The temple is further differentiated into three internal spaces according to degrees of sacredness. First, there is the innermost room (*garbhagṛha,* Tam. *mūlastāṉam*, or sanctum sanctorum), where the stone image (*mūlamūrti*, Tam. *mūlamūrtti*) of the main deity is located, and which only the priest can enter. Next there is a room called *ardhamaṇḍapa,* where women are not allowed to enter. The rest of the temple is accessible to all except the impure.

The *karakam* pot is placed at the entrance of the sanctum sanctorum, while the *kumpam* pots are kept inside it. The *karakam* serves primarily to represent Bhadrakālī in the procession, and the *kumpam* pots are given priority over it. Bhadrakālī is brought from the sea or water-world, and grows up in the *kumpams*. As her divine power gradually flows out, it is stored in the sacred water in the *karakam* pot. The weapons, used by the *cūrapulis*, are placed in front of the lion, Bhadrakālī's mount, close to the entrance. Their proximity to the lion is suggestive of the *cūrapulis*' relationship to Bhadrakālī. They are submissive, obedient devotees, but like the lion they are not entirely free from animality (*puli* means "tiger").

There are normally two kinds of image of the main deity at Hindu temples. One is a fixed (usually stone) idol in the sanctum sanctorum, and the other is a portable image (*utsavamūrti,* Tam. *uccavamūrtti* or festival image) used in the festival procession. Functionally, the *kumpam* and the *karakam* correspond to these two kinds of image. The *karakam* is placed in the same room as the festival image, while the *kumpams* are kept in the sanctum sanctorum. As is the case with the festival and fixed images, the *karakam* and *kumpam* are respectively movable and fixed. But whilst the mobile festival image represents the ordered aspect of the goddess, the *karakam* pot represents her more active, or ecstatic nature. This nature can be called the lower form of the goddess, as opposed to the higher form represented by a stone image (Frasca 1990 : 137; Fuller 1988 : 24-27; Moffatt 1979 : 252-66). In fact, the presence of the *karakam* and *kumpam* (and the *cūrapulis*' weapons) marks the special nature of the festival time, when Bhadrakālī's active power stirs in the everyday life of the village.

The second day has no special ritual, but worship is conducted in the morning and evening.

On the third day the *karakam* pot procession starts from the Bhadrakālī goddess temple and goes to the Muttumāri goddess temple in Adipetti, following the main bus route from Cattiyur to Adipetti. It then heads for the Pārtasārati temple, going past the Bhadrakālī temple. Finally, the medium and the other people return to the Bhadrakālī goddess temple and attend the daily worship.

Before the procession, the medium and *cūrapulis* bathe in the sea and in a temple well, and put on clean clothes. They tie margosa leaves around themselves, and smear ash, sandalwood paste and red powder on their bodies. The medium enters the sanctum sanctorum, with the two *cūrapulis*,[72] and, after the smoke from the incense that he burns has filled the room, the latter two jump out from the inner sanctum, shouting, shaking, and jumping around in front of their weapons. The medium remains inside, holding a cane in front of his chest. Gradually he himself starts to sway. Finally, his whole body shakes, indicating *caṉṉatam* (divine possession). The devotees in the temple shout "Arohara!" The medium then comes out of the sanctum sanctorum and puts the *karakam* on his head, supporting it with his left hand while holding the cane in his right. The medium walks to the temple gate, where the *cūrapulis* wait impatiently for the medium. Carrying their weapons, they join the medium and circumambulate the temple. The medium and the *cūrapulis*, following the Sinhala drummers and Cattiyur musicians, head for the Muttumāri temple in Adipetti. Various devotees and members of the Hindu Temple Administrative Committee follow behind (pl. 9).

PLATE 9. *KARAKAM* POT PROCESSION

At the Muttumāri goddess temple, a priest burns camphor inside the shrine and brings it to the medium.[73] He takes sacred ash from the plate and gives some to the *cūrapulis*, as a sign of cooling and blessing. The performance is repeated at the Pārtasārati temple. This *karakam* pot procession is held to pay homage to the two other main goddesses in Cattiyur (cf. Good 1985 : 131).

Although the medium and the *cūrapulis* return to the temple exhausted, daily worship follows without a break.

On the fourth day there is no special ritual but daily worship is conducted as usual.

On the fifth and seventh days the *karakam* processions are identical. Each participant performs in much the same way as in the first *karakam* procession. Their route is, however, more complicated than the

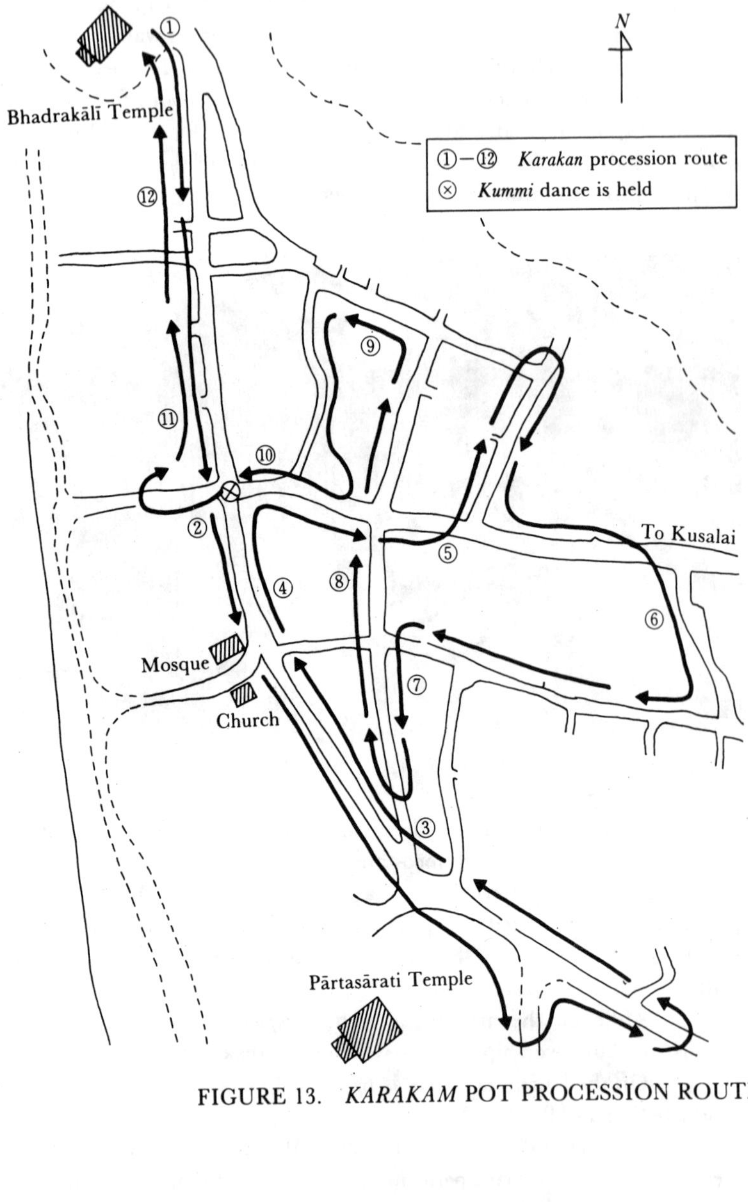

FIGURE 13. *KARAKAM* POT PROCESSION ROUTE

first *karakam* procession, and is restricted to Cattiyur proper. These processions go along not only main streets, but also some narrow lanes. As is clear from figure 13, the procession aims to cover the old and central sector of Cattiyur, making its traditional and ritual boundary clear rather than to reach some particular place. Along the way, several pots (*kumpaṃ*) containing turmeric water with margosa leaves are left on small stools covered with a white cloth outside the houses. As they pass, one of the devotee processants pours the water from these pots over the medium's feet or over the heads of the *cūrapuli*s, again indicating their hierarchical relationship. Some of the pots may have a coconut placed on them, in which case it is smashed at the medium's feet. Sprays of margosa leaves and hibiscus flowers are hung at the entrances to the houses after the procession has passed by (pl. 10).

PLATE 10. MARGOSA LEAVES ON THE FENCES

Generally speaking, when in a trance, Hindus are believed to become extremely hot. The medium and the *cūrapuli*s are no exception. The margosa leaves and turmeric water which are poured over them are believed to be cooling and help to control their ecstatic movements.

Here a brief account of margosa should be given. When somebody in a family suffers from smallpox (*periyammai*), or chicken pox (*cinṉammai*), margosa leaves are hung on the fence. This indicates that the Māri goddess is visiting the house and that an impure person should not enter the house. Smallpox and chicken pox are believed to be caused by the

Māri goddess and are equivalent to possession by her. She is present in the patient, whose house becomes her temporary abode, a temple in which devotional songs are sung to her every evening. Consequently no impure persons are allowed to enter the house. Nobody, however, wants the goddess to remain in their home. The patient should be cured. Margosa leaves indicate the visit of the goddess, but they also show human effort to employ their cooling effect to control the dangerous fever caused by the goddess.

Similarly, the hanging of margosa leaves on the fence during the *karakam* pot procession implies the presence of Bhadrakālī, or more concretely the attack of an epidemic disease on the village. As the use of cooling agents suggests, Bhadrakālī's power must be cooled and controlled before reaching the households. The ambiguous nature of village goddesses in South India has often been pointed out (e. g. Brubaker 1978). Men need to tap their divine power, but it should be contained. In our case, Bhadrakālī's dangerous power, the excess of which can result in epidemic disease, must be turned into protective power. The village is animated by her due to her wandering. With proper control, however, her power can serve to revitalise both the village and each household within it, protecting them from evil forces. As illustrated here, in village festivals there is a balance between two concerns : divine power that must be activated, and the control of that power once it is active. This seems the essential key to understanding the village goddess festival.

The *karakam* pot procession is not just about the chance for one deity greeting others ; it also aims to provide the villagers with direct communication with Bhadrakālī. They do not need always to approach the priest to worship Bhadrakālī ; during the festival she goes out and visits them. What is contained inside the temple at ordinary times flows out and over towards the village.

To sum up, the *karakam* pot procession mediates between the temple (sanctum sanctorum) and the village (households). It is a dangerous intrusion of Bhadrakālī into the village, but at the same time it provides an occasion when such a violent power can be transformed into a manageable and protective power.

The sixth day proceeds with regular worship, and the seventh day is the same as the fifth day.

The eighth day of the festival starts with a ritual regarding vow making. This is called *akkiṉiccaṭṭi* (fire pan). Only four men participate. One man starts from the Muttumāri goddess temple in Adipetti and the other three from the Bhairava temple in Kusalai, the neighboring Muslim dominant village. From these small shrines they move to the Bhadrakālī temple and offer the fire pans.

The *karakam* pot procession on the eighth day is different from those on the fifth and seventh days in two ways. Firstly, when Bhadrakālī comes out from the sanctum sanctorum for the procession, one of the village elders, a school principal and M. M. N.'s younger brother, formally asks her to protect the entire village :

> Our Mother, please save our village and people!
> (*tāyē, inta ūraiyum makkaḷaiyum vaittu kākkavēṇum*)

To this the medium answers :

> You do not need to fear!
> (*oṉṟukkum payappaṭātē*)

At which he takes sacred ash from the elder's plate, and throws it in the air.

On this occasion, however, the medium did not give the usual favourable reply to the villagers. Instead, he asked the President of the Hindu Temple Administrative Committee, who was standing by the elder, for a blood sacrifice. A few weeks earlier a village meeting had been held in front of the Pārtasārati temple. About one hundred men attended it to discuss whether a blood sacrifice should continue to be performed for Bhadrakālī, or not. A bill regarding the prohibition of blood sacrifice was passed in 1979. Since then the villagers have sacrificed only two goats on each festival occasion. The Hindu Temple Administrative Committee now proposed a total ban of the blood sacrifice for two reasons. The first concerns the social tension between the majority Sinhalese and the Tamils at that time. Violent communal disturbances had broken out in July 1983, just two months earlier, and many Tamils were massacred, so they did not wish to provoke a confrontation with the government on an ethnic matter such as a Hindu ritual. They feared that it would give the government an excuse to interfere in village affairs. The second reason is more religious. At the temple consecration ceremony held in January 1983, the Jaffna Brahman had strongly recommended that blood sacrifice should not be performed at the new Bhadrakālī temple. The educated villagers agreed with the Brahman. The village meeting decided that blood sacrifice would not be performed this time.

The medium's demand for a blood sacrifice was, therefore, interpreted as Bhadrakālī's rejection of the decision made at the meeting. The President of the Committee, young and sceptical, was reluctant to accede, but the elder pressed him to show obedience to the medium's command for the time being. After the favourable reply of this young man, he took the ash from the elder, and threw it into the air, an act which was welcomed with the cries of "Arohara!"

The second difference between this *karakam* pot procession and the earlier ones is that a dance (*kummi*) is performed by the main participants at a crossroads towards the end of the procession (see fig. 13). This dance is led by a village singer reciting the original legend of Bhadrakālī and praying for her help. The singer is a fisherman with a small estate. His father is said to have written devotional songs for Cattiyur goddesses. The participants make a circular movements around the *karakam* pot and the weapons.

The song refers to the origin of the Bhardrakālī temple and relates it to the present situation of the village, and the villagers' wish for Kālī's protection.

Evening worship is held after the *karakam* pot procession. The new canopy (*pantal*) is erected in front of the temple at night.

On the ninth day, following a small act of worship at the temple, Bhadrakālī and the *cūrapulis* start the procession. The medium, in a trance, takes an *akkiṉiccaṭṭi* (fire pan) with him, instead of the *karakam* (pl. 11). The elder asks for Bhadrakālī's blessing again. This procession follows the same route as that of the *karakam*, and turmeric water is again poured on the way.

When the *akkiṉiccaṭṭi* procession returns to the temple, the *karakam* pot procession starts immediately, in the same way as on the fifth day. It is followed by worship at 11:00 a.m.

The Hindu Temple Committee members collect various kinds of vegetables, eggs and rice from the villagers for the following day's offering (*paṭaiyal*). They are cooked by about ten village women at night after the evening worship.

At 8:30 p.m. a band of musicians plays in front of the temple, signalling that two large pots of *poṅkal* or rice gruel, one sweet, one plain, have been put on to cook. A village goat is then sacrificed in front of the temple gate. This sacrifice (*vēḷvi*) is for the offering of *paṭaiyal* to Kālī. This offering is displayed on the floor of the temple before being distributed as *prasāda* to the villagers next day. As the procedure of this sacrifice is identical to the one held next day, I shall give a detailed account and interpretation later.

The main ritual in the tenth day's morning is "guarding the village (*ūrkkāval ceyyal*)." This is a variant of the *karakam* procession in that the medium goes into trance and walks around with the *karakam* pot on his head. It differs, however, from other *karakam* processions in the following

PLATE 11. *AKKIṈICCAṬṬI* PROCESSION

four respects. First, the procession route is along the village boundary and not inside the central area of the village (see fig. 14). Secondly, four cocks are sacrificed to evil spirits at the four cardinal points of the village territory. Thirdly, there is no act of pouring turmeric water over the medium or *cūrapuli*s. Finally they dance a *kummi* dance at the end of the procession in front of the temple.

The medium and the *cūrapuli*s go into a trance at the Bhadrakālī temple, and then go towards the sea accompanied by the chief priest of the Bhadrakālī goddess temple, a band of musicians, a washerman with a white cloth, a few devotees, and members of the Hindu Temple Administrative Committee. At each cardinal point, the *karakam* pot and weapons are placed on a stool covered with white cloth. After the priest conducts worship, a temple assistant cuts off the cock's head and throws it

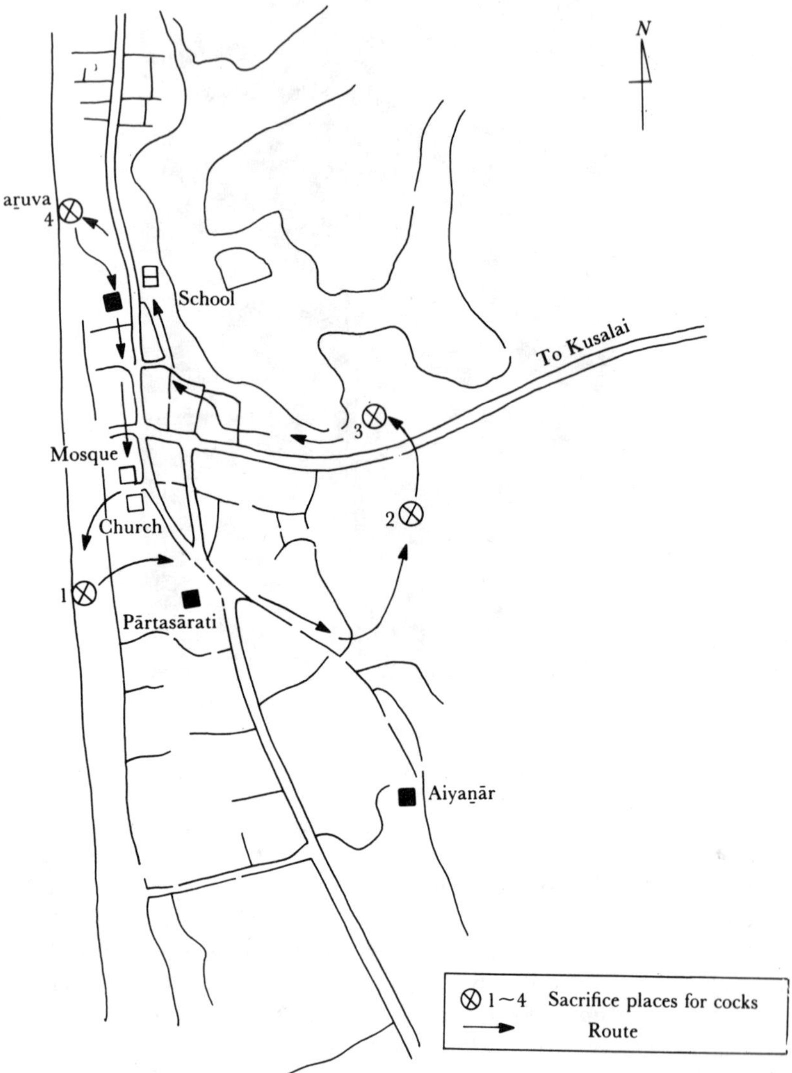

FIGURE 14. *KARAKAM* PROCESSION TO THE VILLAGE BORDERS

away. One of the *cūrapuli*s grabs the decapitated bird and sucks the blood from its neck. The procedure of the sacrifice is the same as that of the goat, which I will describe later. When the four cocks have been sacrificed in this way, they return to the Bhadrakālī temple. Before entering the temple, they perform a *kummi* dance to the accompaniment of a devotional song.

Unlike the earlier processions, this is concerned with evil spirits wandering on the village borders, and women are not expected to follow it. The sacrifices are conducted on the seashore (the first and the fourth sacrifices) or in places away from inhabited areas (the second and the third sacrifices), clearly demarcating the village boundary (not the administrative, but the ritual one). The method and motivation of the demarcation are different from those of the previous *karakam* pot processions. In this case the boundary is marked in relation to exernal evil forces, while in the earlier processions it was demarcated from the inside using Bhadrakālī's power. The sacrifice of the cocks will be seen to contrast with the goat sacrifice, held later at the temple in the centre of the village.

While the final procession is in progress, the villagers gather at the temple. Women start cooking *poṅkal* (rice gruel) around the temple (pl. 12). Inside the temple the villagers form a queue and offer plates of *arcanā* offerings to Bhadrakālī.

I have already discussed the meaning of *arcanā* in chapter 4. Here I give a brief explanation of *poṅkal*. *Poṅkal* offering is very popular among

PLATE 12. *PONKAL* COOKING

the Tamils, and has attracted much attention from anthropologists.[74] The well-known festival celebrated in the month of Tai (January - February) is called Tai Poṅkal, when the renewal of the sun is celebrated with new rice. The *poṅkal* is first offered to the sun.

However, the *poṅkal* ritual is also held at other times, and so its significance must be seen in a wider perspective. Broadly speaking, it is held at transitional times and is associated with renewal and fertility (Good 1983 : 235).

In Cattiyur, *poṅkal* is related to the hauling of fish in the net. When a shoal is caught in a beach seine, it is dragged to the beach, and the surface of the sea bubbles, as the fish struggle in vain to escape the net. The boiling *poṅkal* reminds the villagers of this bubbling, and is linked with abundance in the fisherman's mind.

It should be recalled that the central part of the fishing ritual called Maheśvara Pūjā is the preparation of a huge amount of *poṇkal* for Murukaṉ. The *poṅkal* offering marks the start of the new fishing season.

Poṅkal is also prepared at various other times in the fishing cycle : it is offered as vowed at small temples on the fishing grounds, and net-owners' wives prepare it on the day of a ceremonial anointment (*nīrāṭutal*) and blood sacrifice for a *pātai*-boat on the beach, or in the fish-curing yard (*vāṭi*) on the first day of fishing. The general interpretation of *poṅkal* as a transformative ritual (concerned with the renewal of time) is thus applicable in the Cattiyur case.

By the time the *poṅkal* rite is over, the medium and the others have returned to the temple. Private offerings (*arcanā*) continue to be made inside the temple. The next rite starts under the canopy in front of the temple. It is focused on a pot of boiling turmeric water for "bathing" (*mañcaḷ kuḷittal*). The pot of turmeric water was prepared early in the morning and kept since then on the fire. The medium and the *cūrapuli*s go around the pot in a clockwise direction. They wave coconut shoots up and down in front of themselves, and go into a trance. The elder stops them and again asks Bhadrakālī for her divine protection. The medium accepts his wish, and blesses the village by throwing the sacred ash in the air. Bhadrakālī and the *cūrapuli*s suddenly splash hot turmeric water over themselves with the coconut shoots, and they collapse on the spot. Bhadrakālī is said to be manifest in the boiling yellow water, which is a symbol of fertility. At the same time, Bhadrakālī and the *cūrapuli*s expiate themselves for having contacted the evil forces by pouring the hot turmeric water over themselves.

When the medium and the *cūrapuli*s recover, the blood sacrifice (*vēḷvi*) begins. This is the climax of the festival and its Tamil name derives from this blood sacrifice. A large black village goat (*ūr āṭu*) is taken to the front of the temple entrance. The President of the Hindu Temple Administrative Committee, representing the village (*ūr upayakkāraṉ*), pours a jar of water over the goat's head and back, and hangs a garland on it. The priest pours consecrated water over the goat and waves burning incense over it. The medium and one of the *cūrapuli*s bring a sword (*vāḷ*) from the temple. Spectators wait impatiently for the goat to tremble, showing that Bhadrakālī has accepted it as her offering, and that it has received her grace-power. Significantly, its shaking is called *caṉṉatam* or divine possession. The two *cūrapuli*s stand by trembling. As the goat starts to shake, the villagers keep shouting, "Arohara! Arohara!" while the temple assistant raises the sword and cuts the goat's head off. One of the *cūrapuli*s, in a trance, grasps the goat's body and sucks the blood pouring from the neck. The head is placed on the ground, facing the Bhadrakālī image in the sanctum sanctorum.

Whilst the villagers said only that goat sacrifice was performed as an offering to the goddess to gain her protection for the village, there is a substantial interpretive literature which suggests further meanings. Thus, the goat represents an evil spirit, but is actually Bhadrakālī's devotee husband, and the sacrifice symbolises their marriage. At Cattiyur, the garlanding of the goat, the erection of a canopy (*pantal*) are suggestive of the marriage ceremony. Furthermore the word of *vēḷvi* has a connotation of marriage.[75]

In this case the demon devotee surrenders himself to Bhadrakālī in the sacrifice, and in so doing he becomes her devotee husband. Their union is made possible by his voluntary, humble death. The demon was first represented in confrontation with Bhadrakālī along the borders of the village, but was defeated by her, and is now publicly accepted by her as her devotee at the temple in the centre of the village. The shift from exclusion to inclusion of evil force suggests the goddess's encompassing nature or "totality" (Clothey 1983 : 109).

However, this process can also be interpreted as a transformation occurring in the goddess herself. Over the course of the festival she changes from a fierce deity confronting evil forces into a relatively benevolent deity who accepts them.[76] If we interpret the evil forces as Bhadrakālī's *alter ego*, the blood sacrifice demonstrates her conquest over her own negative aspect of epidemic fever and animality. Such a transformation is the transformation or rebirth of the village as a whole, that is from the epidemic-ridden place to a place graced with divine protection.

After this sacrifice on behalf of the village, several votaries also present goats and cocks. Because of the government's prohibition they are no longer killed, but are auctioned in the afternoon.

At the *balipīṭha* outside the temple, a five foot long stick (*kaḻumaram*) is set up, and the priest gradually works a cock on to the stick through its anus to its mouth. It is left at the *balipīṭha* for four hours. It is removed from the stick at about 3:00 p.m. and revives as if nothing had happened to it. This bird is an offering to the Pēcci goddess, who does not like blood at sacrifice.

When the *arcanā* offerings are over, worship begins. The curry of mutton , boiled eggs, chicken, and vegetables cooked the previous night is covered with a white cloth on the temple floor. The medium performs the worship. Finally the medium raises some burning camphor towards Bhadrakālī, and the cry of "Arohara!" concludes the worship. Some villagers take *poṅkal* home with them, but others including many children partake of the offerings in the temple.

At 4:30 p.m. the medium and the *cūrapulis* take the *karakam* pot, sword and trident respectively. They go close to the Kantacāmi temple at Adipetti with many villagers. They leave the *karakam* and the weapons on the sand, and start *kummi* dancing to a devotional song (pl. 13).[77] This time, many girls join in the dancing. The same dance and song are repeated shortly afterwards on the beach. The medium and the *cūrapulis*, who are now in a mild trance, rush into the sea with the *karakam* and the weapons, and collapse. When they recover, they return to the temple. The two *kumpams* are removed from the temple and thrown into the

PLATE 13. *KUMMI* DANCING

sea at the *aṟuva*.

Several rites in the Bhadrakālī festival are related to female fertility. In the month of Cittirai (April - May) young women praise the Māri goddess by dancing through the night in the same manner as is found in *kummi* dancing. This celebration, called Cittirai Cevvāy, is explicitly intended to increase female fertility,[78] by removing *cevvāy tōṣam* (Skt. *doṣa* or disorder), which is caused by *cevvāi* (the planet Mars) and which causes delay in marriage. The circular movement of the dance has strong connotations of creative power. The *karakam* pot in the centre of the circle is said to infuse the girls dancing around it with Bhadrakālī's fertile power.

The *karakam* pot, weapons and *kumpam*s are all destroyed in the sea, putting an end to what I would call "the ecstatic phase" of the festival. During the festival, these items represent active and dangerous divinity, and provide direct and concrete channels of communication with divine power. Bhadrakālī comes from the sea at the start of the festival, and returns there at the end. This does not, however, mean that there is no deity in the temple after the festival : it is the fierce aspect of a goddess which is discarded at the end of the festival, while her benevolent aspect remains at the temple (cf. Moffatt 1979 : 266).

Next, ten barren women consult and take *käyam* or medicine from the medium in front of the sanctum sanctorum (pl. 14). Women are not usually allowed to enter this part of the temple, and those who attend this session should have refrained from eating meat for the preceding three days. The medicine is a brown coloured paste, made by the medium's father, Muttaiya, to a secret recipe, and has been kept inside the shrine overnight.

One woman at a time comes in and sits down before the medium, who speaks a few words gently to her, and makes her swallow three portions of the medicine. She backs out of the room, and then prays to Pēcci, who is said to be in charge of women's fertility.

The treatment of barren women, one by one inside the temple, contrasts with the *kummi* dance performed collectively by unmarried girls on the beach. By this time in the festival, the medium no longer incarnates Bhadrakālī, and gives each woman the secret medicine in a practical manner. Bhadrakālī's power does not reach the women directly, and this session is more like exorcism, in which Bhadrakālī is often a central deity.

When night falls, the Bhadrakālī festival image is extravagantly adorned with jewels and garlands for the village procession (*ūrppavaṉi*). She rides on the wooden image of lion, carried on a tractor owned by a net-owner, and driven by the owner's seventeen-year-old son. The procession is a triumphant one. Following a bus road, it goes to the

PLATE 14. GIVING MEDICINE

Pārtasārati temple, and then to the Muttumāri temple. The tractor stops several times, and the medium on it receives private offerings (*arcanā*). *Āratti* is performed against evil forces by girls at the main crossroads. Crossroads are believed to be dangerous. Two girls stand face to face waving a burning camphor three times to remove evil forces, and the fire is simply discarded on the ground. This indicates that Bhadrakālī represented by the festival image is no longer a dangerous being, but a beautiful and vulnerable one. The procession lasts several hours, before it returns to the temple.

After the procession, the medium conducts the final act of worship in the festival. This only differs from the normal daily worship in that worship of Bhairava is more elaborate than usual. Therefore it is called Bhairava *pūjā*. Among the items offered are bottles of arrack, ganja and cigars. They are appropriate offerings to fierce deities. *Poṅkal* or milk rice, already prepared before the start of procession, is now served to him. Worship of Bhairava is incorporated into a larger sequence of normal worship, and is followed by the usual worship of the lion. Finally, each *upayakkāraṉ* (patron) from among the net-owners and the other wealthy men receives *prasāda*, consisting of *poṅkal* in a coconut shell cup (*kāḷāñci*). This is the only occasion that patrons are singled out as such throughout the festival, despite their substantial financial support to it.

Cosmological Themes of the Festival

Several cosmological themes emerge during the course of the festival. These can be grouped around two themes : first, a topographical theme, in which the village is opposed to the sea and the forest ; secondly, the opposition between the goddess and evil forces.

Village, Sea and Forest

The festival starts with the setting-up of the ritual pots representing Bhadrakālī. The *karakam* is filled with the underground water considered equivalent to that from the sacred rivers, and the two *kumpams* contain sea water. In topographical terms, Bhadrakālī could be considered to come from the sea (or more generally the water world), and resides at the temple during the festival in the two earthen pots. From there she is taken around the main part of the village in the *karakam*, infusing the village with her power. On the last day she goes to the village borders where she confronts evil forces, then returns to the temple to receive the village goat. Bhadrakālī comes from "nature" (the sea or river), and encounters evil forces again in "nature" (forest). So, nature as opposed to the human world (village) is divided into two, the sea and the forest.

In traditional Hindu thought the forest (Skt. *āraṇya*,Tam. *kāṭu*) has important symbolic connotations and merits special attention (Reiniche 1979 : 229-30). It is the antithesis to humanised space, that is, the village (Skt. *grāma*, Tam. *ūr*). The word "forest" actually connotes wilderness, including swamp, marsh, desert, and uncultivated land in general, where blood-thirsty evil spirits wander and only the fools (*mūṭan̲*) or barely humanised people such as hunters (*vēṭan̲*) live. It is full of dangerous beings and powers. In brief, it is the antithesis of the social world of the Hindus.[79]

The forest, however, is also a source of sacred power, as is often the case in other cultures where it represents a world antithetical to the everyday reality of society. It is often said that the small temples (*kāṭṭukkoyil* or forest temple) scattered around the borders of the village are more powerful than the village temples. Ambiguity characterises the forest : it is a place of danger and ignorance, and yet also the place of sacred power and revelation, all in opposition to the mundane human world.

In the Bhadrakālī goddess festival, nature is not left undifferentiated, but is conceptually divided into the fertile sea and the dangerous forest (wilderness). The sea is the abode of village goddesses, a place where there is no threat from evil spirits. In Cattiyur, unlike many other fishing communities, fishing is not an especially dangerous activity, and the fishermen do not fear the sea. They spend most of their working time on the beach, pulling in the net. For the labourers, the sea is the source of fertility and life, and their work involves direct communication with the Hindu divine beings. Fishing is not a sinful activity in Cattiyur ; on the contrary, labour can be a means of communication with the goddesses, who are in charge of the fertility of the sea.[80] Whilst pulling in the nets, the fishermen face the sea and collectively recite devotional songs called *ampā*.[81]

We have seen the fishermen's conception of space. During the festival, however, the goddess crosses over the boundaries of the conceptual mapping of everyday life. She does not remain at the temple. This enables the villagers to have direct access with the divine being, and the neat distinctions between the sea, the forest and the village disappear. The forest in its negative sense is finally incorporated into the new realm which the goddess suffuses with her presence. Such a dynamic and encompassing nature of the festival is the nature of the goddess herself.

The Goddess and Evil Forces

The procession to the village borders of Cattiyur has no water pouring rites. Whilst it is in progress, all the villagers gather at the temple, where they cook *poṅkal* and offer *arcanā*. The procession is considered too dangerous for women, or children, to follow, and they are also not allowed to witness the sacrifice of the cocks at the four points. This is an example of the clear opposition of the temple and the village borders. This contrast corresponds to the opposition between Bhadrakālī and evil spirits. When Bhadrakālī ventures to the village border, the villagers gather at the temple.

The concern with the borders in this procession is reminiscent of rites of exorcism. In fact the whole festival can be considered as an exorcism rite of the village as a whole. A typical exorcism rite proceeds as follows (see chapter 3 for more details).

In the evening an exorcist is invited to the house of a patient suffering from demonic possession. He sets up a *kumpam* (ritual pot) of Bhadrakālī, or Bhairava, in the room used for the domestic rites. Then he inquires into the cause of suffering by divination. After making offerings to the *kumpam*, the exorcist buries four stakes with magical inscriptions around the house, and one at the entrance. Finally the *kumpam* and offerings are taken away and burned at the village border. The exorcist returns to the house and ties *kāppu* cords on the patient and other family members.

In contrast to the exorcism rite, however, in the festival the logic of inclusion, or encompassment, is more predominant than that of exclusion. Here the expelled evil spirit is considered to reappear as a goat at the temple. This becomes more obvious when we consider how the perceived nature of goddess changes.

The festival is not simply an enactment of the conflict between good and evil, or a celebration of the former's victory over the latter. Indeed, Bhadrakālī herself is not totally benign. She actually poses a problem ; for the goddess is the bearer of epidemic disease. It is her fierce aspect that the villagers appease in the final outcome of the festival. They demonstrate their submission to her, and, by so doing, they transform her dangerous power into a more benign, protective power. The active goddess, as represented by the three pots must be immersed and cooled in the sea towards the end of the festival. The procession to the village borders objectifies Bhadrakālī's own evil aspect——villagers say that she must be at her most fierce when she sets out. The four cock sacrifices implicitly aim to "desacralise" the goddess. Through these sacrifices her character is transformed from the dangerous to the benign. The sacrifice of the village goat involves——as we have seen——controlling the dangerous aspect of the goddess ; for it can be seen at a more esoteric level to represent the control of Bhadrakālī's own animality. The most crucial element, however, is, as the original myth suggests, the villagers' total submission or devotion to Bhadrakālī. Here, the goat to be sacrificed to Bhadrakālī, whether it is a village goat or votive offering, becomes a substitute for each villager and a symbol of his or her submission. The goat represents not only an evil spirit, but also the evil in each of the villagers. By their total submission, as represented by the sacrifice, they are accepted by the goddess, and their evil is removed.

It is also understandable why votive rituals such as *akkiṉiccaṭṭi* are held in the festival. They include a process of sacrificial transformation, which is most effective in a greater cycle of transformation, that is the festival. Bhadrakālī herself is a suffering being, and through ritual transformation she overcomes her suffering and becomes capable of saving the villagers.[82] It is not difficult to understand that votaries and other devotees can empathise with her fully, for her transformation is what they desire for themselves : they want release from their own afflictions, the causes of which are comparable to Bhadrakālī's negative aspect. Taking a broad view, the festival can thus be seen as a process, culminating in the climactic victory of the goddess over evil, and over her own animality. In the final village procession Bhadrakālī is a benign deity, free from the ambivalence which was part of her perceived nature. The goddess is moderated by a series of acts of appeasements, and less likely to be a threatening force. The evil of the goddess is not entirely eliminated, but rather it is incorporated into the encompassing divine order. The festival is a process in which the village and its residents undergo transformation. It is a process of rebirth. In this regard we can understand why *poṅkal*, the ceremonial cooking of rice gruel, which is associated with transitional time, is performed at the festival.

Structure of the Festival

In this final section I describe how the festival progresses in two major phases : an ecstatic and a non-ecstatic phase, and that their hierarchical relationship is closely related to the political function of the festival. The disposal of the pots marks the end of the ecstatic phase of the festival. I hold here that after this the festival enters a new phase. Especially, Bhadrakālī's persona alters ; her fierce perilous aspect transforms into a more benign protection. What is dangerously dynamic is brought under control, but only after it has vitalised an order (Brubaker 1978 : 247, cf. Pfaffenberger 1982 : 109).

During the ecstatic phase of the festival the village is often expressed as an undifferentiated community. The village as such is represented by the President of the Hindu Temple Administrative Committee, who acts as village patron (*ūr upayakkāraṉ*). He is elected at a village meeting in which any adult male of the Karaiyar can participate. This is not to say that he does not reflect the power structure of the village in some way or other. Historically, the Hindu Temple Administrative Committee has been drawn from the elite group of net-owners and their relatives. In the festival context, however, the President represents the village as a whole, or at least the Karaiyar caste as a whole in relation to the other service castes, and not, at least in theory, a particular sector of the village. This is most obvious in the prayer made by the elder, who stands beside the President, to the medium (Bhadrakālī) for her blessing. The elder is also considered as the representative of the village, and, as such, makes frequent use of the words "village" and "people." To sum up, the initial ecstatic phase, in which Bhadrakālī is represented by the *karakam* pot and considered as the perilous being of epidemic disease, is concerned with notions of community. This is an undifferentiated community, and "a community of suffering" (Turner 1957 : xxi). In tandem with affliction, however, such a community must also, in a way, be

TABLE 13
THE STRUCTURE OF THE BHADRAKĀLĪ GODDESS FESTIVAL

	Ecstatic phase	Non-Ecstatic phase
Main ritual	*karakam* procession	festival image procession
Communication	possession	priesthood
Kālī's nature	multiplex	benevolent
Village	community of suffering	community of victory
Effect	epidemic, death	prosperity
Negative force	dangerous to evil spirits	vulnerable to evil spirits
Icon	water, margosa temporal natural	brass, jewel permanent artificial
Patron	village	net-owners

overcome.

After the pots have been discarded in the sea, the politico-economic differentiation in the village becomes gradually more evident. The festival image is carried around in the final procession on a net-owner's tractor, and the *prasāda* of the final worship is distributed only to the net-owners. They are the festival patrons and their names are recited by the medium. So whilst this procession might function to reinforce village "solidarity", and whilst it celebrates the victory of the goddess and the village as a whole, over malign forces, the financial cost of victory is borne by the net-owners. The mundane order based on economic dominance of the net-owners is articulated with the cosmological narrative of the festival. The villagers' communal effort in transforming the divine is overshadowed by the material support given to the festival by the net-owners. Submission to Bhadrakālī in order to gain her protection also involves the villagers' recognition of the beach seine owners' legitimate financial assistance and their superiority as evidenced by the exclusion of non-sponsors from the final *prasāda*. It appears as if the beach seine owners support only the non-ecstatic phase, and not the ecstatic phase, which is set up to be denied at the end of the festival. The net-owners seem to take over the collective effort of the villagers in transforming Bhadrakālī, and to insist that, without their financial support, neither the village festival nor the transformation of the goddess would ever be possible. This kind of logic can lead to the conclusion that it is through their contributions that the village is saved from the epidemic. This articulation of local politics with the festival process will be examined further in the next chapter on the Draupadī goddess festival, where the net-owners act as more visible patrons. Table 13 schematises the two distinctive phases, showing the oppositions between them.

Conclusion

In this chapter I have analysed the Bhadrakālī goddess festival, which is, from other anthropological works, considered as one of the typical Tamil village festivals. From a structural-functional point of view the village festival enforces "village solidarity" by representing it as a community of suffering at the beginning and as a community of triumph over the epidemic at the end. During the festival the village is clearly demarcated by a series of processions.

Symbolically, the village festival provides an occasion when the village is infused with the divine power of Bhadrakālī and renewed. The villagers make every effort to cool her down and propitiate her, whereupon her suffering is removed and she is transformed into a benevolent deity.

Likewise each votary, who performs some votive rite has been released from affliction. In a sense the votaries have cleared their accounts with the goddess and can call her again. There is also a kind of reciprocal relationship between the goddess who ameliorates human suffering, and humans who release the goddess from a similar condition.

From a political point of view the festival legitimates and demonstrates the politico-economic domination of the wealthy sector of the village, especially the net-owners. In return for generous financial support of the festival they enjoy exclusive rights to receive *prasāda* at the end of the festival. In comparison with the Draupadī festival, however, the emphasis on communal solidarity during the Bhadrakālī festival remains far greater than on the legitimation of the local political structure. But, before going to analyse the Draupadī goddess festival, it is necessary to consider in the following chapter *abhiṣeka*, which, in my opinion, makes this festival more complex than the Bhadrakālī festival. This will be done in the next chapter.

CHAPTER SIX

THE CREATION AND DISTRIBUTION OF POWER

The aim of this chapter is to analyse a consecration ritual known as *abhiṣeka* and the worship conducted as part of it. An analysis of *abhiṣeka* is a necessary preliminary to the understanding of the difference between the Bhadrakālī goddess festival covered in the preceding chapter and the Draupadī goddess festival to be discussed in the next chapter, and, more generally, the relationship between secular power and rituals. Here I will discuss a case of *maṇḍalābhiṣeka,* or the consecration of a stone image in detail. We shall see that the *abhiṣeka* includes sacrificial rituals, and generates divine power, and that its patron undergoes a series of transformations involved with gaining divine power. *Abhiṣeka* is a typical Brahmanical ritual and provides an occasion on which men of power can effectively convert their secular power into divine power. As with the analysis of the Bhadrakālī goddess festival, the following discussions on *abhiṣeka* and the Draupadī goddess festival show that political elements of the rituals can be well comprehended through symbolic analysis.

Introduction to *Abhiṣeka*

Definitions and Varieties

The original Sanskrit term of *abhiṣeka* (Tam. *apiṣēkam*) refers to the consecration of an image, object or person through ritual anointment. These definitions are offered by the *Tamil Lexicon* (1982 : s. v. "*apiṣēkam*") : i) bathing of an idol with water (oil, milk, honey and other substances) ; ii) inauguration of a king by anointing, consecration of a priest ; iii) a crown. The first two meanings were frequently given to me in the field. Given that the ultimate aim of *abhiṣeka* is consecration and not simply bathing, it is little wonder that royal coronation (Inden 1978) and initiation of a priest novice (Fuller 1985) are classified as *abhiṣeka*. Both rituals have a common aim : to imbue a new king or a novice with sacred power or vitality, and to consecrate him.

In contemporary Hindu society, the most common objects of *abhiṣeka* rites are idols at temples. I had the opportunity to observe eight kinds of such *abhiṣeka* rites in Sri Lanka (see table 14).

TABLE 14
LIST OF *ABHIṢEKA*S

Name
unmarked *abhiṣeka*
snānābhiṣeka
rudrābhiṣeka
mahākumbhābhiṣeka
kumbhābhiṣeka
maṇṭalābhiṣeka
śaṅkhābhiṣeka
caṇṭālaprāyaścittābhiṣeka

The list that follows is not comprehensive, and I do not propose to discuss each *abhiṣeka* in detail. On the other hand, a brief discussion may shed light on the general idea of the *abhiṣeka*.

(1) Perhaps the simplest *abhiṣeka* is that performed in the course of daily worship. On these occasions the term is linguistically unqualified ; *abhiṣeka* is simply used. The rite consists of anointing, or bathing an image with milk, fruit,[83] clarified butter, and finally consecrating it with holy water. This simple form of *abhiṣeka* can be performed for different objects on different occasions by both Brahman and Paṇṭāram priests. For example, a flagstaff may be an object of this simple *abhiṣeka*, in preparation for a flag hoisting ceremony on the first day of the village festival (see chapter 7). A portable brass image may be the object of *abhiṣeka* prior to a procession around the village.

In contrast, the following *abhiṣeka*s stand by themselves as independent rituals, and are not considered to be part of the normal course of worship although, as they are usually followed by worship, it is difficult to entirely divorce the *abhiṣeka* from worship. Except for *caṇṭālaprāyaści-ttābhiṣeka*(Tam. *caṇṭāḷapirāyaccittāpiṣēkam*), or expiatory *abhiṣeka*, which is not always followed by worship, and the purpose of which is not consecration, but expiation, these *abhiṣeka* rites have similar structures, in spite of differences in the objects, ritual instruments, *mantras* they employ.

(2) *snānābhiṣeka*(Tam. *snāṉāpiṣēkam*) is performed for every deity in a temple, and is held daily for the seven days of the Draupadī goddess festival. In this case *snānābhiṣeka* is an obligatory ritual incorporated into the overall structure of the village festival.

(3) *rudrābhiṣeka*(Tam. *uruttirāpiṣēkam*) is a fairly large *abhiṣeka* with special *mantra*s for Śiva or Rudra. The *rudrābhiṣeka* was performed on the tenth day of the above village festival in 1982, but was a personal votive ritual, and this ritual is not part of the fixed structure of the festival.

Temple consecration rituals fall into three types of *abhiṣeka* : (4) *mahākumbhābhiṣeka* (Tam. *mahākumpāpiṣēkam*), or its simpler form, (5) *kumbhābhiṣeka* (Tam. *kumpāpiṣēkam*) ; (6) *maṇḍalābhiṣeka* (Tam. *maṇṭalāpiṣēkam*) ; and (7) *śaṅkhābhiṣeka* (Tam. *caṅkāpiṣēkam*). I had the opportunity of observing the whole sequence of these at the time of the consecration of the Bhadrakālī goddess temple. In this case the *mahākumbhābhiṣeka* was held from 27 to 31 January, 1983, followed by a daily *maṇḍalābhiṣeka* for forty three days from 1 February to 15 March, and concluded by a *śaṅkhābhiṣeka* on 16th March.

In addition, a small scale *kumbhābhiṣeka* was held at the Draupadī goddess temple on 12 July 1983, and was followed by a daily *maṇḍalābhiṣeka* for ten days in July, and finally a *śaṅkhābhiṣeka*. In this case, the *abhiṣeka* was not concerned with the consecration of the temple as a whole, but was held on the occasion of the completion of repairs to the damaged pedestal of the Draupadī goddess.

Strictly speaking, the (*mahā*) *kumbhābhiṣeka* consecrates the pinnacle pots (Skt. *kumbha*, Tam. *kumpam*) on the top of a temple tower (cf. Clothey 1983 : 189). But it generally involves the consecration of newly installed idols. Without the *abhiṣeka* rituals, the temple would not be a place of worship and an idol would be nothing but stone. Deities would not be considered to be housed there. The (*mahā*) *kumbhābhiṣeka* should be conducted at twelve year intervals.

Many days of *maṇḍalābhiṣeka* follow the *(mahā) kumbhābhiṣeka*. The popular concept of *maṇḍala* is a mystical figure of circles and squares representing the universe. It also includes, however, a calendric element, based on units of forty. Winslow defines the *maṇḍalābhiṣeka* as the *abhiṣeka* conducted for forty days after the consecration (Winslow 1979 : s.v. "*maṇṭalāpiṣēkam*").[84]

The *śaṅkhābhiṣeka* marks the end of the sequence of temple consecration. Named after the *śaṅkha* (Tam. *caṅku*) or conch-shell, which is enployed as a receptacle of the holy water used for anointing the idol, the *śaṅkhābhiṣeka* requires 1008 or 108 shells. The water in a conch shell is said to be as pure as that of the sacred rivers in India.

In spite of differences in detail, I believe that the aim of each *abhiṣeka* is identical in that it generates power (*śakti*), sacralises an idol with it, and finally channels it to the devotees.

(8) The expiatory *abhiṣeka* is held when an impure person enters a temple sanctum sanctorum, or a villager dies during the festival time. The main aim of this *abhiṣeka* is to rearrange and normalise the relationships between deities and human beings which have gone wrong because of the latter's sinful activities, mistakes or whatever. Therefore, this expiatory or reparatory *abhiṣeka* can be classified as a ritual of "desacralization" as opposed to "sacralization" (Hubert and Mauss 1964 : 56-58).

In the following section *maṇḍalābhiṣeka* held at the Bhadrakālī goddess temple is taken up for detailed analysis.

Ritual Participants

As *abhiṣeka* rituals, except for simple unmarked ones, require a knowledge of Sanskrit *mantras,* they are conducted by a Brahman priest. Though the chief priest of the Bhadrakālī goddess temple belongs to the Paṇṭāram caste, the *maṇḍalābhiṣeka* was conducted by the elder son of Kumaracami, assisted by his younger brother. The Bhadrakālī goddess temple priest (in this case Parandaman's elder brother) usually assists the Brahman priest when the Brahman conducts the *abhiṣeka* in his temple, and is in charge of daily worship after the *abhiṣeka*. During my observation, however, he was absent because of an ongoing problem between him and the Hindu Temple Administrative Committee, and the younger brother of the Brahman had to perform the worship as well. In this chapter I refer to him as an assistant priest, and his elder brother as the chief priest.

In Cattiyur most of the *maṇḍalābhiṣeka*s were individually sponsored, and the list of patrons was less exclusive than for the festival. Of the forty-three *abhiṣeka*s, thirty-nine were allocated to the Karaiyar caste members. Net-owners or groups of net-owners and their relatives accounted for twenty-four (60%) of these, the others were sponsored by the village, or more precisely, the Karaiyar caste as a whole (two days), by teachers (two days), by estate-owners (two days). Other groups of the villagers were responsible for a further nine days of *abhiṣeka* (see table 15).

Four days were allocated to non-villagers. They were : a Colombo merchant of Indian origin who is a regular patron of the village festival ; a group of the Munnesvaram villagers ; a group of the Ācāri caste

TABLE 15
PATRONS OF THE *MAṆḌALĀBHIṢEKA*

Patron	Day
Net-owner	24
Village	2
Teacher	2
Estate-owner	2
Hindu Temple Adminstrative Committee members	1
Fibreglass boat owner	1
Accountant	1
Lagoon fisherman and trader	1
Singing group	1
Other	4
Non-villager	4
Total	43

(sculptors) who came from the east coast to restore the temple ; and myself and three other villagers.

Everyday a group of several musicians also came to perform during the period of *abhiṣeka*, playing the drums, pairs of small cymbals and the harmonium. The band was drawn from the Cattiyur Karaiyar, one of whom was a vocalist who sang devotional songs accompanied by the music.

A Washerman caste member prepares white cloths and the temple assistants help the priest. Patrons give *dakṣiṇā,* or a fee, and *dāna,* or a gift of clothes to the two Brahman priests, and some money to the musicians, but not to the Washerman or the temple assistants, who are paid by the Hindu Temple Administrative Committee.

The size of the audience depends on the importance of the *abhiṣeka* and the publicity given to it. As a reference point in any villager's life, the *mahākumbhābhiṣeka* is a special and rare occasion when the whole village celebrates the completion of a new temple. On the other hand, an *abhiṣeka* held as a personal votive rite is important only for the votary, or patron and his family. The audience is correspondingly small, especially if it is held on a normal day. Spectators, if they come, particularly boys and girls, usually come to the temple with small pans and nylon bags in the hope of getting a handful of *prasāda* (consecrated offerings), such as boiled rice, Bengal gram, or the fruit used for the anointment.

Space and Instruments

The ritual space of the *maṇḍalābhiṣeka* consists of two areas ; one is the space called *yāgaśālā* reserved for fire sacrifice, *homa* (Tam. *ōmam*) and the other is the sanctum sanctorum where the idol of main deity (Bhadrakālī goddess) is installed. A room called *ardhamaṇḍapa* is used for the *yāgaśālā* in the *maṇḍalābhiṣeka*, and it is not necessary to construct a new hut as in the case of the *mahākumbhābhiṣeka*. This room is located just outside the sanctum sanctorum, and women are not allowed access to it (see fig. 15).

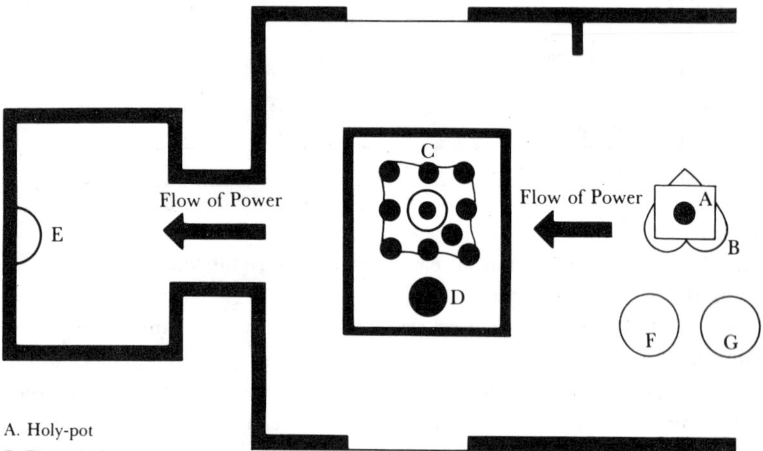

A. Holy-pot
B. Fire sacrifice pit
C. *Kumpams* (pots) for Bhadrakālī and others
D. Gaṇeśa *kumpam*
E. Stone idol of Bhadrakālī
F. Brahman priest
G. *Upayakkāraṉ* (patron)

FIGURE 15. LAYOUT OF THE *MAṆḌALĀBHIṢEKA* (PART OF FIG. 5)

There the Brahman priest sets up the pit for a fire sacrifice, and places a small table called *pīṭha* (Tam. *pīṭam*) between the main idol and the altar. He arranges several pots (Tam. *kumpam*) on the *pīṭha*-table.

The fire pit (Skt. *homakuṇḍa*) for fire sacrifice is a heart-shaped receptacle three feet across and four inches high, made out of cast concrete. The priest winds a thread around the edge of the pit three times, and spreads some white sand inside it. The pit is then completely covered with a large brass tray which has a thin layer of rice grain spread over it. A cup of milk, three sets of *tāmbūla*, and a pot called *puṇyakumbha*, or holy-pot, are set on the rice.

The *tāmbūla* is a collective noun referring to a set consisting of a couple of betel leaves and areca nuts with an optional banana. Two out of the three *tāmbūlas* are offerings to Gaṇeśa, the other is for Varuṇa (the Water God), who will later be present inside the holy-pot. The priest prepares eleven pots (*kumpam*) on the *pīṭha*-table between the pit and the temple sanctum sanctorum, and offers one *tāmbūla* to each ritual pot.

Chewing areca nuts with slaked lime wrapped in a betel leaf (sometimes with a dried tabacco leaf) is very common in South and Southeast Asia. It is a luxury for both men and women, but it also has ritual implications.[85] On auspicious occasions, such as weddings and house-opening ceremonies, two trays are always passed around among the guests. Each guest takes some sacred ash (Tam. *tirunīṟu*), sandalwood paste (Tam. *cantaṉam*), and vermilion powder (Tam. *kuṅkumam*) from small cups on one of the trays and makes the mark (Tam. *poṭṭu*) of the Śaivites on his or her forehead, by drawing three horizontal lines of the ash on the forehead and applying the dot of the sandalwood paste, and the vermilion powder on a spot above the bridge of the nose. After this the host sprinkles rose-water (Tam. *paṉṉīr* or fragrant water) over the guest, who then takes areca nuts from the other tray, wraps them in a betel leaf, and chews the package. The *tāmbūlas* offered to the ritual pots suggest that the deities are the guests who are invited on this occasion. This impression is reinforced, when the priest makes the *poṭṭu* mark of Śaivites on the ritual pots and later sprinkles rose-water over them.

Kumpam (Skt. *kumbha*) generally means a water pot, but in a ritual context, it is a term applied to a special pot which acts as the temporary abode of a deity, or as a representation of the deity. Five mango leaves, a symbol of auspiciousness, are set upright in the mouth of a pot, and a coconut is placed on the top of it. A thread is coiled around the pot, which is filled with water, rose-water and turmeric (Tam. *mañcaḷ*) powder.[86] A pot full of water is an auspicious symbol in itself, especally in contrast to an empty pot, which is considered inauspicious.

This is the basic form of a ritual pot, but additional decoration varies according to the kind of ritual and the deity involved in it. Some pots are decorated with cloth (particular colours are specific to particular deities) or embroidered with gold threads, garlands and three branches of dried, reed-like, *darbha* grass (Tam. *taruppai, Poa cynasuroides*). The grasses are tied together at one end and are left open at the other to make a tripod shape. They are put on top of the coconut. *Darbha* grass is said to have been born from sacrificial fire, and to retain strong purificatory power. In the case of the *maṇḍalābhiṣeka,* both the pot for Bhadrakālī and the pot for Gaṇeśa are decorated with cloths and big garlands, and the arrangements of *darbha* grass are put on the former. The other pots have a small garland of jasmin flowers.

In a similar way to stone idols or *karakam* pot, the *kumpam* represents a deity, its form reminding us of a body. The pot is a body, the coconut a head, and the *darbha* grasses hair.[87] As I have already pointed out, a water pot has rich symbolism. It symbolises the womb, fertility and vitality. Unlike the *karakam* (see chapter 5) the *kumpam* represents both male and female deities.

Five banana leaves are laid on top of one another on the *pīṭha*-table. Sandwiched between are unhusked and husked rice, and other kinds of grain. They will serve as seats for the deities who will be invited into the eleven pots on the banana leaf seat. The largest ritual pot is for the main deity, in this case Bhadrakālī. It is surrounded by nine small ritual pots. At a little distance another large pot (slightly smaller than Bhadrakālī's) is placed for Gaṇeśa. The nine small pots are for the Sun, the Moon, Fire, Water, Wind, Sky, the Earth, soul (*ātman*, Tam. *āttuman*) and the sacrificer (*yajamāna* Tam. *ecamāṉaṉ*). These identifications are, however, highly ambiguous. One villager told me that they suggest the nine planetary deities (*Navagraha*) : the Sun, the Moon, Mars, Mercury, Jupiter, Venus, Saturn, the Caput draconis and the Canda draconis. Another said they were for Bhadrakālī's nine traditional guardian deities.

As we shall see later, formless divine power (*śakti*) is generated through fire sacrifice, and when it is temporarily stored in the ritual pots, it becomes half-formless in the sense that it is still on the way to the idol, which is its full form in this world. Fluidity is another property of the power in the ritual pots. Just as water requires a receptacle to contain it, so too does power. This in-between nature of the power contained by the pots is also emphasised by their location : the ritual pots are placed on the *pīṭha*-table between the altar and the stone idol. The thread coiled around the pot further symbolises a bound and relatively tamed power, in contrast to uncontained, wild power.

Description and Interpretation of the *Maṇḍalābhiṣeka*

With some exceptions *abhiṣeka* rituals feature at least the following five sequences : 1) a set of preparatory and purificatory rituals ; 2) *homa,* or fire sacrifice ; 3) the procession of the main ritual pot ; 4) the consecration of an idol ; 5) giving of *dakṣiṇā* or fees to the priests. Usually, however, they are followed by temple worship and distribution of *prasāda.* I shall consider the *abhiṣeka* and subsequent worship together as one sequence so that we may gain an understanding not only of *abhiṣeka,* but also temple worship in general. Simple unmarked *abhiṣeka* and the expiatory *abhiṣeka* are the exceptional cases. The former is incorporated as part of worship, rather than *vice versa* and is not dealt with here. The expiatory *abhiṣeka* lacks the last two sequences : worship and the distribution of *prasāda* as is consistent with the fact that it is essentially a rite of desacralization.

My analysis will focus primarily on the generation of power and its movement to the idol, and the transformation of the patron in an *abhiṣeka.* These two aspects are actually two sides of one process, i.e. the process of establishing communication between a patron and a deity, the former disaggregating his soul from his body and moving from the profane world to the sacred, while at the same time the power of the deity is embodied or located in a tangible form such as a ritual pot, or a stone idol, thus becoming accessible to the human world.

Preparatory and Purificatory Rituals

Both priest and patron sit cross-legged in front of the holy-pot. First the chief priest declares the purpose of the rites to follow on behalf of the patron. With this, he makes a mental resolve (Skt. *saṅkalpa* or engagement) on behalf of the patron. The patron then receives sacred ash from the priest and smears it on his forehead. The patron, then, puts a ring of *darbha* grass on the ring finger of his right hand and places a sprig of *darbha* grass under his right leg. He places his left hand, palm upwards, on his right thigh with his right hand, palm downwards over it and closes his eyes for a while.

The *darbha* grass ring is a sign of engagement in a particular ritual as well as having the function of purifying one's body and protecting it from malevolent influences (cf. Fuller 1985 : 110-11).

This protective power of *darbha* grass ring is very suggestive for an understanding of the sacred power which protects the person from malevolent or negative beings and impure substances. Here I would like to discuss the case of *kāppu,* which has roughly the same effect as the *darbha* grass ring, but is more popular and considered stronger : while the *darbha* grass ring is rarely used by specialists other than Brahman priests, the *kāppu* appears in various ritual contexts such as village festivals and healing rituals.

More precisely called *mañcaḷ kāppu*,[88] the *kāppu* is a yellow cord dyed with turmeric which is tied around the right wrist of men, and the left, in the case of women. It is an amulet powerful enough to ward off evil influences and protect a person from them.[89] In similar way to the *darbha* grass ring, the *kāppu* is tied around a participant's wrist at the commencement of rituals. As it has a stronger and more long-lasting effect than the *darbha* grass, healing or exorcist rituals often end with the tying of *kāppu* cords around the wrists of the afflicted person and the members of the patient's household. The power of these amulets derives from *mantras* chanted by the priests and exorcists. *Mantra śakti*, or the power of sacred verses, is infused into the cord through their sound (*oli*). To put such a cord on one's wrist is to place oneself within the protective zone of sacred power. Here we can cite a case in which a *kāppu* cord is strong enough to avert death pollution (*toṭakku*).

> The chief priest of the Draupadī goddess temple is a Brahman, but at the time of the Draupadī festival it is a member of the Paṇṭāram caste who is the main figure in whom the goddess incarnates. At this time the medium can even enter the sanctum sanctorum, to which only Brahmans normally have access. It is the ritual of tying a *kāppu* (*kāppu kaṭṭi*) on the first day of the festival which enables the Paṇṭāram to do so (see chapter 7). In 1968, Muttaiya was the medium. His mother, however, died on the third day of the festival. But, since the *kāppu* had already been tied by the chief Brahman priest, he was able to continue to serve the festival without being disturbed by death pollution. When the festival was over and he took off the *kāppu* cord, he became impure, and joined the other mourners. He resumed the pure status on the thirty-first day of his mother's death.

This case clearly demonstrates the power of the *kāppu* against pollution. To return to a more theoretical issue discussed in chapter 1, it casts doubt upon the prevalent thesis that the pure is always vulnerable to the constant threat of pollution, and that, therefore, the impure is more powerful than the pure.

The *darbha* grass sprig placed under the right leg of the patron is a metonymic representation of a mat woven from sacred *dharba* grass. Such mats are used by ascetics during penance. According to the chief Brahman priest, it keeps users off the earth and detaches them from worldly desires, helping them to control their five senses. With the help of the ring and the symbolic mat of *darbha* grass, the patron temporarily transforms his profane status as a householder into the sacred one of ascetic.

The chief priest quickly repeats the same purificatory ritual acts for himself. In so doing, he himself successfully achieves the pure status of an ascetic. It may seem contradictory for the priest to become "a renouncer," but, as I shall show, his transformation stops at this point. The priest, as a mediator, has to be purified, but he cannot enter the sacred world with the patron, as one of his roles is to ensure the patron's safe return from the sacred realm.

The following set of rituals is concerned with the worship of Gaṇeśa. He is considered so jealous that every Hindu ritual should start with his worship. Gaṇeśa is represented by a cone made from turmeric paste into which a stem of a grass called *arukaṇi (Vitis quadrangularis)* is stuck. If shown the proper respect, he will remove any obstacle in the way of fulfillment of the rituals. The turmeric representation of Gaṇeśa is placed on the appropriate *tāmbūla*. *Arukaṇi* is believed to be prolific, because it is the first grass to be seen after the initial rain that ends the long dry season.

The priest invokes Gaṇeśa by ringing the bell to ward off evil spirits in his left hand, and chanting *mantras*. He then offers him : (1) a seat with a hand gesture ; (2) water for washing his hands ; (3) water for washing his feet ; (4) water for rinsing his mouth ; (5) water for bathing. Each time the priest sprinkles a few drops of water over the cone of turmeric paste which embodies the deity. He then makes a *poṭṭu* mark by applying (6) sacred ash, (7) sandalwood paste, (8) vermilion powder on the cone. In this way the priest invites Gaṇeśa to the ritual place. After this he entertains the god by : (9) offering flower petals accompanied by the chanting of his names ; (10) burning incenses in a special stand ; (11) lighting a single-wick oil lamp ; (12) halving a coconut ; (13) offering rice grains ; (14) again offering water and flower petals. Lastly the priest (15) waves a burning camphor tablet to perform *āratti*, over which the patron quickly puts his hands, and (16) bids the god farewell by putting out the camphor.

In comparison to the daily temple worship discussed in chapter 3, the worship of Gaṇeśa has a clear beginning and ending of ritual process. A god is invited from the outside and given a form to take, he is then entertained, and, finally he leaves. This is why I consider the temple worship as not presenting a complete set.

I have already discussed the meaning of coconut sacrifice in relation to *arcanā* offering, but here the main points bear repeating. To be more precise about the breaking of the coconut, the priest picks up a coconut, and the patron spreads both his hands over it and lightly touches it. The priest then hands it over to one of the temple assistants, who splits it and pours the milk into a bowl. The priest takes the two halved coconut shells (*kāḷāñci*) and places them inside upwards on both sides of the cane of turmeric paste, the representation of Gaṇeśa. What is important here is the clear identification between the patron and the coconut. As in the case of the *arcanā* presenter, by removing three kinds of evil, the patron becomes as pure as the white flesh of the coconut. This is a symbolic self-sacrifice.

The attention of the chief priest shifts from the lump of turmeric paste to the holy-pot. He invokes Varuṇa, the Water God, to be present in the pot and consecrates the water by chanting *mantras*. When the consecration of the water is over, the priest removes the coconut on the top of the holy-pot. Then he bunches up the five mango leaves from the pot, and uses them to flick the consecrated water over the items to be used in the rites that follow, and around the area in which they will be performed. The patron receives some of this holy water and drinks it. Then a temple assistant takes the holy-pot and goes around the inside of the temple sprinkling it with holy water.

This consecrated water is called *puṇyatīrtha*. *Tīrtha* (Tam. *tīrttam*) originally means pilgrimage centre, ford or crossing-point. The purification of the ritual space with the *puṇyatīrtha* does create a crossing space between the sacred and profane. It should be noted that the holy water was consecrated by *mantras*, and that it differs from ordinary water which is both vulnerable to pollution and capable of absorbing it.

Fire Sacrifice

Sprinkling the holy water concludes the first set of purificatory rituals. The tray on the pit is removed, after which the chief Brahman priest stretches a thread from the main ritual pot of Bhadrakālī to the pit. He invokes Gaṇeśa, Bhadrakālī and the other nine deities to be present in their respective pots.

The priest draws a *yantra* or a mystical design, on the sand in the pit, into which he places blades of *darbha* grass to purify it. Then he piles several twigs for the fire sacrifice,[90] and drops *nei* (clarified butter) on them, and sets the pile alight with burning camphor. After the fire is lit, he continues dripping *nei* on it, and also sprinkles parched rice (*neṟpori*) and the nine auspicious grains and seeds(*navadhānya*, Tam. *navatāṉiyam*)[91] over the fire so that it may "grow" (*vaḷarttal*).

Whilst the chief priest is looking after the fire sacrifice, the assistant priest enters the sanctum sanctorum. With the help of the temple assistants, who remain outside the room, he begins the bathing rituals preparatory to the consecration of the stone idol of Bhadrakālī. First he dashes a bucketful of water over the idol, and rubs it with a variety of fruit(*pañcāmṛta*, Tam. *pañcāmirutam*) : banana, jack fruit, and pineapple, all cut into pieces and mixed with honey (*tēṉ*) and sugar. After washing these fruits off the stone idol with water, the assistant priest applies milk, water, and young coconut juice in that order.[92] These "bathing" acts are identical to some of the services performed merely for the deity's entertainment, but they can be interpreted in this context as preparatory and precautionary acts of cooling the idol in order to make the "hot" *śakti* or divine power more easily accessible to human beings.[93]

When the bathing ritual is over, the patron stands at the eastern side of the pit, facing the idol, and puts various offerings into the sacrificial fire, while the priest offers drops of *nei* with a pair of two foot long ladels. This is called *pūrṇāhuti* (Tam. *pūraṇākuti*). The offerings here consist of a coconut, a *tāmbūla* including a ripe banana, and rice. At this point the drums and cymbals are beaten loudly and the temple bell struck, indicating that the fire sacrifice has reached its climax.

The priest invokes Agni, the God of fire to come to the pit, and Agni consumes the offerings and transfers them (or their essence) through the thread stretched from the pit to the other deities who have been already invited to the ritual pots. Because of this, Agni has been described as a messenger god (cf. Knipe 1975 : 124-30). If, however, we take the fundamental basis of Hindu divine beings to be power, and that this power can be generated by the burning of sacrificial offerings, we could say that divine beings in the pots are regenerated or revitalised during the fire sacrifice. In brief, divine power is created through the destruction of the offerings by fire (*agni*, Tam. *akkiṉi*,), and is transferred to the deities by Agni. With regard to the process of destruction of the offerings, and regeneration of power, we can see two kinds of symbolism in the fire sacrifice. One is the symbolism of digestion——fire or Agni consumes the offerings——and the other is the symbolism of procreation. Fire is the god's mouth in the former, while it is a vagina (Tam. *kuṇṭi*), and offerings are seeds (*vindu*, Tam. *vintu*) in the latter.[94]

The power which was generated at the pit is transferred to the ritual pots on the *pīṭha*-table. In the same fashion, the patron undergoes a new phase of transformation by identifying himself with the offerings he has made to the fire. Symbolically he sacrifices himself as they are devoured by fire (Clothey 1983 : 154 ; Knipe 1975 : 131-132). His soul becomes disembodied, and takes a temporary abode in one of the nine small ritual pots. It should be remembered that one of them is for the sacrificer or patron. By contrast divine power becomes embodied and is stored in the pots.[95]

Finally, when the sacrificial fire goes out, the priest picks up the black ashes from the pit and mixes these into paste with the remnants of the *nei* on a betel leaf. This black paste is called *ōmappoṭi* (Tam.), literally powder of fire sacrifice. The paste is first smeared on Bhadrakālī's ritual pot, and then on the foreheads of the patron and other onlookers.

As with the case of the sacred ash applied to the forehead, this paste is believed to have a strong cooling effect on the body and to calm one's spiritual state when applied to the brow, which is one of the hottest points of the body. This effect of the paste derives from the belief that it is the leftover of the offerings after the fire burns out the three evils. We can see the same idea at work here as that we saw in the coconut sacrifice (see chapter 4) : the idea that one can purify oneself through self-sacrifice or destruction of one's evil aspects.

Procession of the Main Ritual Pot

After divine power is created through fire sacrifice and transferred to it through the thread, the main ritual pot of Bhadrakālī is henceforth the focal point of ritual activity. The chief priest holds a long stem of *darbha* grass in his right hand and a bell in the left, and the assistant priest carries the main ritual pot. Headed by two torch carriers and a group of musicians, and followed by a big ceremonial umbrella, and some devotees, the procession goes around the temple clockwise. A coconut is smashed on the threshold by the patron, just as the pot is about to be taken on its round. As is the case with the coconut sacrifice we have examined in the context of *arcanā* offering and Gaṇeśa worship, this coconut sacrifice suggests the self-sacrifice of the patron, and is a mark of his further transformation. His union with the divine is further reinforced by this second coconut sacrifice.

Though small in scale, the procession of Bhadrakālī's ritual pot recalls a royal procession. Here again, we find a series of identifications between the king, the divine being and the ritual patron. Interestingly, however, it is not the patron, but the Brahman assistant, who carries the Bhadrakālī pot around the temple building. Even with his purified ritual status after having undergone several purificatory and transformative rituals, the patron can neither touch the Bhadrakālī pot nor enter the sanctum sanctorum. There are three possible interpretations of this fact. They are : (1) the patron, as a member of the Karaiyar caste, is not pure enough to touch the ritual pot ; (2) what has undergone a transformative process is his soul, while his body remains unchanged ; (3) the *śakti* in the ritual pot is so dangerous that only the Brahman may cope with it by virtue of his knowledge of *mantra* or sacred verses. None of them seems wrong, and all are somehow interrelated, although the last interpretation seems the most relevant. During the *mahākumbhābhiṣeka* (temple consecration ritual) at the Bhadrakālī goddess temple, the main pot was set up at the centre of the *yāgaśālā,* and the thread was stretched from the pot to the newly installed stone idol in the inner room. In this case, when the priest induced divine power, which had been accumulating in the pot during the five days of fire sacrifice, it flowed through the thread. I was warned several times not to stand right under the thread. The villagers' concern was not about my impure status, but about the dangerous power running through the thread from the pot in the *yāgaśālā* to the idol in the sanctum sanctorum. This power was said to be hot, like blood, and dangerous, like high voltage current. Indeed, blood and electric current are popular metaphors which were frequently used by my informants to explain *śakti* to me.[96] Control of this potentially dangerous *śakti* is maintained by the power of *mantras*.

From this discussion, we can infer that two kinds of power are in operation : one is generated from sacrifice (destruction of a victim), and the other derives from *mantras*. The former becomes tamed and benevolent only when it is under control of the latter. Divine power generated through sacrifice is too dangerous for ordinary people to approach, and they need the help of the priest's *mantra śakti.* Here it should be recalled that possession is effectively controlled by *mantra śakti* (see chapter 4). Furthermore, the threads coiled around the pit for fire sacrifice, and around the pots, are imbued with *mantra śakti*, which should control the divine power generated and now present in the pots.[97]

Consecration through Anointment

The main ritual pot is placed by the side of the stone image of Bhadrakālī in the sanctum sanctorum after the procession. One of the Gaṇeśa idols is the first object of anointment. The ritual pot of Gaṇeśa, which has remained on the *pīṭha*-table, is now taken to the small shrine dedicated to him inside the temple. The chief priest pours consecrated water from it over the idol of Gaṇeśa. Then he enters the sanctum sanctorum, and stands in front of the Bhadrakālī pot which has been set before the stone idol of her. First he touches each corresponding part of the pot and the stone idol in alternation with the long stem of *darbha* grass. Then he takes off the cone-shaped bunches of *darbha* grass, the garlands, and the cloth from the pot, and puts them on the stone idol exactly in the same fashion. He removes the mango leaves and coconut from the pot and pours the consecrated water from it over the idol. The nine pots are taken inside the sanctum sanctorum and the water from each is poured, one by one, over the idol. In this way, the idol is charged with divine power. Finally the priest draws down the curtain. The idol will be decorated with new cloths, garlands and jewels by the priests for subsequent public worship.

Dakṣiṇā to the Priests

Outside the inner room, the patron gives each Brahman priest some money (twenty-five rupees) as *dakṣiṇā* (Tam. *taṭcaṇai*), and a white sarong for ceremonial occasions. At the same time he returns the *darbha* grass ring he put on at the beginning of the purificatory rituals. In return the chief priest conducts *āratti* for the patron with a single-wick lamp. Then he distributes to him and the other people present sacred ashes and the *apiṣēkattaṇṇīr,* or holy water (Tam. *taṇṇīr* or water), which was used for the consecration (*abhiṣeka*) of the stone Bhadrakālī idol. They receive these items in cupped hands, draw three horizontal stripes on their foreheads with the ashes, and sip the holy water. The priest gives the patron and the representative of the Hindu Temple Administrative Committee a *tāmbūla* and the fruit used for the preparatory bathing ritual. These items are handed over in the coconut halves (*kāḷāñci*).

The above five sets of ritual activities, from the purificatory rituals to the fee-giving to the Brahman priests, constitute the *maṇḍalābhiṣeka* sequence *per se*. The patron enters the sacred world through a series of purificatory rituals and sacrificial acts (coconut sacrifices and fire sacrifice), aiming at a union with the divine, and returns to the profane world. Therefore the *abhiṣeka* not only consists of sacrificial rituals, but also, as a whole, contains the general structure of Hindu sacrifice as delineated by Hubert and Mauss (1964 ; cf. Clothey 1983 : 97-98) : rites of entry, immolation and rites of exit. Beginning with purificatory rites, followed by sacrificial rites, and concluded by fee-giving and other subsequent rites. As Logan points out (1980 : 132), the final *āratti* directed at the patron by the Brahman priest suggests a dangerous and transitional phase, in which he passes from the sacred to the profane, and which is so threatening that he requires the protection of an *āratti.* Divine power will also be activated by the worship which follows, but the main purpose of this is the communication between the divine and devotees in general ——

rather than with the patron's own transformation and his individual accumulation of divine power. The patron remains, however, the principal actor, and the public nature of worship effectively shows his power to the worshippers.

Worship

The assistant priest starts by worshipping Gaṇeśa at the shrine outside the temple, then he prays at the Gaṇeśa shrine inside the temple, followed by worship at the beautifully decorated stone image of Bhadrakālī in the sanctum sanctorum, then at the Pēcci goddess image outside it, at Bhairava, the lion, and the *balipīṭha* or sacrificial altar. The assistant priest offers one rice ball on the *balipīṭha*. He then enters the sanctum sanctorum once more and conducts *pañcāratti*. The procedure of worship at the *maṇḍalābhiṣeka* is identical to the daily worship held at 11:00 a.m. and 8:00 p.m (see chapter 3). The priest repeats the following acts in front of each idol : he offers water and flower petals with appropriate *mantra*s, then waves burning incense, an oil lamp, and a cake of camphor. He sprinkles water and petals over *naivedya* (offerings) on the floor in front of the idol to consecrate them. Finally he performs *pañcāratti* with the seven flames of camphor.

The priest consecrates *arcanā* (private offerings) after the *naivedya* (public offerings). In this case only Bhadrakālī receives *arcanā* from the patron of the *maṇḍalābhiṣeka*, and from other devotees (as votaries). First the patron's name and then the names of the other donors are recited by the priest inside the sanctum sanctorum, and the prosperity of their households is prayed for.

Distribution of *Prasāda*

This phase begins with the priest passing the fire of the *pañcāratti* among the devotees. The patron, and then the other devotees, hold their hands over the flame. After this sacred ash, sandalwood paste and vermilion powder are passed round among the patron and other devotees. This is followed by the holy water used for the consecration. The devotees receive it and sip a little. Finally the priest puts some of the mixed fruit used for the anointment ritual, and one rice ball in each of about thirty coconut halves (*kāḷāñci*), for distribution, first to the patron, and then to the representative of the Hindu Temple Administrative Committee, the musicians, village elders and others. Sometimes the patron himself distributes the *prasāda*. There seems to be no conscious effort to construct a hierarchy (for example in accordance with the caste hierarchy) on the occasion of distributing the *prasāda*, only the patron is given obvious priority, but the hierarchical order between male and female, and between seniors and juniors remains recognisable.

It is necessary to reiterate that *prasāda* is charged with divine power. In the analysis of *arcanā* offering we have seen that coconut sacrifice is performed (see chapter 4), but *arcanā* includes other items such as a bunch of ripe bananas, betel leaves and so on, and these are also destroyed by a priest. If we consider these items carefully, we can see that the items given over in *arcanā* are very similar to those offered to the fire by an *abhiṣeka* during a *homa*. After *arcanā* the priest returns some sacred ash to the *arcanā* donor in exchange for the *arcanā*. This is symbolically equivalent to the *ōmappoṭi*, or fire sacrifice powder, which the priest makes from the black ashes remaining after the fire sacrifice. *Prasāda* is also usually distributed in the coconut halves which remain after coconut sacrifice.

Naivedya is cooked in a temple kitchen called *yāgaśālā*, which is the same term used for the place of fire sacrifice, and which is located at the southeastern corner of the temple, the direction associated with Agni, the Fire God (Fuller 1984 : 4). Furthermore in this case, rice balls are cooked : they are called *pali uruṇṭai* (Tam.), which literally means "sacrificial ball." Here again, the act of cooking of the public offerings is redolent with the imagery of sacrifice (Fuller 1979 : 440-41).

From these examples, we can define *prasāda* as the leftovers of sacrifice. Certainly there are some items, such as fire, holy water, fruit and so on, which are not direct products of sacrificial acts. On the other hand, they are involved in the process of generating divine power in the first half of the *abhiṣeka* sequence, which has the structure of sacrifice as a whole. In other words, the mediating items, which are essential in generating power and transforming the patron in the first half of the *abhiṣeka*, are distributed as *prasāda*, which, in turn, mediates between the deity and the devotees.[98]

Stating the facts generally, whether the leftovers of a sacrificial offering are distributed among the devotees as *prasāda*, or not, depends on the aim of the ritual. If the purpose of a ritual is sacralization, the leftovers will be shared by the devotees after *pūjā*. By contrast, if the purpose is desacralization, the leftovers are simply discarded, and not shared. This happens at the expiatory *abhiṣeka*.

This *maṇḍalābhiṣeka* which I observed started at about 10:00 a.m. and the whole sequence ended just before 1:00 p.m. The patron had to meet all the expenses of the above rituals, and also of the worship to be held at 8:00 p.m., for which he prepared fifty pounds of Bengal gram (*payaṟu*). This gram will be distributed among the devotees as the main *prasāda* after evening worship. It is not cooked in the temple kitchen, but is considered a public offering or *naivedya*. Every evening about three hundred devotees with small pans and vinyl bags gathered at the evening worship for the distribution of this large amount of *prasāda*. A large bag of gram is provided every day by patrons drawn from among the wealthy villagers. The total cost of the *maṇḍalābhiṣeka* is about Rs. 1,300.00——that is about three times as much as a beach seine fisherman's monthly income.

Transformation of Patron and the Flow of *Śakti*

In this section I look at the structure of *maṇḍalābhiṣeka* by focusing on the transformation of the patron and the flow of power.

I have included the *maṇḍalābhiṣeka* along with the temple worship. The whole sequence could be analysed as follows : (1) preparatory and purificatory rituals ; (2) fire sacrifice ; (3) procession ; (4) consecration ; (5) fee-giving. This is followed by : (6) worship ; and (7) distribution of *prasāda*.

The *abhiṣeka* starts with preparing the ritual status of the patron, the chief priest, and the ritual space. After this the fire sacrifice (*homa*) is perfomed. Through this act divine power is created, and passes through a thread to the pots. The main pot representing the main deity, Bhadrakālī, is carried in procession around the temple. Her stone idol in the sanctum sanctorum is consecrated with the water from the main pot and from the other pots, and the idol is adorned for the subsequent worship. The patron returns the *darbha* ring, pays a fee (*dakṣiṇā*) and makes gifts to the priests. Finally, the worship starts, after which *prasāda* is distributed.

In the above description and analysis of the *maṇḍalābhiṣeka*, the main focus has been first on the transformation of the patron, and secondly on the flow of *śakti*. The *abhiṣeka* establishes the identification between the patron and the victims, in this case offerings, which is brought about by sacrificial rituals involving coconut and fire sacrifices. It accomplishes a symbolic transformation of the patron, and the eradication of his evil aspects, followed by a rebirth, or consecration involving a passage from the visible to the invisible, from the body to the soul, so that he can join the divine. Underlying his transformation is a principle of substitution. After the patron is identified with an offering or victim, the latter is physically transformed, a substitute for the former. Following this destruction in proxy the patron comes close to the divine being. In this sense the offering is a mediator between the patron and the divine.

Considering the flow of power (*śakti*), we can also see that *abhiṣeka* and worship are radically different in terms of the direction of flow : in the former, *śakti* is generated in the fire sacrifice, and transferred to the stone idol through the pots ; during worship the *śakti*, which has been embodied in the idol and fully identified with Bhadrakālī, is activated in worship, and finally reaches the devotees in the form of the consecrated leftovers, *prasāda*. *Śakti* is created in the fire, or is brought in from the outside world.[99] It is then transferred to the sanctum sanctorum, the purest place in the temple, and finally moves back again to the village. In short, divine power moves from the outer world to the village through the temple. In the process power is successively brought into being in fire, then embodied and located in the pots of consecrated water and finally is transferred to the immovable stone idol. That is, it moves into progressively more containable, tangible forms, from the uncontrollable to the controllable, from hot to cool.[100]

Śakti can be considered as a fertile power underlying the natural world, but its excess would threaten the human world (see chapter 5). One of the main aims of *abhiṣeka* rituals is to gain control over this equivocal power. The human world needs divine power for its prosperity and reproduction, but, in essence, it is dangerous.

A parallel process of embodying power can be found in the distribution of the various items of *prasāda* : divine power is first transferred to the devotees in the camphor fire, then in the holy water, and finally food. Again there is a sequence of passage from fire to liquid to solidity—— this transformation suggests another dimension of movement, from the dangerous to the edible. Power is gradually absorbed and internalised within the devotee's body. At the same time it is transformed, from something hot, dangerous and wild, into "grace" (the root meaning of *prasāda* in Sanskrit). If ritually controlled and tamed, this power is a blessing which brings prosperity to the human world.

The progressive disembodiment of the patron seems to be the inverse of the progressive embodiment of divine power. Symbolically, he moves from village to forest, changing his social status from a householder to an ascetic in a set of purificatory rituals, ultimately to leave behind the profane body and attain union with the divine through fire and coconut sacrifices. As with the embodiment of divine power in a stone idol or a pot, the disaggregation of the patron's soul from his body is, however, of a temporary nature.

It should be noted that there are some discrepancies in the ideologies surrounding the *abhiṣeka* and the worship which follows it. For example, the *maṇḍalābhiṣeka* is concerned almost exclusively with the transformation of the patron, while during the latter just as in ordinary worship, the emphasis is on the congregation in general. In the *abhiṣeka* sequence, the main theme is the regeneration, and acquisition, of divine power by a man with secular power (wealth and social status). On the other hand, worship concerns spiritual communication between the villagers in general and divine beings ; the receipt of divine grace (*aruḷ*) through devotion (*bhakti*) is the central interest.

These differences are congruent with the differences in the conceptualisation of the divine being. In the *abhiṣeka, śakti*, abstract divine power, is emphasised, while in worship the object of devotion is a personified divine being able to bestow grace on the devout.[101]

In spite of these differences, the patron, however, remains a central figure through the whole sequence of the *abhiṣeka*. It is the patron who meets the expense of worship and, especially, prepares the substantial public offering of Bengal gram at the evening worship, which, as *prasāda*, provides the only material link between the other devotees and the deity, symbolising their own acquisition of divine grace. From a slightly different point of view, the patron is a mediator between the god and the devotees. He achieves union with divine power, and with its acquisition, he successfully becomes a source of power for the devotees. We could even argue that the patron is a more important mediator than the priest between human and divine beings. So although there are egalitarian elements in the worship following personal consecration, they are subject to a pervasive hierarchical ideology, which emphasises material wealth and its possessor. The same argument may be relevant to regular temple worship, that is worship not preceded by *abhiṣeka*. In as much as temple worship is financially dependent on patrons, temple owners, trustees, and so on, when in attendance they usually receive the first *prasāda* : subsequently the egalitarian ideology of religious discourse remains subordinate.

Conclusion

This chapter consisted of a lengthy analysis of *maṇḍalābhiṣeka*. First, I repeat that *abhiṣeka* is a significant Brahmanical ritual that demonstrates the close relationship between man of power and man of purity. With the latter's help, the former undergoes a series of transformations to approach divine power which takes an increasingly concrete form as the ritual proceeds. A disembodiment of the patron's soul and the embodiment of divine power occur during the ritual. At worship, divine power embodied in the patron's offerings is distributed to the villagers through *prasāda*. The man of power is less prominent during subsequent worship and, in this sense, worship is more egalitarian and shares some common features with ecstatic rituals such as firewalking. It is conducted for the devotees. Even here, however, the patron remains the main figure.

As we shall see, *abhiṣeka* is one of the important rituals the Brahman priest performs during the Draupadī goddess festival. If we consider the function of the *abhiṣeka* within it, the political nature of the Draupadī goddess festival will become clearer.

CHAPTER SEVEN

PASSING OVER FIRE TO GODDESS

In this chapter I would like to describe and interpret a village festival for Draupadī. First I examine the *Mahābhārata* epic on which the festival is based, the historical development of the Draupadī goddess (now Pārtasārati) temple, the divine beings housed in the temple, and the main participants. Then, a detailed description of the festival follows. In the final section I analyse the structure of the festival as a whole and discuss some of its symbolic and political dimensions.

I should give a brief account of the festival here before going into a detailed description. It is held for twenty days. With *śānti* (appeasement) rituals and the tying of a *kāppu* cord to the Paṇṭāram medium's wrist by the Brahman priest, the festival begins. After this the medium goes to the sea to induce Draupadī to be present in a *karakam* pot. Every other evening he carries the pot on his head to the temple. Draupadī's divine power, after propagation, is eventually transferred to the stone image of her inside the temple. From the eleventh day onwards the Brahman priest conducts *abhiṣeka* to create power and transfer it to the stone images of both Pārtasārati and Draupadī. On the morning of the eighteenth day, the priest creates a sacred fire. The medium goes into trance in front of the stone image and transfers the fire to the firewalking pit. In the evening the medium walks over the fire, the first of about one thousand male devotees. The next day the festival image of the Draupadī goddess is taken out from the temple on a village procession. At midnight the Brahman priest removes the *kāppu* from the medium's hand. On the twentieth day, the festival is concluded with *śānti* and *prāyaścitta* (expiatory) rituals.

Introduction to the Draupadī Goddess Festival

The *Mahābhārata*

The *Mahābhārata* is one of the most famous Hindu epics. It is said that the *Mahābhārata* was put into its present form between four hundred B.C. and four hundred A.D. A Tamil translation was made in the ninth century (Hiltebeitel 1988 : 14).

The central theme of the story is the rivalry for the throne of the Kuru dynasty between two groups of cousins, the Pāṇḍava brothers and the Kaurava brothers. Draupadī is the common wife of the five Pāṇḍava brothers. They undergo a series of hardship and suffering, but, after a great war with the Kauravas, the eldest Pāṇḍava brother, Yudhiṣṭhira, becomes the king and Draupadī the queen (see fig. 16).

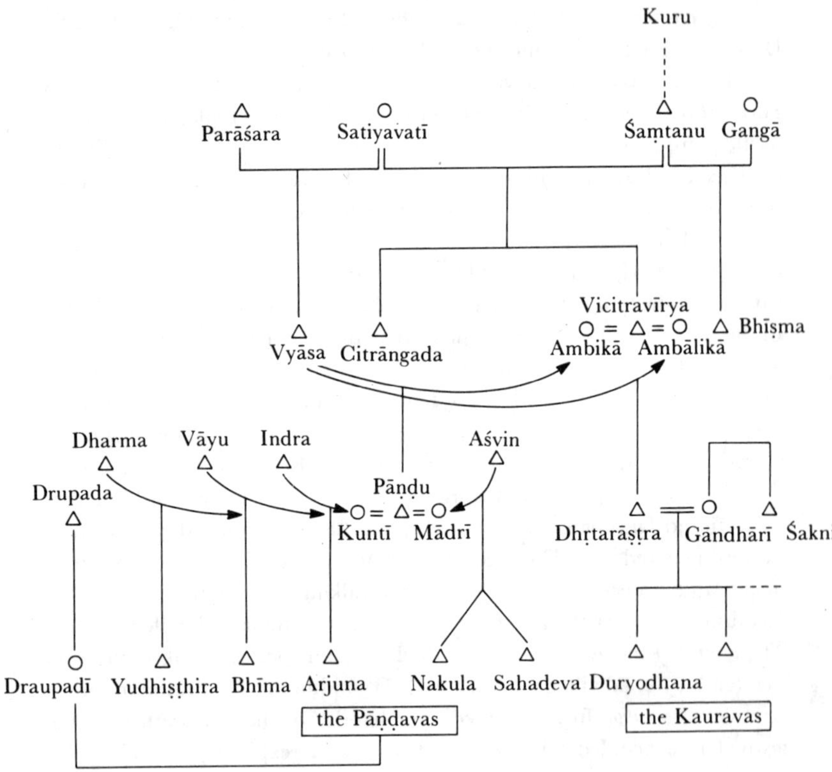

FIGURE 16. CHARACTERS IN THE *MAHĀBHĀRATA*

During the festival the *Mahābhārata* story is recited by the medium through a public address system. As the *Mahābhārata* story is the basis of the Draupadī goddess festival, I provide here a brief synopsis based on the Tamil texts recited at the festival.

At the beginning, the role of the moon in cosmogonical activities is related. Out of these Budha is born, then his son, Purūravas is born. This is the origin of the Kuru (Lunar) dynasty. The marriage of Purūravas, his grandson Yayāti, the conflicts between Yayāti's wife Devayānī and Śarmiṣṭā, the birth of Duḥṣanta, the first son of Yayāti with Śarmiṣṭā are subsequently narrated. Duḥṣanta meets Śakuntalā and has Bharata with her. Then the story of Śaṃtanu, one of Bharata's descendants, begins.

One day king Śaṃtanu marries Gangā. She kills their seven babies one after the other. Śaṃtanu intervenes, but only one son survives among their eight children. He is called Bhīṣma. After Gangā leaves him, Śaṃtanu meets Satyavatī, a daughter of the fishermen, and wants to marry her. Her father says that he will allow her to marry Śaṃtanu on the condition that only her children will succeed him. Śaṃtanu, thinking of Bhīṣma, is perplexed. After hearing this story, Bhīṣma is prepared to give up his right to the throne. Śaṃtanu has two sons with Satyavatī, Citrāngada and Vicitravīrya. The former dies unmarried, and the latter takes two wives, Ambikā and Ambālikā, but dies without issue.

Before having Citrāngada and Vicitravīrya, Satyavatī had had a son called Vyāsa with Parāśara, a saint. She asks him to impregnate the widows, Ambikā and Ambālikā. So ugly is he, that when he approaches them at night, Ambikā closes her eyes, while Ambālikā's face becomes pale with fear. Thus, they respectively give birth to blind Dhṛtarāṣṭra and pale-faced Pāṇḍu.

Dhṛtarāṣṭra becomes king and marries Gāndhārī, while Pāṇḍu has two wives, Kuntī and Mādrī. Before marrying Pāṇḍu, Kuntī had received a magical spell from a sage. This spell gave Kuntī the power to conceive the child of a god. She tried the spell, praying to Sūrya, the Sun God, and had his son, Karṇa. At the time she was still unmarried, and too ashamed to bring him up, left him on the bank of the Gangā.

One day Pāṇḍu goes out hunting, and shoots two mating deer with arrows. It turns out that they are actually a sage and his wife. The sage curses Pāṇḍu saying that he will die when he sleeps with a woman. He decides to live an ascetic life but wants a son. Kuntī tells Pāṇḍu that she knows a magical spell and can have a son with its power. In this way she has Dharma's son, Yudhiṣṭhira.

At this time Gāndhārī is pregnant. She is so upset about the news of Yudhiṣṭhira's birth that she hits her belly to cause a miscarriage. Vyāsa suggests that she should keep the blood from this in one hundred pots and put milk and clarified butter into them every day. As a result ninty-nine boys and one girl are born from these pots. They are called Kauravas, the eldest of whom is Duryodhana.

Pāṇḍu wants more sons when the news of the multiple birth of the Kaurava brothers reaches him. Kuntī has two more sons, Bhīma with Vāyu, the Wind God, and Arjuna with Indra, the king of gods. Mādrī asks Kuntī for the spell, so she can also have sons. She has twins, Nakula and Sahadeva with Aśvin. These five brothers are known as the Pāṇḍavas.

Pāṇḍu finally dies after having sex with Mādrī, and she throws herself into his burning fire. Kuntī and the Pāṇḍavas move to Dhṛtarāṣṭra's palace. The text mentions several attempts by Duryodhana to kill the Pāṇḍavas. But the plots always fail.

Both the Pāṇḍavas and the Kauravas learn archery with Droṇa. He has trouble with Drupada, the king of Pāñcāla, for a while. When young, Droṇa and Drupada had studied with a *guru,* and Drupada promised Droṇa that he would give him half a kingdom someday. Sometime later, he completes the study, and Droṇa's wife has a son called Aśvatthāman with Śiva. Droṇa decides to bring him up as his own son, but he does not have sufficient resources. So, remembering Drupada's promise, Droṇa goes to meet Drupada, but is turned away. After this unexpected humiliation he decides to conquer Drupada's kingdom to make him feel the same degree of humiliation. Having taught them archery for many years, Droṇa asks the Kauravas and Pāṇḍavas to invade the Pāñcāla kingdom. The Kauravas fail, and only Arjuna succeeds, but leaves Drupada alive. Drupada vows that his son will kill Droṇa and his daughter marry Arjuna. Sometime later, a son and a daughter are born out of the fire of a *homa,* fire sacrifice, at the palace. This daughter is Draupadī. She is also known as Pāñcālī (the daughter of the king of Pāñcāla) or Kṛṣṇā (the dark one), because of her dark complexion. At the time of her birth, there is a voice from the heavens, saying that Draupadī, born from the fire of Śiva's third eye, will destroy the dynasty in the same way that Sītā destroyed the dynasty of *asura,* Rāvaṇa.

As Yudhiṣṭhira's fame increases, so does Duryodhana's jealousy burn. He plots to build a lacquer palace and to invite the Pāṇḍavas to stay there. At night when they are fast asleep, Duryodhana sets fire to the palace. Six seriously burned bodies are found in the ruins, and it is thought that the Pāṇḍavas and Kuntī have all perished. Bhīma, however, had got wind of Duryodhana's plan in advance and carried his mother and brothers to safety through a secret tunnel at midnight. Thus they all survive unhurt.

The Pāṇḍavas do not return to Dhṛtarāṣṭra's palace, and remain in the forest. Here Bhīma has heroic adventures. He fights with a ferocious *asura*, Hiḍimba, and has a son with his sister, Hiḍimbā. He also saves Brahmans by killing another *asura* called Baka.

Meanwhile Draupadī grows to marriageable age, and her father, Drupada, decides to hold a *svayaṁvara*. This is a traditional method of selecting a bridegroom. Young men display their martial skills in competition, the winner of which gains the hand of the bride. Being a rare beauty, she attracts many princes as suitors, including the Kaurava brothers, from all over India. The Pāṇḍavas also come, but disguised as Brahmans. Only Arjuna is able to string a giant bow and shoot a mark. Draupadī garlands him, a sign that she accepts Arjuna as her legitimate bridegroom. Mistaking Arjuna for a Brahman, the other suitors consider that it is improper for Draupadī, of Kṣatriya origin, to marry a Brahman. They try to prevent the couple from leaving, but they are all defeated.

When the Pāṇḍavas return to the hut where Kuntī is waiting, she misunderstands that her sons have brought fruit, and she tells them to share it. Thus Draupadī becomes the common wife to the five brothers.

There is a grand wedding ceremony and the Pāṇḍavas remain in the kingdom of Pāñcāla, but it becomes widely known that they are alive. So they are asked to return to Dhṛtarāṣṭra and govern half the kingdom.

Kṛṣṇa builds a beautiful palace for the Pāṇḍavas there. The sage Nārada visits them and suggests that in order to avoid any conflict among the brothers with regard to Draupadī, she should stay with each husband for a year at a time. At the end of the year Draupadī should walk through fire to purify herself before moving on to the next husband. Yudhiṣṭhira has the privilege of the first year. Arjuna, however, while looking for a weapon, happens to see Draupadī in Yudhiṣṭhira's room. In order to expiate this sin, he decides to go on a pilgrimage to various sacred places. On this trip he meets many girls and has sons with them.

One day Duryodhana is invited to the Pāṇḍavas' palace, where he has a vision, and cowers with fear. Seeing this, Draupadī mocks him. Duryodhana wants revenge for this humiliation. He sees a way to do this through a gambling session in the assembly hall, where Draupadī can be publicly humiliated.

It is obvious that Yudhiṣṭhira will succeed Dhṛtarāṣṭra, so, one day, Duryodhana invites Yudhiṣṭhira to a game of dice. With the help of his maternal uncle, Śakuni, Duryodhana tricks Yudhiṣṭhira, and keeps winning. Yudhiṣṭhira is eventually left with nothing but his wife. Desperately he stakes even Draupadī, and once again loses. Duryodhana's younger brother, Duḥśāsana, fetches Draupadī from the women's quarters and tries to insult her by pulling off her sari. But, with Kṛṣṇa's help, no sooner is one sari pulled off, then another appears in its place. Bhīma, the second Pāṇḍava brother, vows that he will kill Duḥśāsana and Duryodhana. Draupadī takes a binding oath (Tam. *capatam*) that she will leave her hair dishevelled until she can wash and dress it with dead Duryodhana's blood. Draupadī is menstruating at that time.[102] King Dhṛtarāṣṭra intervenes, and the results of the dice session are cancelled. As part of a compromise the Pāṇḍavas have to endure an exile in the forest for twelve years.

The Pāṇḍavas and Draupadī experience various events in the forest. During this exile, Arjuna performs *tapas* (austerities) to gain Pāśupata, the strongest weapon, from Śiva.

Another important episode during the exile is an abduction of Draupadī, by Saindhava, Duryodhana's sister's husband. Bhīma and Sahadeva rescue her and try to kill Saindhava, Yudhiṣṭhira intervenes, and saves the life of the kidnapper. Smarting with humiliation, however, Saindhava vows to kill the Pāṇḍavas. Just before the onset of the war, the Pāṇḍavas get to know about a fort built by Saindhava. They have to destroy the fort, guarded by four warrior deities —— Kālī, Aiyaṉār, Bhairava and Vīrabhadra —— in order to win the coming war with the Kauravas. Kṛṣṇa, disguised as an old lady, approaches these guardians. They recognise that she is Kṛṣṇa with their powerful vision and agree to help him. Consequently, the fort is taken by the Pāṇḍavas.

The fort has to be kept, so, Kṛṣṇa asks one of the guardians, Vīrabhadra, to remain. In return, he demands to marry Yudhiṣṭhira's half-sister Caṅkuvati. Kṛṣṇa had saved her, when her mother, Mādrī, threw herself on the funeral fire of Pāṇḍu. The pregnancy had continued for two years at that time. Kṛṣṇa preserved the womb and foetus in a conch-shell (*śankha*), from which Caṅkuvati was born. Vīrabhadra demands an extraordinary dowry, part of which is a goat as big as a palmyra tree. Kṛṣṇa meets his demand presenting him with a goat on top of a palmyra tree.

After the period of exile, a fierce battle starts between the Pāṇḍavas and the Kauravas, and their followers. The war lasts eighteen days. On the seventeenth day Bhīsma and Karṇa, members of the Duryodhana camp, are killed. On the eighteenth day Śalya of Mitra, Mādrī's brother, becomes the commander in chief and fights against Yudhiṣṭhira. Arjuna and Nakula fight against Aśvatthāman, the son of Droṇa, and sons of Karṇa respectively. Bhīma slaughters the Kaurava brothers one after the other. Eventually Yudhiṣṭhira kills Śalya, and wins the war. Sahadeva kills Śakuni. Duryodhana leaves the battle field and hides in a lake. He is thinking of using a magical spell, Sañjīvanī *mantra*, which would bring his warriors back from the dead. The Pāṇḍavas discover him, and he is killed by Bhīma. Draupadī fulfils her vow to dress her hair with the blood of Duryodhana. After the battle, the Pāṇḍavas and Draupadī cross a fire to expiate the sins they have committed during the battle. The Cattiyur *Mahābhārata* ends with the coronation of Yudhiṣṭhira.

Historical Development of the Temple

Draupadī is a popular village goddess in Tamilnadu State of South India, especially the northern part of the state.[103] As mentioned in chapter 2, the Cattiyur villagers emigrated from India to Sri Lanka in the seventeenth century. They first arrived at Mannar and gradually moved south to the present site of the village. It is claimed that they built a temple for Draupadī at each place at which they stayed. In fact, however, only two Draupadī temples survive in the Western Province of Sri Lanka. The other is located in Mannur across the lagoon from Cattiyur. The ancestors of the Cattiyur villagers had stayed in Mannur, just before their migration to Cattiyur. There are some other Draupadī temples around Batticaloa in Eastern District, but I have never visited them.

The villagers presumably built a small shrine for Draupadī when they came to stay in Cattiyur. A local chronicle refers to the laying of the foundation stone for the new brick temple in 1905. It was completed in 1908 and the *mahākumbhābhiṣeka* (consecration) was performed by the chief Brahman priest from the Munnesvaram Śiva temple. The sandalwood image of Draupadī was replaced with a sculpted stone image on this occasion. This was followed by another restoration in 1929.

1950 is a crucial year because the Draupadī temple was transformed into a Pārtasārati temple. Pārtasārati (Kṛṣṇa) and his two consorts, Rukmiṇī and Satyabhāmā were installed in the sanctum sanctorum, and Draupadī's image was reinstalled in the small room (*ardhamaṇḍapa*) between the sanctum sanctorum and *pūjāmaṇḍapa* (see fig. 9). Furthermore two small shrines for two prominent Śaiva deities, Gaṇeśa and Murukaṉ, were added to the temple in the same year, thus showing a kind of syncretism of Vaiṣṇava and Śaiva traditions. The temple had two small restoration ceremonies in 1961 and 1972, and *mahākumbhābhiṣeka* were performed in 1974 and 1980. In 1974 the stage hall (*vasantamaṇḍapa*) for festival images was added at the northeastern corner.

The reason why the Draupadī goddess temple became the Pārtasārati temple is not difficult to guess. Kṛṣṇa is the presiding deity in the *Mahābhārata* story. He is disguised as the chariot driver of Arjuna, one of Draupadī's husbands.

Divine Beings

There are now no blood sacrifices offered in the Pārtasārati temple. Draupadī's nature is less fierce than the other village goddesses, Bhadrakālī and Muttumāri, at whose temples blood sacrifices are offered. Nor are margosa leaves, which have a cooling effect during epidemics, used in her festival. Instead, mango leaves or coconut shoots are used in the *karakam* pot representing Draupadī. This implies that Draupadī has no relationship with smallpox and other diseases. She is, in fact, considered *paricuttam* (absolutely pure), and I have never heard villagers speak of violent possession by Draupadī, except for a case in which she was said, along with various other supernatural beings, to have possessed a pregnant girl. Otherwise possession by Draupadī occurs only during the festival. Draupadī is often identified with Śrī Lakṣmī, Viṣṇu's wife. Furthermore, Draupadī is said to be both Kṛṣṇa's wife and his sister as well.

Cattiyur Draupadī's general character is also indicated by the caste of the chief priest at her temple, that is, a Brahman. It is fairly common for blood sacrifice to be absent from temples cared for by Brahman priests. Generally speaking, deities served by the Brahman caste are benevolent, have strong connections to Sanskritic deities, do not possess villagers or cause affliction to them, and are strongly associated with ritual purity (Srinivas 1952 : 185-86). The first Brahman priest started serving the Draupadī goddess at the end of the last century, and it is reported that blood sacrifice was performed until the early twentieth century (cf. Modder 1908 : 137). In other words the present-day Draupadī has been significantly Sanskritised due to the presence of the Brahman priests.

Draupadī, however, is not as high in status as Kṛṣṇa and his two consorts, even if she is an incarnation of Śrī Lakṣmī. She is not housed in the same room with them. The position of her statue between the sanctum sanctorum and its entrance to the main hall indicates her relatively lower status. She also stands alone, without any image of her husbands, which is reminiscent of fierce village goddesses. Unmarried goddesses are generally fierce in nature, for their sexuality is not under the control of male deities (Fuller and Logan 1985 : 91). Draupadī's mount is a lion, as is that of Kālī.[104] Another indication of Draupadī's equivocal nature is the central role a non-Brahman medium plays in the festival.

It is superfluous to repeat the explanations of Gaṇeśa and

Murukaṉ here. One feature that seems unique to the Draupadī temple is that the sanctom sanctorum is protected by two guardians. On the left hand side stands Pōttirācaṉ, holding the head of an exorcist (*mantiravāti*). The other guardian, called Muttālarācaṉ, is mounted on a horse. At the main entrance of the temple is a shrine to Viṣṇu's snake-like incarnation Cantāṉa Kōpālaṉ. Another guardian, Vīrabhadra stands in front of the flagstaff, and Garuḍa (Viṣṇu's mount) is next to the *balipīṭha*.[105] It is not surprising to find Vīrabhadra here, as in the local version of the *Mahābhārata,* mentioned above, the guardian has an obviously emphasised role. Muttālarācaṉ and Pōttirācaṉ appear in a myth not included in the *Mahābhārata.* It goes as follows :

> After forty generations from Yudhiṣṭriṛa, there is a king called Cunītaṉ. His kingdom is under threat from the powerful *asura.* One day he has a dream, in which Draupadī appears and tells him that she will save him, as he is a descendant of the Pāṇḍavas. Next day the king performs *homa,* from which Draupadī is born. In the fight against the *asura,* Draupadī is helped by Pōttirācaṉ and his close relative, Muttālarācaṉ. After winning the fight she tells Cunītaṉ that, if he builds a temple for her, and arranges an annual festival with firewalking on the eighteenth day, anybody who takes part in the firewalking will receive her blessing.

As Hiltebeitel argues (1988 : 90), the myth of Cunītaṉ, rather than the *Mahābhārata,* is directly related to the origin of the Draupadī goddess temple and her festival.[105]

Main Participants

The significant figures in the festival are Kumaracami, the Brahman priest, and Parandaman, the Paṇṭāram medium. As I have already described them, I introduce other people.

During the festival the *Mahābhārata* is recited by the medium with the help of an assistant from the Karaiyar caste. The story teller of the *Mahābhārata* is usually from the Paṇṭāram caste. The first narrator was Cokkalingam, and he was followed by his daughter's husband (see fig. 11). Now his grandson, Parandaman, who began public recitation in 1971, annually carries on the family tradition. Now he is both a narrator and a medium. Most villagers feel that they should find somebody else to recite the *Mahābhārata,* as playing both roles during the festival is too much for Parandaman.

Parandaman does have the support of one villager, who sits opposite him, and responds to the recitation with interpretations. He also dances with him in his role as medium at the *karakam* procession. This role is not hereditary. The present incumbent called *pakkam* or assistant is a semi-retired fisherman, who was interested in the *Mahābhārata* and decided of his own accord to become the assistant. The story teller and the assistant are entitled to payment by the Hindu Temple Administrative Committee, but the assistant refused to accept it because, he said, his involvement was out of *bhakti* (devotion) to Draupadī. This is a typical expression of *bhakti* used against material interests.

There is an attendant to the medium. He is a votary and plays the role of Arjuna (one of Draupadī's five husbands) at one of the *Mahābhārata* enactments. Arjuna must remain under various taboos in the temple, as does the medium. He must always stay close to the medium. Structurally, he occupies the same position as the *cūrapuli*s (Bhadrakālī's attendants), but he shows no sign of trance. Draupadī is said to remain benign as long as the medium and Arjuna do not meet their wives.

In addition there are some villagers who play various roles in the enactments of the *Mahābhārata* story during the festival. They are votaries and selected by lottery.

The Washermen provide white cloths and the Goldsmiths present Draupadī with a gold necklace at her wedding with the Pāṇḍavas on the twelfth day. There are also three groups of musicians involved in this festival. One consists of the Karaiyars, who sing accompanied by drums and cymbals during the *karakam* pot procession and worship. The second group is a trio from a professional caste (Mēḷakkāraṉ) from Munnesvaram. They play drum, harmonium, and an oboe-like instrument (*nākasvaram*). Two or three Sinhalese drummers from the outside also usually perform. Both of the latter groups play music at the processions of festival images, but the Sinhalese are not allowed to enter the temple.

Description and Interpretation of the Festival

The Draupadī goddess great festival (*Tiraupatai Tēvi Mahā Uccavam*)[106] is held for twenty days in the months of Āṉi (June—July) and Āṭi (July—August).[107] The fifth day should fall on the new moon day of Āṭi. The following description is based on the 1982 festival, which started on 18 July and ended on 5 August.

The first rite called Vāstu *śānti* (Tam. *cānti*) and *grāma śānti* (1.1)[108] in the festival starts in the evening (see table 16). It is a combination of two

TABLE 16
THE DRAUPADĪ GODDESS FESTIVAL SCHEDULE

Date	No	Time (approx.)	Ritual
1	1.1	17 : 30	Vāstu *śānti* and *grāma śānti*
	1.2	18 : 30	*karakam* procession
	1.3	21 : 00	the *Mahābhārata*
	1.4	23 : 30	flag hoisting and *kāppu* cord tying
	1.5	1 : 00	worship
2	2.1	6 : 00	worship
	2.2	11 : 00	worship
	2.3	19 : 00	worship
3	3.1	6 : 00	worship
	3.2	11 : 00	worship
	3.3	19 : 00	worship
4	4.1	6 : 00	worship
	4.2	11 : 00	worship
	4.3	19 : 00	worship
5	5.1	6 : 00	worship
	5.2	9 : 00	hoisting of the Hanuman flag
	5.3	10 : 00	village meeting
	5.4	11 : 00	worship
	5.5	17 : 00	*karakam* procession
	5.6	19 : 00	worship
	5.7	21 : 00	the *Mahābhārata*
6	6.1	6 : 00	worship
	6.2	11 : 00	worship
	6.3	19 : 00	worship
	6.4	21 : 00	the *Mahābhārata*
7	7.1	6 : 00	worship
	7.2	11 : 00	worship
	7.3	17 : 00	*karakam* procession
	7.4	19 : 00	worship
	7.5	21 : 00	the *Mahābhārata*
8	8.1	6 : 00	worship
	8.2	11 : 00	worship
	8.3	19 : 00	worship
	8.4	21 : 00	the *Mahābhārata*
9	9.1	6 : 00	worship
	9.2	11 : 00	worship
	9.3	17 : 00	*karakam* procession
	9.4	19 : 00	worship
	9.5	21 : 00	the *Mahābhārata*
10	10.1	6 : 00	worship
	10.2	11 : 00	worship (after votive *rudrābhiṣeka*)
	10.3	19 : 00	worship
	10.4	21 : 00	the *Mahābhārata*
11	11.1	6 : 00	worship
	11.2	10 : 00	*snānābhiṣeka*
	11.3	12 : 00	worship
	11.4	20 : 00	Gaṇeśa's procession
	11.5	22 : 00	worship
	11.6	23 : 00	the *Mahābhārata*
12	12.1	6 : 00	Gaṇeśa's procession
	12.2	6 : 30	worship
	12.3	10 : 00	*snānābhiṣeka*
	12.4	12 : 00	worship
	12.5	17 : 00	*karakam* procession
	12.6	20 : 00	Pārtasārati's procession
	12.7	22 : 00	worship
	12.8	23 : 00	the *Mahābhārata* (Draupadī's wedding)

13	13.1	6 : 00	Gaṇeśa's procession
	13.2	6 : 30	worship
	13.3	10 : 00	*snānābhiṣeka*
	13.4	12 : 00	worship
	13.5	20 : 00	Pārtasārati's procession
	13.6	22 : 00	worship
	13.7	23 : 00	the *Mahābhārata*
14	14.1	6 : 00	Gaṇeśa's procession
	14.2	6 : 30	worship
	14.3	8 : 30	votive rituals
	14.4	10 : 00	*snānābhiṣeka*
	14.5	12 : 00	worship
	14.6	17 : 00	*karakam* procession
	14.7	20 : 00	Pārtasārati's procession
	14.8	22 : 00	worship
	14.9	23 : 00	the *Mahābhārata*
15	15.1	6 : 00	Gaṇeśa's procession
	15.2	6 : 30	worship
	15.3	8 : 30	votive rituals
	15.4	10 : 00	*snānābhiṣeka*
	15.5	12 : 00	worship
	15.6	16 : 30	scene from the *Mahābhārata*
	15.7	20 : 00	Pārtasārati's procession
	15.8	22 : 00	worship
16	16.1	6 : 00	Gaṇeśa's procession
	16.2	6 : 30	worship
	16.3	8 : 30	votive rituals
	16.4	10 : 45	consecration of the firewalking pit
	16.5	11 : 00	*snānābhiṣeka*
	16.6	13 : 00	worship
	16.7	16 : 00	scene from the *Mahābhārata*
	16.8	18 : 00	*karakam* procession
	16.9	20 : 00	Pārtasārati's procession
	16.10	22 : 00	worship
17	17.1	6 : 00	Gaṇeśa's procession
	17.2	6 : 30	worship
	17.3	9 : 30	invocation of guardian gods
	17.4	10 : 30	consecration of the firewalking pit
	17.5	10 : 45	consecration of the *Mahābhārata* scene site
	17.6	11 : 00	*snānābhiṣeka*
	17.7	13 : 00	worship
	17.8	17 : 00	scene from the *Mahābhārata*
	17.9	20 : 00	Pārtasārati's procession
	17.10	22 : 00	worship
18	18.1	6 : 30	*grāma śānti* and *agniyāga*
	18.2	7 : 30	the *Mahābhārata* (goat offering)
	18.3	8 : 30	consecration of the *Mahābhārata* scene site
	18.4	9 : 00	the *Mahābhārata*
	18.5	9 : 00	*arcanā* offering
	18.6	11 : 00	worship
	18.7	16 : 45	scene from the *Mahābhārata*
	18.8	19 : 00	firewalking
19	19.1	6 : 30	worship
	19.2	13 : 00	worship
	19.3	19 : 00	Draupadī's procession
	19.4	23 : 00	*māviḷakku* offering
	19.5	0 : 30	the *Mahābhārata*
	19.6	1 : 00	lowering the flags and untying *kāppu* cord
	19.7	2 : 30	worship
20	20.1	11 : 00	Vāstu *śānti* and *prāyaścitta*
	20.2	12 : 30	worship
	20.3	18 : 00	worship

PLATE 15. THE MEDIUM AND THE PRIEST (RIGHT)

appeasement (*śānti*) rituals concerning Vāstu, the deity of residence, and evil spirits, who must be kept away from the village (*grāma,* Tam. *kirāmam*) during the festival. They are actually combined in a single sequence which consists of the following rites : preparatory and purificatory rites ; fire sacrifice (*homa*) ; Vāstu *śānti* in its narrow sense. After these rituals a protective *kāppu* cord is tied around the medium's right wrist, who sits on the seat of the *upayakkāraṉ* (patron), next to the Brahman chief priest (pl. 15).

The ritual setting for Vāstu *śānti* and *grāma śānti* is more or less identical to *abhiṣeka.* A raised sacrificial pit is made of bricks inside the temple, and nine pots representing the nine planetary deities (*Navagraha*) are set up, between it and the sanctum sanctorum. Draupadī's weapon, a hand-knife (*camcapaṭu*) with a lime on the tip, a two foot long cane and *karakam* pot are placed near these pots. First, the chief priest declares his resolve (Skt. *saṅkalpa*) to perform the rituals which follow. This is done in the name of the village. A series of preparatory and purificatory rituals are carried out. The medium places a *darbha* grass ring on his ring finger ; Gaṇeśa is invoked and worshipped ; the water in holy-pot (*puṇyakumbha*) is consecrated and Varuṇa is invoked ; and finally, this water is sprinkled around. The medium receives the sacred water and applies it to his neck and head. One of priest's sons picks up the holy-pot and sprinkles the water in it on the stone images of Gaṇeśa, Pārtasārati and his consorts, Draupadī, Murukaṉ, and other deities.

Then the nine planetary deities are invoked to come into the nine pots and *homa* is prepared. Towards the end of the fire sacrifice the medium stands at the eastern edge of the pit, and offers a set, consisting of a coconut, unhusked rice, a banana, areca nuts and betel leaves. Since this is not an *abhiṣeka,* the stone images are not anointed.

The fire sacrifice is followed by Vāstu *śānti.* The garlanded straw figure is carried near the pit. First a temple assistant cuts an ash-pumpkin (*pūcaṉi*) into halves, smears them with vermilion powder, then the priest scoops some flesh from the freshly cut surfaces with a wooden spoon and puts it into the fire. He ignites the end of the straw figure with the fire. The temple assistant carries it, together with the halves of ash-pumpkin, inside the temple, and goes out to the lagoon. The other assistant follows him, sprinkling around consecrated water from the holy-pot. These ritual acts serve both to appease Vāstu, the residence deity, and to pacify supernatural beings in the village. It ensures the success of the festival.

Now the priest ties a *kāppu* cord three times around the medium's right wrist which concludes the first set of festival rituals. Now he has been consecrated. He can approach dangerous divine power and is immune to the pollution, even that resulting from the death of his close relatives. After this cord is tied, he can enter the sanctum sanctorum, where only Brahman priests are usually allowed. During the festival the medium refrains from eating non-vegetarian food and going home to see his wife. He must stay at a hut temporarily built in the temple precincts until the firewalking ceremony is over.

After the consecration a *karakam* pot procession takes place (1.2). The Brahman priest starts by paying homage to Gaṇeśa, and then Pārtasārati and his consorts in the sanctum sanctorum. Following this, the medium enters the sanctum sanctorum and venerates Draupadī, Pārtasārati and his consorts, and again Draupadī. Coming out with a cane, a hand-knife and a *karakam* (a large pot with mango leaves) representing Draupadī, he goes to the Muttumāri goddess temple in Adipetti. This time there is no elaborate rite for setting up the *karakam* pot. The Brahman priest remains in the temple. A group of twenty devotees, including a pair of torch holders, a band of six village musicians, the Hindu Temple Administrative Committee members, and Arjuna accompany the medium.

When the procession reaches the Muttumāri goddess temple, the medium and Arjuna bathe in the temple well inside the precincts, smear their bodies with sacred ash, sandalwood paste, and red powder, and then change into new ceremonial loin clothes (Tam. *vēṣṭi*). In front of the temple gate the assistant narrator decorates the *karakam* with flowers and *poṭṭu* marks. The medium goes into a trance (*caṉṉatam*) there, in the same

PLATE 16. THE MEDIUM GOING INTO TRANCE

way as he does in the Bhadrakālī goddess festival (pl. 16). Arjuna is, however, not possessed. Bearing the *karakam* pot on his head the medium enters the temple with Arjuna. After taking sacred ash from the temple priest and receiving *āratti,* he briskly sets off with the others to the Pārtasārati temple, on the way passing by the Kantacāmi temple, and the Bhadrakālī goddess temple, where the medium also takes sacred ash from the priest. As in the *karakam* procession during the Bhadrakālī goddess festival, several pots full of water are prepared on the route, and water from them is poured over the medium's feet in order to cool him.[109]

When the medium returns to the Pārtasārati temple and enters the sanctum sanctorum, the curtain is closed behind him, but it soon reopens. The villagers who have gathered in the temple shout Viṣṇu's other name, "Govinda! Govinda!" as they see the sword (*vāḷ*) miraculously standing upright on the curving side line of the *karakam* which is placed in front of Draupadī's stone image. This is repeated at the conclusion of every *karakam* procession. The sword is the weapon of Bhīma, one of Draupadī's husbands, and represents him, whilst the *karakam* represents Draupadī. More generally speaking, the sword is a phallus and the pot a womb. Thus this ritual act implies the symbolic union of Draupadī and Bhīma during the festival.

According to the medium, he formerly would enter a trance at dusk on the beach, but since a few years back this now occurs at the Muttumāri goddess temple. He said that some fish-curing yards were built at the beach, which thereby became polluted, so, it was no longer an appropriate place to enter a trance. Thus the medium used to become possessed by Draupadī as he faced the sea at dusk. At this liminal time, she is believed to walk on the sea. Every time the medium goes into trance, Draupadī or her power comes into him, as well as into the pot. Her power, thus stored in the pot, increases to its maximum at the end of the festival.[110] The power in the pot is represented by the sword standing on the pot. The medium told me that more the power is stored in the pot, the longer the sword would stand upright in it. It is also the sign of Draupadī's reply to the prayers for protection by devotees who are going to participate in the firewalking.

With a notebook on his lap, the medium proceeds with the recitation of the *Mahābhārata* story (*katai*) inside the temple (1.3). The

PLATE 17. THE *MAHĀBHĀRATA* TELLING (THE MEDIUM ON THE RIGHT)

assistant sits in front of the medium (pl. 17). Their exaggerated expressions, gestures and, of course, the contents of the story attract the audience.

The medium calls on various deities, such as Rāma and Draupadī, for protection. He does this at every recitation. The story today is a rough account of the negotiations preceding the outbreak of war up to the duel between Duryodhana and Bhīma. The first day's recitation goes on for about two and half hours from 9:00 to 11:30 p. m. Usually it lasts less than two hours.

The audience is composed of about 130 women, 20 men and 50 children. Women are in overwhelming majority, and this tendency remains the same for the rest of the festival. For less educated Hindus, listening to religious stories such as the *Mahābhārata* is a merit-earning activity.

The five flags for the festival are prepared (1.4). Four of them are hoisted on the first day. The one for the temple flagstaff is called *uṭkoṭi* (*uḷ* or interior, *koṭi* or flag) and represents the Kaurava brothers. This is contrasted to *veḷikkoṭi* or the outside-flag, which is hoisted outside the temple next day. The *uṭkoṭi* is emblazoned with a large painting of a cobra (*nākam*).

The Pāṇḍava flag is only a piece of red cloth. The pole is seven foot long, and is like a fork with five prongs. Five limes are transfixed on the prongs of the pole (pl. 18),[111] and a rope or whip (*cattaikayiṟu*) is hung loosely on it. This Pāṇḍava flag is called *kontaṉ* (cross-cousin) *koṭi,* and is usually accompanied by two other flags of the sun and the moon. The former is said to represent the Pāṇḍavas and the daytime, while the latter the Kauravas and the nighttime. They are placed together in front of the temple flagstaff for the Kaurava flag, or carried when necessary. Usually the Pāṇḍava flag is carried by Arjuna, and the others by any two of the devotees.

Why is the Pāṇḍava flag called "cross-cousin" flag? It is said that the villagers call the brothers cousins in a euphemistic way. The ideal marriage is the cross-cousin marriage in this area, and unlike husbands, one can have more than one cross-cousin. Therefore it is more suitable to call the Pāṇḍavas Draupadī's cross-cousins rather than husbands. Or, as one villager suggested, Draupadī remained virgin even after the marriage with the Pāṇḍavas, thus her relationship with them is more like the one between cross-cousins before marriage. The outside-flag is painted with an image of Hanuman, the monkey god, famous for his assistance to Rāma in the *Rāmāyaṇa*, and a half brother of Bhīma. Therefore it is considered to be his flag. It is said to have been used as a standard in the battle with the

PLATE 18. THE PĀṆḌAVA FLAG (CENTRE)

Kauravas.

Abhiṣeka and worship are performed for the flagstaff by the medium. Initially the Kaurava flag is hoisted, and then the Paṇḍava, the sun and the moon flags are also tied to the poles. Subsequently *kāppu* cords are tied around them. The medium goes on to tie *kāppu* cords to other objects : an image of Vīrabhadra in front of the flagstaff ; a book of palmyra leaves of the *Mahābhārata* ; a hand-bell for the *Mahabharata* recitation ; the stone image of Draupadī ; the *karakam* ; and her festival image. With the tying on of the *kāppu* cords these items are consecrated for the festival.

A likely interpretation is that, following *abhiṣeka* and the binding of *kāppu* cords to the flagstaffs, the *Mahābhārata* heroes and their enemies, who have no fixed images inside the temple, come to be present in the flags. The five prongs of the Pāṇḍava flag are said to represent the five brothers (cf. Babb 1974 : 6). Arjuna carries the flag of the Pāṇḍavas, while the medium in trance (Draupadī) holds the *karakam* pot and her hand-knife. Every time the pot goes out in procession, the Pāṉḏava flag follows it. The flag is the counterpart of the pot. But the final union between the goddess and her husbands is symbolised by the pot and the sword, which is kept in the sanctum sanctorum. Here we can recognise an already familiar dichotomy between the mobile and the immobile. The *karakam* and the three flags move outside, while the sword and the Kaurava (cobra) flag stay inside the temple. But all are prepared for the festival and represent active power in contrast to the stone idols. Some say that when the cobra flag is hoisted, evil forces are trapped inside it and stay there during the festival, until the flag is lowered. Thus they cannot disturb the festival. I am not certain if this is a general view of the flag hoisting, or it relates specifically to the flag of the Kaurava brothers, which is the symbol of evil. If we accept this interpretation, the flag hoisting has a similar function to that of *śānti*. However, in general terms the flagstaff is *axis mundi* which connects the mundane world to the divine world, and through the pole the deified heroes of the *Mahābhārata* descend to the ground.

Worship at the temple is always conducted by the Brahman priest (1.5). It starts as usual with homage to Gaṇeśa, and then moves on to Pārtasārati and his consorts, Draupadī, and her main festival image in the sanctum sanctorum ; Murukaṉ ; Pōttirācaṉ and Muttālarācaṉ and the festival images of Gaṇeśa, Pārtasārati and his consorts, and, again, Draupadī ; Pārtasārati's vehicle, Garuḍa ; Vīrabhadra and ends with Cantāṉa Kōpālaṉ. It thus progresses in a clockwise direction around the inside of the temple. The worship of the stone image of Draupadī is the most elaborate.

The first *prasāda,* known as village (*ūr*) *kāḷāñci,* is proffered to the medium in a half coconut shell (*kāḷāñci*). In relation to the Brahman priest and deities the medium represents the village. Next two portions of *prasāda* are given to the musicians. The fact that the medium is the first recipient of the *prasāda,* especially the village *kāḷāñci,* is congruent with his role as the village *upayakkāraṉ* (patron) at the festival's first rituals ; Vāstu and *grāma śānti,* and *kāppu* cord tying. With these rituals he assumes the role of village representative. In other situations, the village *kāḷāñci* goes to the representative of the Hindu Temple Administrative Committee, which, ideologically, is the collective body of the villagers, but more practically, serves the Karaiyar caste as patrons. As we shall see later, the medium is not a patron or representative in any real sense, but "a victim" to be sacrificed on behalf of the village. This makes sense because the patron, or sacrificer, is identified with sacrificial objects. Consecration transforms the medium into a suitable victim on the first day. To follow through the symbolic implications of this, however, we must analyse the whole structure of the festival, and how he is "killed."

For the next three days nothing but daily worship is conducted at 6:00 a. m., 11:00 a. m. and 7:00 p. m. The early morning worship occurs only during the festival from the second to the nineteenth day.

On the fifth day, after early morning worship, the outside-flag (*veḷikkoṭi*) of Hanuman is hoisted (5.2). It is just 9:00 a. m. First a thirty foot long flag pole is prepared and ceremonially erected at the eastern corner of the temple plaza, across from the temple (see fig. 17). After this

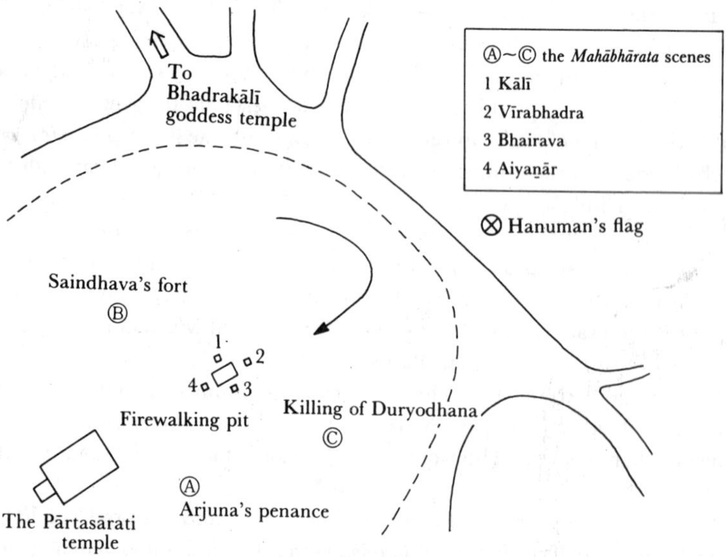

FIGURE 17. THE AREA AROUND THE PĀRTASĀRATI TEMPLE

the villagers hoist the Hanuman flag. The medium again prays at the pole and then ties a *kāppu* to it.

A lottery is held to select three groups of people to enact several episodes from the *Mahābhārata*, and four men to invite the four guardian gods to the firewalking pit (5.3). About thirty groups applied to the Hindu Temple Administrative Committee to perform these three scenes (Tam. *kāṭci*), for which the Committee will provide them with six hundred rupees for their preparations. Generally, those who have made vows to Draupadī that they would play acts at her festival bid for participation. Some roles in the enactments are, however, taken on by elder devotees. The groups of votaries apply to perform a particular act, and the more popular acts are subject to strong competition. The medium draws a lot for each. After this meeting, midday worship is conducted.

The medium goes into trance in front of the Muttumāri goddess temple and starts the *karakam* pot procession to the Pārtasārati temple (5.5). The only difference from the first *karakam* procession is a dance (*kummi*) performed by the medium and his assistant narrator at a cross-roads. Unlike the dance in the Bhadrakālī goddess festival, only the medium, now Draupadī incarnate dances with his partner to a devotional song.[112] The same Cattiyur musicians play in both goddess festivals. The dancing couple face each other, making slow circular movements, with the partner taking the lead, as if entertaining the goddess and inviting her to the temple. Some villagers go into trance, while watching the dance. After the dance, the procession starts again and when the men return to the temple, they again pray.

At about 9:00 p. m. the medium and the assistant sit face to face under the canopy in front of the temple, and relate the first chapter of the epic concerning cosmogenesis, and various stories of the ancestors, especially Yayāti, of the Pāṇḍavas and Kauravas. The audience numbers from two to three hundred, mostly comprised of women and children.

From the sixth to the tenth day there are no new rituals. Daily worship and the *Mahābhārata* recitation are carried out on the sixth, eighth and tenth, while a *karakam* pot procession with *kummi* dancing is added on the seventh and ninth days.

On the morning of the tenth day *rudrābhiṣeka* is conducted by the priest. This *abhiṣeka,* briefly mentioned in chapter 6, was sponsored by Cellamuttu, one of the big net-owners operating on the east coast and on the Manakkulam coast, north of Cattiyur. It is a votive *abhiṣeka.* For the *rudrābhiṣeka,* Gaṇeśa, Draupadī, Pārtasārati and his consorts are represented by large ritual pots. Conducted on a fairly large scale, the setting and procedure are essentially similar to other *abhiṣeka* rituals.

This *abhiṣeka* is followed by worship as usual. During the worship in the sanctum sanctorum, a prominent net-owner and Cellamuttu's best friend, M. M. N., sings devotional hymns. When the worship is concluded, the chief priest brings from the sanctum sanctorum "Viṣṇu's feet (*śrīpāda,* Tam. *tiruppātam*)," or, in this context, Pārtasārati's feet, an object which resembles a crown, and puts it on Cellamuttu's head.

Viṣṇu's feet are used to symbolise devotion to Viṣṇu or one of his incarnations. Respect is demonstrated in various contexts by bowing to the feet of others, divine or human. Young men touch the elders' feet on some special occasions to show their respect, and the elders in turn bless the youths.[113] By placing his head under the divine feet, the patron publicly demonstrates his total surrender to Pārtasārati. A devotee is called *aṭiyāṉ* in Tamil, a word deriving from *aṭi*, or foot. Here, the concept of *bhakti* is explicitly invoked in the context of the *abhiṣeka* ritual. In other words, the communication with the divine through the mechanism of elaborate and costly rituals is articulated with the idea of *bhakti* based on spiritual devotion rather than ritualism.

On the sixth day the stories of Śaṃtanu and Gangā, the birth of Bhīṣma and Satyavatī are told. On the seventh day how Dhṛtarāṣṭra and Pāṇḍu are born with Vyāsa's assistance, and how the Pāṇḍavas and the Kauravas are born is told. Every time the births of the Pāṇḍava brothers are mentioned, a hand-bell is rung by the medium. On the eighth day the death of Pāṇḍu and conflicts between Bhīma and Duryodhana are related. On the ninth day the attack on the kingdom of Drupada by both Kauravas and Pāṇḍavas is recited. The tenth day's episodes are about the escape from the lacquer palace by the Pāṇḍavas and Bhīma's heroic adventures in the forests.

From the eleventh to the sixteenth day all ritual expenses are met by groups of patrons (*upayakkāraṉs*) who are listed on the board near the temple kitchen. In the morning of the eleventh day *snānābhiṣeka* is performed. A representative of each group occupies the seats set aside for *upayakkāraṉ* adjacent to the Brahman priest (11.2). The consecration of the stone images of Pārtasārati and his consorts, Gaṇeśa and Draupadī is the main purpose of *abhiṣeka*, and they are anointed with water from the ritual pots. After this, the idols are decorated for the worship which follows. Nine musicians now perform, three of whom are Sinhalese. The procedure is much the same as that of the *maṇḍalābhiṣeka* discussed in chapter 6.

In the evening the festival images move to a hall, called *vasantamaṇḍapa*, near the entrance to the temple. That night the Gaṇeśa image is carried outside by the day's patrons and the members of the Hindu Temple Administration Committee (11.4). This is the first village procession of Gaṇeśa. This procession involves only Gaṇeśa, who is, as has been already mentioned, the god of beginning. This procession goes along the main bus road and is restricted to Cattiyur proper.[114] There are about twenty five stops on the way for the Brahman chief priest's son, who rides on a jeep driven by a member of the Hindu Temple Administrative Committee, to receive offerings (*arcanā*) from devotees.

After the Gaṇeśa procession, evening worship and the *Mahābhārata* recitation are performed. Today's episode is about Draupadī's selection of a bridegroom, *svayaṁvara*. When Arjuna wins the archery contest, the bell of the Pārtasārati temple starts ringing and the son of the Brahman priest garlands the festival image of Draupadī.

Some votaries start staying in the temple overnight, cooking their daily meals outside. Subsequently they will take part in votive rites, including firewalking.

Early on the morning of the twelfth day the *upayakkāraṉs* of the day before parade the Gaṇeśa image around the temple on their shoulders (12.1). Worship follows. It is considered an honour to have such direct contact with the deity. Then *snānābhiṣeka* and midday worship are conducted, and in the evening a *karakam* pot procession is held.

From the twelfth day in addition to Gaṇeśa's festival image, the festival images of Pārtasārati and his consorts are taken out (12.6). A tractor owned by M. S. T., one of the leading Cattiyur net-owners, is used to carry Pārtasārati and his consorts (pl. 19). It is driven around the village

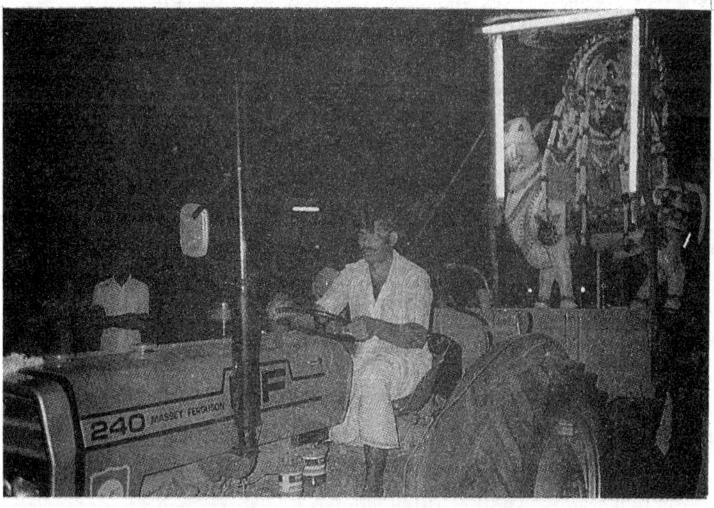

PLATE 19. NET-OWNER CARRYING THE PĀRTASĀRATI IMAGE

by M. S. T. himself. The procession is accompanied by a pair of torch bearers and professional musicians, both Tamil and Sinhalese. Before the procession begins, two girls perform *āratti* for Pārtasārati, against the evil eye. Worship takes place when the procession returns to the temple.

Draupadī's wedding to the Pāṇḍavas is the topic of tonight's narration (12.8), and the wedding ceremony is actually enacted inside the temple. The *upayakkāraṉs* (patrons) of this ceremony are the fifteen households of the Cattiyur Goldsmith caste. They are exclusive patrons of the entire ceremony and also present a *tāli* (golden necklace for marriage) to Draupadī. Draupadī and the Pāṇḍavas are represented by two pots and the Brahman priest officiates at their ceremonial union.

In addition to the *tāli* given by the Goldsmiths, three other *tāli*s are also given to Draupadī by votaries.

The schedule of the thirteenth day is the same as the preceding day except for the absence of the *karakam* pot procession. The events from the *Mahābhārata* are about Duryodhana's jealousy of the Pāṇḍavas, and Arjuna's pilgrimage.

Votive rituals begin from the fourteenth day (14.3). About thirty votaries and their family members have stayed at the Pārtasārati temple for several days, have taken only vegetarian foods and abstained from sexual intercourse, and have been bathing in the sea. They gather at the Murukaṉ shrine of the Muttumāri goddess temple in Adipetti at about eight thirty o'clock in the morning. A few go to other small shrines around the village.[114] Men perform *pāṟkāvaṭi,* while women perform *pāṟcempu,* (see chapter 4).

When the *kāvaṭi,* the pole that the men will use to cary milk to the temple, has been decorated, Gaṇeśa, represented by a lump of turmeric paste, is worshipped. All male participants, and some of the women, wear necklace garlands of *rudrākṣa* (Tam. *urttirāṭcam, Eloeocarpus ganitrus*) beads, which are believed to be the third eye of Śiva or Rudra. All participants tie their sarongs, or saris tightly around themselves, and the women also arrange flowers and margosa leaves on their heads. In turn, they bathe at the well in front of the temple,[116] where each has a jar of water poured over them by their relatives, after which their bodies are covered with ash, and smeared with sandalwood paste and vermilion powder. At the well two women start trembling in a trance. One of them begins jumping with hands clasped above her head and her tongue protruding from her mouth.

After bathing, the votaries enter the temple, where the medium conducts worship. Another three women and three men are possessed by the Muttumāri goddess and start dancing, in front of the temple. If participants show little sign of entering a trance, their relatives try to induce one by burning incense just under their noses. Some Sinhala musicians accompany the votaries to the Pārtasārati temple, but this is not a well organised procession ; rather each participant independently heads there with his, or her, relatives. On the way, they pass by the small Kantacāmi temple and the Bhadrakālī goddess temple, and the name of the deity their devotional prayers are addressed to changes, as they pass each temple, from Māriyammā, Kantacāmī or Murukā, to Kāḷiyammā, finally, as they approach the Pārtasarāti temple, it changes to

Tiraupataiyammā. About one third of the participants are seized in a violent trance, and some have backs and cheeks pierced with hooks, skewers, or small lances by their relatives.

As the votaries enter the temple, the medium puts ash on their foreheads, whereupon they immediately collapse. They are carried out of the temple, in a state of exhaustion. Their friends and relatives give them lemonade, lime juice, coconut juice and other cool drinks. The milk the votaries have carried from the Muttumāri goddess temple is collected in a large pot to be used at the *abhiṣeka* rite, and the decorated poles for *kāvaṭi* are returned to the temple.[117]

Other votive acts also take place on this occasion : *akkiṉiccaṭṭi* (fire pan), rolling along the ground by men, and various other kinds of self-mortification. Such votive rituals are also held collectively on the fifteenth and sixteenth day. About 120 villagers and a few outsiders participate in them, including a Buddhist trader who visits Cattiyur daily.

The attempted humiliation of Draupadī by disrobing her after the gambling session and the exile of the Pāṇḍavas to the forest are the subjects covered in the *Mahābhārata* session.

Fishermen working on the east coast break their activities to come back temporarily to Cattiyur for the festival by the fourteenth day. The Draupadī goddess festival is one of the two occasions when the fishermen return home, the other being the Munnesvaram Śiva temple festival. Those who remain in the village and work on the Cattiyur beach stop fishing for the last three or four days of the festival.

From the fifteenth day, various stories from the *Mahābhārata* are enacted by votaries (15.6), and the main road from the Bhadrakālī temple to the Pārtasārati temple is adorned with branches of the Bo-tree (*Ficus religios*). At four o'clock in the evening a group of twelve actors have *kāppu* cords tied around their wrists by the medium, all, except for the person playing the female role of Draupadī, who has a *kāppu* cord on the left wrist, wear their *kāppu* cords on the right (pl. 20). After worship at the Bhadrakālī goddess temple, which is conveniently close to their starting point, they head for the Pārtasārati temple, enacting several episodes of the Pāṇḍavas and their bride Draupadī in exile in the forest. the street decorated with greenery is the set for these scenes (*vaṉampuṭkāṭci*). They do not speak, but at locations on the way, the medium and his assistant narrate appropriate parts of the *Mahābhārata*. Eventually they enter the Pārtasārati temple, return the *kāppu* cords to the medium, and receive sacred ash from him.

The rite of *kāppu* tying signifies that the enactment of the *Mahābhārata* has entered a special liminal phase in the consecration. The tying of the *kāppu* often precedes relatively institutionalised divine

PLATE 20. SOME VOTARIES AT THE *MAHĀBHĀRATA* SCENE

possession or access to divine power, seen when the medium has his wrist bound at the beginning of the festival. It is also considered to protect against pollution and divine power. Playing the role of figures of the *Mahābhārata* denotes their temporary personification or possession. A hierarchical order is also manifest in the *kāppu* tying ritual: the Brahman priest ties a *kāppu* on the medium ; then the medium ties *kāppu* cords on the wrists of votaries and on various other items.

On the sixteenth morning (16.4) the medium goes to the firewalking site (*pūṇiṭam*, or sacred place) where, he digs three points on the ground and puts yellow powder, *paṇṭārattūḷ* (powder of the Paṇṭāram caste), into them. The rope tied to the flag pole is removed and placed on the ground. As both the powder and the rope contain *mantra śakti,* these activities are regarded as the consecration of the firewalking pit, and constitute part of the precautions against pollution, and against, more importantly, divine power in the form of fire.

The *Mahābhārata* is enacted at 4:00 p. m. In this scene (*Aruccuṉaṉ tavacilaik kāṭci*), Arjuna, still in exile, singing hymns, climbs up the tree and observes a severe penance (Skt. *tapas*) at the top of the tree in order to gain a weapon from Śiva. The role of Arjuna in this scene is acted by the medium's attendant. Śiva and Śakti are played by ordinary votaries.

From the sixteenth day onwards, the main village roads and the temple plaza are lit with tube lights. This helps to enhance the festive atmosphere.

Early in the morning of the seventeenth day, about six inches deep, fifteen foot long and four foot wide, a rectangular pit is dug for the firewalking. Four small *mēṭais*, or mounds, representing the shrines of Kālī (north), Vīrabhadra (east), Bhairava (south) and Aiyaṉār (west), are raised at points around the pit. These deities are all *akkiṉikuṇṭakāvals*, guards of the fire pit. They are embodied in four *kaḷikampus* (sticks of joy), which are inserted in the mounds by four villagers (17.3).

These four villagers must first bathe in the sea, at about nine thirty o'clock in the morning, and cleanse themselves at the well outside the Muttumāri goddess temple. The medium ties *kāppu* cords around their wrists and the sacred powder of the Paṇṭāram is smeared on the *kāppu*. When the temple bell is struck, three of them fall into a deep trance and dance outside the temple with short sticks in their hands. A small hourglass-shaped drum (*uṭukkai*) is rhythmically beaten. This is a common instrument for increasing *mantra śakti* and a means of controlling the possessed.

Upon reaching the firewalking site, they dance for a while in a row facing the east, with a large audience of villagers. The mounds are decorated with coconut shoots and a *tāmbūla* set of a betel leaves, areca nuts and a banana ; two half coconut shells (*kāḷāñci*) are also placed on them, as if they were small shrines. Then one of the entranced dancers dashes onto the mound of Kālī, drives his stick into the mound and collapses. At this point the medium uses the rope from the Pāṇḍava flagstaff to lash the wrist of this possessed person three times, and then removes the *kāppu* cord from his wrist (pl. 21), thus releasing him from Kālī's fierce possession. The three others follow suit, and, in the same fashion, the medium whips each with the rope. In this way the four guardian deities are brought into the mounds to guard the fire pit.

The whip used by the medium is of the same kind as that used in some rituals of exorcism.[118] In other words, the actors are ambivalent about the nature of possession in this ritual. The guardian deities in general are all equivocal in nature (see chapter 3), because they stand on the border between the outside and the inside. Nobody wants to remain possessed by the four guardian deities, and yet being possessed is a necessary precondition for installing them on the mounds around the pit. Divine possession is here aimed at localising divine beings around the pit. Because possession by guardian deities is very dangerous, the *uṭukkai* drum is beaten, and the *kāppu* cords used are smeared with specially prepared sacred powder.

In this respect, it is similar to *abhiṣeka*. Possession by the guardian

PLATE 21. WHIPPING

deities and the *abhiṣeka* both aim to fix divine power in concrete objects—in the former case a human body, then a sand mound, and in the latter a ritual pot, then a stone image. A sacrificial logic underlies both rituals. The votaries here are like sacrificial victims : the deities use them as their mounts, to go to the sand mounds around the firewalking pit. In fact the Tamil word for mount, *vākaṉam,* is also used to refer to the victims of blood sacrifice. The votaries are, however, like patients suffering from demonic possession and they get rid of the possessing beings in a way reminiscent of exorcism. Such a procedure is appropriate to the supernaturals concerned on this occasion. After the guardian deities are installed, the medium steps into the fire pit, digs three holes and puts sacred powder in them (17.4). Hereafter, the fire pit is roped off.

The medium then goes to the northwestern corner of the temple plaza, which is used for one of the scenes from the *Mahābhārata,* and consecrates this place with the Paṇṭāram's sacred powder (17.5). He does this because the scene played there features a homicide, and this enacted death is believed to be the result of divine action. The sacred powder is used to control divine power and to ensure the revival of the actor.

Snānābhiṣeka is, today, sponsored by the village (*ūr upayam*). The position of the *ūr upayakkāraṉ*, the patron representing the villagers, is taken by the President of the Hindu Temple Administrative Committee.

In the evening the scene of the attack on the fort of Saindhava or Tēttarācaṉ (*Tēttarācaṉ kōṭṭaip piṭittal*) is enacted by another group of votaries, in which Kṛṣṇa disguised as an old lady visits the fort guarded by four deities; Kālī, Vīrabhadra, Bhairava and Aiyaṉār. They are the same guardians as are invited to the firewalking pit. They agree to help Kṛṣṇa and Saindhava loses the fort. He is killed, but is revived later with Draupadī's grace.[119]

On the eighteenth day the temple has a *cikaram*, a false facade of a royal palace erected. No Hindu works, and village schools are closed. The firewalking site is decorated with flowers (pl. 22). In the early morning the

PLATE 22. FIREWALKING PIT

second *grāma śānti* and *agniyāga* (Tam. *akkiṉiyākam*), or the fire-setting ritual, are performed by the chief Brahman priest's son near the temple entrance (18.1). The medium sits next to the priest. The ritual is very similar to Vāstu *śānti*. It consists of: preparatory and purificatory rites, *homa*, and the cutting of an ash-pumpkin. After sprinkling sacred water and igniting the end of a straw figure, the medium enters the sanctum sanctorum and goes into trance in front of the Draupadī stone image. Significantly this is the first occasion in the festival that he is possessed by Draupadī at the temple. White cloth is laid out by the Washermen all the way from the sanctum sanctorum to the fire pit of *homa*, and on to the firewalking pit.

N. M. M., who is an influential net-owner, asks the medium to protect the village and the villagers. He answers that they should have no fear (see chapter 5), and blesses the villagers by throwing sacred ash into the air. They cry, "Arohara ! Arohara !" The medium as Draupadī grasps some burning embers from the *homa* pit with his bare hands and puts them in a pan. The medium walks like an *akkiṉiccaṭṭi* votary around the temple on the white cloth and reaches the firewalking pit (pl. 23). He steps into it, places the pan in the pit, then prays to the guardian deities at the four corners of the pit.[120]

PLATE 23. CARRYING FIRE TO THE PIT

After this the villagers start piling firewood over the burning embers in the pan and pour coconut oil on the wood. The fire is kept fuelled until the evening, when, just before the firewalking, any wood that is still burning is cleared away, and the remaining embers are raked flat inside the pit. Wood is donated by a few of the wealthy villagers, while the coconut oil is donated by some poorer villagers.

The movement of the medium, in a trance, from the sanctum sanctorum to the firewalking pit suggests that Draupadī is now residing in the temple after the repetitive *karakam* pot processions, which I interpret as a beckoning of Draupadī to come to the temple from the sea. A close link between the *homa* prepared by the Brahman priest, and firewalking led by the medium is suggested by the *agniyāga* ritual. Firewalking is *homa*, a form of fire sacrifice, as the name of its site, *agnikuṇḍa* (pit for *homa*) suggests. As we shall see, firewalking is a ceremony of symbolic death and rebirth in which the medium and the votaries he leads sacrifice themselves. Although the medium plays the crucial role of transferring the fire from the pit inside the temple to the firewalking pit outside, that is, from the relatively closed space to the open space of mass devotion outside, the fire itself is created by the Brahman priest. This parallels the kind of hierarchical relationship found in *kāppu* tying. It is the direct contact of the entranced medium with the goddess which enables him to grasp the burning embers with his bare hands, but such a feat would be impossible if the *kāppu* tying ceremony were not performed on the first day by the Brahman priest, who charges the cord with his *mantra śakti*.

The medium, standing between the temple and the firewalking pit, starts reciting the part of the *Mahābhārata* (18.2) which concerns the wedding between Vīrabhadra and Caṅkuvati, who is a younger sister of Yudhiṣṭhira. A goat is brought in as a part of her dowry, and water is poured over it in the same way as it would be before a blood sacrifice. When it shakes its head, it is not killed, but lifted up by a temple assistant and dropped onto a log and the medium places a whip on the body of the prostrate goat.[121] Another goat is brought in as a votive offering, by a net-owner, and auctioned later.[122]

In preparation for the later enactment of the scene from the *Mahābhārata*, the southeastern corner of the temple plaza is consecrated with sacred powder by the medium, just as in the preceding day (18.3) Under the canopy in front of the temple the medium, and then two villagers, N. M. M. (a net-owner) and Kantaiya, representative of the Gramodaya Mandalaya, recite the story of the battle (18.4). This is a good example of powerful men performing as good devotees by reciting the *Mahābhārata*.

While the recitation continues, the villagers gather at the temple to offer *arcanā* (18.5). They pay two rupees to the Hindu Temple Administrative Committee at the temple entrance. About 1,100 households took part in the offering. These personal offerings continue all-day long.

The last enactment of the *Mahābhārata* is performed at five o'clock in the evening (18.7). A villager in the role of Duryodhana first worships the stone image of Draupadī at the temple, and then has a *kāppu* cord tied on by the medium. Later he is killed by Bhīma and his "corpse" is covered with a white cloth. Both roles are played by specially selected votaries (pl. 24). Draupadī appears in the scene, played, or rather embodied by the

PLATE 24. BHĪMA AND DURYODHANA

medium, wearing a yellow sari and carrying the hand-knife. This is the only time the medium plays the role of Draupadī in the enactments. Draupadī goes behind the white cloth to conceal the acts that follow. She is said to cut Duryodhana's chest with the knife and put the blood on her hair. Thus her vengeance is fulfilled. When uncovered, Duryodhana is almost in trance, he cannot walk, and tears run down his cheeks. The whip is hanging around his neck. He is laid down by the temple building to expose his "wound" to the sea wind, then enters the temple and worships Draupadī in the sanctum sanctorum. He returns the *kāppu* to the medium. He has been killed by Bhīma, but has been revived by Draupadī's grace.[123] Such experiences as the death of Duryodhana and Saindhava in the

Mahābhārata scenes are comparable to divine, but dangerous possession, and must be kept well under control, otherwise the actors could die. The presence of the whip, which is used for controlling dangerous possession, further reinforces this interpretation.

Draupadī's festival image is then carried outside and taken around the temple for the first time, together with Gaṇeśa, Pārtasārati and his consorts. The images are left in a row on the seat, *capparam,* in front of the temple all night, so that the votaries walking on the fire may see them directly and have auspicious sight (Skt. *darśana*) of them.

This time the medium goes into trance in front of Draupadī's festival image, not her stone image in the temple, at about 7:00 p. m (18.8). His possession is welcomed with shouts of "Govinda ! Govinda !" He blesses the village by throwing ash in the air in the same way as the blessing at *agniyāga.* He and the followers head for the Muttumāri goddess

PLATE 25. FIRE WALKING

temple, where the medium goes into a trance again and repeats the ash throwing blessing.[124] When he reaches the Pārtasārati temple, the medium walks slowly on the fire (pl. 25). He is followed by Arjuna. The medium holds a colourfully decorated *karakam* pot on his head and Arjuna holds the Pāṇḍava flag. Then the flag of the moon for the Kauravas and the night-time is followed. Only men are allowed to participate in firewalking. About one thousand male devotees then walk the fire. Some walk at a stately pace, while others dash across the pit. A few carry small children on their shoulders or in their arms. Some devotees hold their hands clasped overhead. All are quickly doused with water when they reach the other side of the fire. While the devotees cross the embers, the medium, as Draupadī, and Arjuna keep walking up and down the right side of the pit. When the firewalking is over, she suddenly collapses and is given cooling lime juice outside the temple.

When the medium has recovered from his trance, he attends worship in front of the festival image, and receives sacred ash and a halved coconut shell (*kāḷāñci*) as *prasāda* from the Brahmaṇ priest. After that he goes home, where he has a small feast with the musicians. This is the first time, since the beginning of the festival, when the *kāppu* cord was tied, that he is allowed to meet his wife and eat meat.

Participants in the firewalking are mostly votaries, with personal reasons for participating. Many come from outside Cattiyur, not only from neighbouring villages, but from as far away as Jaffna or Colombo. They stay at the temple for several days before firewalking, and may take part in other votive rituals such as *paṟkāvaṭi* or *akkiṉiccaṭṭi*. They eat only vegetarian food for the week before the firewalking, and, like the medium and Arjuna, they abstain from sexual intercourse. More outsiders now participate, as the fame of the Cattiyur Draupadī is spreading. The rapid expansion of the economic activities of the fishermen outside the village has probably contributed to the increasing popularity of the Cattiyur Draupadī festival.

In contrast, some villagers, especially the young men, walk the fire without any specific reason, and do not strictly observe the above restrictions. In general, they first began firewalking as children, and have continued to do so every year since then. As time passes, the seriousness with which they first participated disappears. For most villagers, however, firewalking is a serious matter, and many stress their fear of it.

Except for the medium, who bears the *karakam* pot, and Arjuna who carries a flag, the firewalkers wear only loin cloths and show no visible signs of social distinction. In this sense the firewalking ceremony is a significant occasion on which secular differentiation in economic power and caste status is dissolved. In other words "communitas" of the devotees is realised.[125]

Firewalking has been generally reported at Draupadī temples or at her husband Yudhiṣṭhira's temples, this is despite the fact that there is no mention of it in Sanskrit sources. I was told that firewalking was held at the Draupadī goddess temple, because, after the war, the Pāṇḍavas, Draupadī, and the Kauravas had to purify their minds and bodies through fire before Yudhiṣṭhira's coronation could take place. A typical explanation from elsewhere, however, is that Draupadī had to walk the fire in order to demonstrate her chastity during her exile with the Pāṇḍavas in the forest.[126] Babb suggests that, from a votary's point of view, firewalking is an ordeal to test one's purity (Babb 1974 : 25). If injured, the votary's mind and body are proved impure. On the other hand, although firewalking does contain an element of self-imposed ordeal, its central theme seems union with Draupadī through purification. The underlying belief is that man is impure, but he can be saved by Draupadī's compassion, purifying himself, receiving her grace through the firewalking, as the myth of King Cunītaṉ points out, and thus undergoing a type of rebirth. This view is congruent with the main theme of *bhakti.* I have already suggested that firewalking should be compared to *homa,* fire sacrifice. The main functions of *homa*, besides the creation of divine power, are the destruction of evil, and union with the divine. Firewalking has the same implications, that is, purification and union with the goddess.

In the version of the *Mahābhārata* recited at the festival, Draupadī's affinity with fire is apparent from the beginning of her life. She is born out of a fire sacrifice, and after marriage to the Pāṇḍavas she goes through fire annually when she moves on to a different husband. Perhaps even more interesting is, however, the changing nature of her hair. According to Modder (1908 : 179), Draupadī's invisible hair is conceived of as being stretched over the fire and the firewalkers thus walk on her hair. It should be recalled that when Draupadī is insulted at the assembly hall, she is said to be menstruating. She curses that she will leave her hair dishevelled. At Duryodhana's death she dresses her hair with his blood. Until that time her dishevelled hair is a visible indication of her fierce curse. Thus the meaning of the state of her hair has changed from a sign of pollution to one representing her vow of revenge and the suffering associated with its cause, and then extended further to include protective power. This is also indicative of the change in Draupadī's character, as well. At first, she is an obedient feminine figure, and then becomes a heroine enduring great ordeals and suffering, but with a firm will to revenge. Finally she is a queen and goddess able to save suffering people with her all encompassing grace (cf. Hiltebeitel 1981).

The climax of the festival falls on the eighteenth day, and many people come from outside Cattiyur in order to participate in the firewalking or just observe it. Policemen from Chilaw are kept busy at the firewalking site. About ninety shops (mostly stalls) are open around the temple, and both villagers and outsiders enjoy shopping after the firewalking ceremony. The stall-holders mostly come from nearby villages, but some even come from as far away as Colombo. Sites are auctioned to a villager by the Hindu Temple Administrative Committee, and the winner to the rights sublets the sites to outsiders for a small fee.

That night the worship is less extensive, only *pañcāratti* to the festival images in front of the temple is carried out, and some devotees offer *arcanā*.

On the nineteenth day morning, after the Gaṇeśa's procession, all the festival images excluding Draupadī's are returned to the temple hall.

At about seven o'clock in the evening the Draupadī festlval image, adorned with flowers and jewels, is paraded round the village on M. S. T.'s tractor (19.3). The medium also joins the procession, but he just sits beside the priest on the tractor. The *karakam* pot, the Pāṇḍava flag, the flags of the sun and the moon, and the hand-knife are placed at the foot of the festival image. The image holds a cane.

Six small huts, at which the Brahman priest receives *arcanā* offerings, are set up along the way from Cattiyur to Adipetti. In front of the huts, young men dance to taped music. *Dharma,* or cosmological order, is finally restored, and this is a triumphant procession after the victory in the battle.

When the procession returns at midnight, young village women gather at the temple to offer *māviḷakku,* rice flour lamp, to the festival image of Draupadī (19.4). Despite its name, it is not a lamp, but a simple offering of rice cake accompanied by three bananas and some joss sticks. This is said to have been Murukaṉ's favourite food, and his second wife, Vaḷḷi, offered it to him whenever they met, so young unmarried women offer it, but to Draupadī, and not to Murukaṉ, with a hope of good marriage. It is also meant to admire her chastity. Some, still childless, recently wedded women also offer *māviḷakku.*

Today in the last episode of the *Mahābhārata* recitation, the coronation (*paṭṭābhiṣeka,* Tam. *paṭṭāpiṣēkam*) of Yudhiṣṭhira, the eldest of the Pāṇḍavas, is described (19.5).

The four flags are lowered and taken off the staff by the medium (19.6), while the remaining outside-flag is lowered on the following day.

He then cuts off all the *kāppu* cords tied around the flagstaffs and other items on the first day.

After this, the Brahman priest performs daily worship (19.7), and then cuts off the medium's *kāppu* cord, receiving a fee from him. The medium receives sacred ash from the priest and touches his feet. Then the medium receives the first village *kāḷāñci* and goes around the temple. Other items of *prasāda* are distributed to musicians and the devotees. At well past three o'clock in the morning, the distribution is over.

On the last day, Vāstu *śānti* and *prāyaścitta* are performed (20.1). These rites are for the expiation of any fault committed by the religious specialists and other villagers during the festival, and the procedure is identical to the ceremonies carried out earlier on the first day. Midday worship is held afterward.

To sum up, the first day features preparatory and purificatory rites (*śānti*, *kāppu* tying, flag hoisting). The *karakam* procession and *Mahābhārata* narration are carried out, but they are performed regularly only from the fifth day. The first *karakam* procession has no dancing, and the first story is a summing-up of the *Mahābhārata* war. The correct sequence of the *Mahābhārata* story is resumed on the fifth day. On this day, the basic daily pattern of the festival—daily worship ; *karakam* pot procession ; and *Mahābhārata* story telling—is established. Ritual acts especially performed by the Brahman priest are added to these basic rites ; for example : the morning procession of Gaṇeśa, the *snānābhiṣeka,* the evening procession of Gaṇeśa, Pārtasārati and his consorts. After the fifteenth day recitation is supplemented with physical enactment, in which certain votaries play the roles of the *Mahābhārata* figures. Focus gradually shifts to the firewalking pit as its consecration proceeds from the sixteenth day onwards. The four guardians are invited to the pit on the seventeenth day and the fire is set early in the morning of the eighteenth day. The medium goes into a trance and carries burning embers in a pan to the fire pit. *Arcanā* offerings are received all-day long. The festival image of Draupadī is set in front of the temple facing the fire pit. Firewalking is held that evening. The medium, in a trance, leads a thousand devotees over the fire pit. This is the highlight of the festival ; hereafter, the medium is released from the restrictions imposed on him during the festival.

On the next day, a procession of the Draupadī festival image is conducted around the village. Draupadī's procession is an inversion of the *karakam* pot procession, which is held to bring her from the sea. Now, Draupadī is conveyed out of the temple and around the village, like a triumphant queen, to ensure the prosperity of the village. Villagers offer *arcanā* to her festival image. Village youths dance on the procession route, rejoicing in her victory. *Māviḷakku* is offered by young women wishing for successful, fertile marriages. The story of the coronation rite for her eldest husband is read inside the temple after the procession. The flags are lowered and the *kāppu* cords are cut. On the last day an expiatory ritual is held for any wrongs committed during the festival. This concludes the festival.

As discussed in chapter 4, ritual acts concerning personal vow fulfilments in the festival provide a way in which individuals can voluntarily participate in the festival. *Pāṟkāvaṭi, pāṟcempu,* and various forms of self-mortification, performed from the fourteenth to the sixteenth day clearly show how seriously individuals are committed to the festival. Enacting parts of the story also gives villagers an opportunity to fulfil their promises. Other vows fulfilled during the festival are a *rudrābhiṣeka,* sponsored by a rich net-owner on the tenth day, the extensive *arcanā* offerings, and the provision of firewood and coconut oil for firewalking. Needless to say, the most important votive rite in the festival is firewalking. Firewalking is thought of as part of the *Mahābhārata*. More generally speaking, however, firewalking in the Hindu context involves the symbolism of sacrifice or rebirth through fire. The votaries are led by Draupadī, embodied as the medium, through fire, and are reunited with her as they cross the fire pit. In this way they receive her grace and are revived.

The Medium as a Sacrificial Victim

In this section I analyse the festival structure and discuss its symbolic meanings.

First I would like to focus on those rituals where the Brahman priest officiates, and the medium participates as a central figure, as the key to understanding the whole structure of the festival. These are the appeasement ritual, *śānti,* held on the first day, the day of firewalking, and the final day.

It is interesting that the medium receives the first *prasāda* for the village (*ūrkkāḷāñci*) on these occasions, suggesting that he represents the village as a whole. It is hard to consider him as representative of the village in its strict sense, as he is not a member of the numerically and economically dominant Karaiyar caste. He is not a representative patron because he is an employee of the Karaiyar caste. It may be enlightening to speculate why he takes the seat of honour as *upayakkāraṉ*. It should be recalled that according to the general theory of sacrifice presented by Hubert and Mauss (1964 : 13), the patron, or sacrificer, should be identified with the victim, so perhaps the medium could be more aptly called a primary victim dedicated to Draupadī. He is a scapegoat to be killed symbolically on behalf of the villagers. But in what way is he killed ?

It is important to understand that the festival as a whole is based on the traditional structure of sacrifice. On the first day after *śānti* ritual the medium is consecrated with a *kāppu* cord by the priest. Then on the eighteenth day he takes part in the firewalking, which is considered as symbolic death. On the nineteenth day, the Brahman cuts off the medium's *kāppu*. *Śānti* and *prāyaścitta* are performed on the last day. The overall structure of the festival thus accords neatly with the general model of sacrifice : it involves a rite of entry ; liminal status, *dīkṣā* ; immolation ; and a rite of exit.[127]

The medium can enter trance only after a rite of entry performed by the Brahman priest. In this liminal state, the medium can fully experience divine power. Subsequently he is sacrificed in the fire ; the vernacular name of the firewalking pit is the same as that of *homa*. Firewalking symbolises immolation and rebirth.[128]

What I refer to as the liminal state here corresponds to the ecstatic phase of the festival (see chaper 5). After the *kāppu* tying on the first day, the ecstatic phase sets in. It is characterised by a series of *karakam* processions and later other activities such as *kāvaṭi* or the *Mahābhārata* plays. Its climax is firewalking. After that the medium goes home, and the ecstatic phase is over. On the nineteenth day, the non-ecstatic phase is resumed, and the procession of the Draupadī goddess is performed.

As in the case of the Bhadrakālī goddess festival, the ecstatic phase is, in a way, somewhat negatively represented. There is no clear association of Draupadī with negative elements such as smallpox or chorela. Nonetheless Draupadī is a fearful and dangerous presence, which is clear in the *Mahābhārata*. She is not firmly under control. It is only after her curse is fulfilled and she purifies herself with fire that her negative aspects are removed.

In the case of the Bhadrakālī goddess festival, the suffering of Bhadrakālī represents that of the village as a whole. During the Draupadī festival the representation of the village as such is not so clear. Instead, Draupadī's suffering can be compared to the personal suffering of each devotee. Because of this, I suggest that the ecstatic phase of the Draupadī goddess festival appears to aim at constructing the world of devotees, where the medium is not a victim on behalf of the village, but both Draupadī herself in relation to ordinary devotees and an exemplary devotee in relation to the goddess. I would like to take up this point again in the following discussion.

Hierarchy in the Festival

Bearing the whole structure of the festival in mind, I would like to analyse the relationship between the festival and power in more detail.

The rituals of the Draupadī goddess festival can, accordingly, be divided into three categories according to the nature of the officiants. These are: (1) rituals officiated by the medium, whether in trance or not; (2) rituals in which the Brahman priest is the officiant; and (3) rituals in which both the medium and Brahman participate (see fig. 18). The first category would be ecstatic rituals, the second Brahmanical rituals, and the third rituals express the relationship between the two, and the wider symbolic role of the medium in the festival. I have already described the nature of the third type.

The medium is the central figure in the *karakam* pot procession, ecstatic votive rituals, the consecration of the firewalking pit, and in various rituals concerning the *Mahābhārata* story such as flag hoisting, story telling and so on. These are, more or less, ecstatic in nature, and culminate in firewalking. The medium, when in trance, is considered to be Draupadī : the participants in these rituals encounter the goddess directly. While not in trance his primary role is to protect festival participants against dangerous divine power by tying *kāppu* cords, or using the sacred powder of Paṇṭāram. During ecstatic votive rites, and while playing parts from the *Mahābhārata*, participants lose their individual identities. The actors do not merely play roles; they impersonate the figures in the epic, and experience their suffering, death and salvation. In a word they participate in the festival as Draupadī's devotees free of any social distinction. As in the case of the Bhadrakālī goddess festival, I propose to use the concept of ecstatic phase in general reference to a period of the festival in which these ecstatic rituals occur. One major difference, however, should be noted : in the Bhadrakālī goddess festival this phase is mainly concerned with the village as an ideal and egalitarian community, while in the case of the Draupadī goddess festival it implies a more universal world, which is not premised on village boundaries.

The salient icons in this ecstatic phase are, initially, the *karakam* pot, and moving flags, while the stone image of Draupadī and her mobile festival image become important only at the end of the festival. *Karakam* represents divine power moving inwards, from the sea, to the temple. The pot brimming with raw power is dangerous and only the medium can approach it.

The Brahman priest performs non-ecstatic rituals, daily worship, receiving *arcanā* offerings, and the *snānābhiṣeka*, and they seem to be directed towards Pārtasārati, even though the festival is dedicated to Draupadī. Their nature is, however, diverse. Daily worship is concerned with the prosperity of the world, effectively the village, and supported by the villagers (the Karaiyar caste) as a whole, while *arcanā* is exclusively personal. As for *snānābhiṣeka*, access to the service of the Brahman priest is determined primarily by economic factors, except for the rite supported by the village as a whole. I would suggest *abhiṣeka* is the most significant ritual performed as a Brahmanical ritual, as other rituals may be performed by the medium on different occasions.

To return to my general points in chapter 6, the *abhiṣeka* has two functions : one is to generate divine power and transfer it to an image, and the other is to transform a patron into a sacred figure and to infuse him with divine power. The patron is a person who meets the expenses of the ritual in exchange for the power the ritual produces. Thus the patron has to be wealthy. Economic means and status are a minimum requirement for taking on this role. As a result, festivals which include the *abhiṣeka* tend to affirm the given social order, that is, the net-owners' economic domination over the rest of the villagers, or to allow the patron to transmute economic power into spiritual strength. With his knowledge of *mantra* and ritual procedures, the priest ensures the patron's acquisition of divine power. The *abhiṣeka* is primarily political, but there are two qualifications to this statement.

First, I must repeat that net-owners do not deny popular devotionalism. Indeed, they present themselves as devotees *par excellence*. It is hard to distinguish between the two types of participants in terms of devotion. Providing firewood, for example, is taken as an explicit sign of the donor's devotion rather than as a mark of his wealth. On the other hand, it is undeniable that few wealthy villagers participate in explicitly ecstatic rituals. They find it more apposite to express their devotion through offering things and donating money. There is no necessity to offer their bodies.

Second, the rituals conducted by the Brahman priest are not necessarily concerned with legitimation of economic power. The worship and *śānti*, that he presides over, have at their core a communal, idealised notion of the village. These rituals are involved with the communal aspects of the festival, in which the medium is sacrificed to the goddess. Similarly, *abhiṣeka* can be supported by the village (the Karaiyar caste) as a group

	Participant (patron)		1) Controller of power 2) Channel of mediation		
Type 1	devotee	⟶	1) medium 2) devotee's body	⟶	goddess
Type 2	net-owner	⟶	1) priest 2) offering	⟶	goddess
Type 3	the Karaiyar	⟶	1) priest 2) medium	⟶	goddess

FIGURE 18.
THREE TYPES OF RITUALS IN THE DRAUPADĪ GODDESS FESTIVAL

sponsor, as occurs in the festival.

As for the rituals of the third category it would seem obvious that the transformation of the medium in the festival cannot be accomplished without the Brahman priest's help. The latter protects him against divine power by binding a *kāppu* cord. Rituals conducted by the priest are prerequisite to the performance of rituals by the medium in the festival. The ecstatic phase is thus encompassed by the Brahmanical rites within the grand framework of the sacrifice. The fact that the *karakam* pot is placed near the nine pots at the Vāstu *śānti* on the first day is suggestive of this relationship. It seems to deny the medium's ability to invite Draupadī from the sea, and to suggest her birth through the fire sacrifice, as the *Mahābhārata* tells us. Further, it suggests the denial of the existence of the active Draupadī embodied in the medium. Draupadī is born from *homa* at the first ritual of the festival, which is performed by the Brahman priest: her power increases by means of a series of *abhiṣeka* rituals, again performed by the priest, and not through the *karakam* pot procession led by the medium. These *abhiṣeka*s are, significantly, supported by the groups of men of secular power. From the Brahman's point of view, and the patrons' too, the medium's role is redundant.

The most striking feature is the participation of the masses in the festival, especially through the dyadic relationship (possession) between men and the divine beings. The medium as an incarnation of the goddess becomes a focal point. The villagers themselves enter this dyadic, ecstatic relationship with the divine. In such a relationship, the ideology of *bhakti*—devotion, love and piety—becomes predominant. We have also noted that this dimension is concerned with personal, existential suffering. This suffering is, however, related to a cosmological dimension, the suffering of Draupadī in the *Mahābhārata*. The festivals are the major occasions of cosmological, and individual renewal in Hindu society. In the votive rituals, the votary's total subordination to the goddess and her compassion are emphasised. Service and possession at the festivals are the outward expression of an inner state of intense devotion. The aspirations of the devotees, however, are not fully realised, but constrained by both caste and economic factors. They are only partially realised.

As we noted in chapter 4, devotion alone is not enough to qualify for mediumship ; only Paṇṭāram caste members have suitable powers for the role. In other words, the hierarchical order of the caste penetrates the ecstatic devotional rituals. This means that to accept the medium as the paramount devotee of Draupadī implies an acceptance of the hierarchical order which underlies his qualification for mediumship, that is, his hereditary caste status. It also indirectly involves accepting the hierarchical relationship between the Brahman and the Paṇṭāram, because the latter acknowledges the former's superiority : without the former's rituals the latter cannot play his role. From the medium's point of view, his subordination to the Brahman priest legitimates his status as Draupadī's medium. For the Brahman, the ecstatic rituals are meaningful only because they are dependent upon him. The medium is more significant as a victim, than as an exemplary devotee. In the final analysis, the devotees would seem ultimately to be subject to men of secular power, because, first of all, the medium depends on the Brahman priest, and the priest in turn is not able to conduct the crucial rituals, such as *abhiṣeka,* without the sponsorship of the net-owners. In brief, the devotees are subjected both to the hierarchical principle of caste, and to politico-economic power. Or to put it less assertively, their world is not fully realised. The festival, therefore, fails to provide a real opportunity to realise what Babb calls "religious individualism" (Babb 1976), or a transcendental, anti-structural world of *bhakti,* in which mutual love and egalitarian values are totally predominant. On the contrary, such a world is, in fact, denied through complex articulations of various rituals and symbolism in the centre of the festival.

Conclusion

In this chapter I have analysed the complex structure of the Draupadī goddess festival in terms of symbolic meanings and political implications. The festival is framed by the *Mahābhārata,* especially focusing on Draupadī's experience of suffering, and has a structure of sacrifice in which the medium plays a role of victim. From the political point of view the ecstatic rituals, whose participants are, in the main, ordinary, impoverished fishermen, are subordinated to the rituals which are conducted by the Brahman priest, who must maintain a close alliance with the wealthy net-owners. In other words, the festival is ironically the place where *bhakti* is emphasized, whilst simultaneously being rendered subordinate to authority of the Brahmans and mundane secular power. In the festival secular power is legitimated without any apparent contradiction to the more devotional and personal themes of the festival.

In the next, concluding, chapter I shall summarise the foregoing discussions by comparing the two village festivals, and put forward arguments concerning the relationship between power and priesthood, ideological constructs of Hindu society as evidenced by religious activities, and the general concept of Sanskritization.

CHAPTER EIGHT

CONCLUSION

Two Village Festivals Compared

In this section, I will discuss the general nature of the Draupadī goddess festival in comparative terms, by referring to the themes I delineated in the analysis of the Bhadrakālī goddess festival ; the relationship of the goddess to evil forces, and the relationship between the ecstatic and non-ecstatic phases of the festival.

Controlling Evil Forces

Both the Bhadrakālī and Draupadī goddess festivals are structured on the theme of sacrifice and control over evil forces. The prevalence of the symbolism of sacrifice in both festivals has been already pointed out. The central ritual of the Bhadrakālī goddess festival is a blood sacrifice ; the Draupadī festival follows the basic structure of the sacrifice, and the *Mahābhārata* story is itself said to be about sacrifice (Biardeau 1984 : 19). The basic function of sacrifice is to negate one's evil element in order to become purified. The two festivals show a similar concern with evil forces in reference to sacrificial symbolism.

The legend of Bhadrakālī's original manifestation in the village shows her appearing to counter an epidemic disease, which is considered to be a dark aspect of herself. The repetitive *karakam* pot processions suggest the attack of the epidemic disease on the village, and show the villagers' effort to cool Bhadrakālī (herself epidemic disease), and to transform her into the protective power. Bhadrakālī's battle against the evil, and her subsequent victory over it, involves her gaining control over her own chaotic character.

In comparison with Bhadrakālī, Draupadī is less fierce, and is considered to have a less ambivalent attitude towards people. With the discarding of the *karakam* pot, the ecstatic phase of the Bhadrakālī festival is clearly demarcated. In the Draupadī goddess festival, it is less clear when the active Draupadī leaves the village for the sea. It seems as if she still resides at the temple after the festival. This implies that Bhadrakālī's departure is more desirable than Draupadī's. The former is more closely linked with evil forces than the latter. Unlike Bhadrakālī, Draupadī does not go to the village border to confront the evil force herself; in fact, it is one of her husbands, Bhīma, who kills Duryodhana, a symbol of evil. Draupadī is, however, according to local accounts, as fierce as Bhadrakālī, but the violence remains latent, is less clearly articulated, and does not seem apparent in the rituals, except when she approaches Duryodhana to fulfil her oath in one of the enactments of the epic.

Duryodhana, who was brutally killed by Bhīma, is finally said to be saved by Draupadī's grace. The logic here is similar to that which sees the sacrificial goat as Bhadrakālī's husband. The evil force is ultimately allowed to unite with the goddess by totally surrendering to her. Thus Duryodhana is comparable to a sacrificial victim. He, however, plays second fiddle to the medium, who remains the most important victim, representing, in a similar way to the village goat, the village as a whole. The place of sacrifice is not a battleground, but a firewalking pit, where the medium, and the votaries, who are functionally comparable to votive offerings made after the sacrifice of the village goat, are symbolically immolated in order to gain divine grace.

Bhadrakālī suffers from cholera, while Draupadī from exile. They are saved only through blood sacrifice and firewalking respectively. Common to both festivals is the idea that only those who have successfully recovered from suffering themselves can save others. The festivals demonstrate such a process of recovery.

In the Draupadī goddess festival more universal themes of devotion and salvation are dominant, while in the Bhadrakālī goddess festival the importance of the village is stressed. The Draupadī goddess festival enacts the pan-Indian epic of the *Mahābhārata* emphasising evil in universal terms, while the Bhadrakālī goddess festival is based on the local legend of her first manifestation in the village as a possessing agent. The Bhadrakāli is consequently concerned with evil spirits on the village borders. In the Draupadī goddess festival the medium is an incarnation of Draupadī and simultaneously an examplar of her devotees, rather than a representative of the village, though he becomes one as the victim. As far as its reputation is concerned, this festival is more concerned with devotion itself than with a village, that is why so many outsiders participate in it.

Festival Structures

The argument in chapter 6 suggests that during the *maṇḍalābhiṣeka,* a patron undergoes a process of disembodiment, while, step by step, divine power becomes embodied in concrete objects. Similar aspects are also apparent in the analysis of village festivals. Through various sacrificial rituals, the villagers approach divine power, while this power radiates from the temple to the village, and beyond. The distinction between the sacred and the secular is temporarily suspended. In spite of these common features there are marked differences between the Bhadrakālī and the Draupadī festivals.

We have noted that the Bhadrakālī goddess festival is divided into two phases, ecstatic and non-ecstatic. The ecstatic phase is governed by a series of rituals, in which the goddess, and other minor deities such as Bhairava, possess the medium and other votaries. This phase starts with the setting up of two *kumpams* and one *karakam,* representing active Bhadrakālī, and differentiating the festival time from ordinary time. I have suggested that the aspect of Bhadrakālī in the ecstatic phase is the epidemic bearing one.

When these pots are discarded in the sea, a more ordered time is resumed, although it is still distinctive from ordinary time. The final night of the festival is marked by the procession of Bhadrakālī's festival image through the village, which represents a more active form of Bhadrakālī than her stone idol in the sanctum sanctorum, but which is less fierce than the *karakam.* The festival has a double structure, involving the time of the *karakam* and the time of the festival image. Both are opposed to the normal time represented by the stone idol.

The Draupadī goddess festival has a similarly duplex structure. After the Brahman ties the *kāppu* cord onto the medium, the ecstatic phase sets in. Unlike the Bhadrakālī goddess festival, however, the duplex structure of the Draupadī goddess festival is not only a lineal sequence from one phase to the other, but it also involves the articulation of one phase with the other in parallel. In tandem with the ecstatic *karakam* procession, *snānābhiṣeka* is held from the eleventh day onwards by the Brahman priest, and is sponsored by the village net-owners and other wealthy men.

In the Bhadrakālī goddess festival, the festival image goes around the village only after the ecstatic phase is over. Similarly in the case of the Draupadī goddess festival, Draupadī's festival image comes out only on the nineteenth day, after the firewalking. In the Draupadī goddess festival, however, the festival images of Gaṇeśa, Pārtasārati and his consorts are carried around the village from the tenth or eleventh day onwards, well before the firewalking ceremony. The first day of this corresponds, more or less, to the first date of *abhiṣeka*.

The way the two phases are articulated in the Draupadī goddess festival is closely related to the division of labour between the medium and the priest. In the Bhadrakālī goddess festival, there is no strong contrast between mediumship and priesthood and the role can be filled by a single individual. The medium resumes the role of priest, receiving *arcanā* offering during the triumphant village procession, when the ecstatic phase is over. This is possible because the two phases are linked in a lineal order, so the same person can play the two roles. In contrast, the synchronic articulation between the two phases in the Draupadī goddess festival inevitably points out a marked division of labour between the medium performing the ecstatic rituals, and the priest performing the non-ecstatic ones. The two types of rituals are found side by side in this festival. In the final analysis, however, the medium's role is encompassed by the priestly one. He cannot simply switch roles, and he is subordinate to the priest.

Another difference in the way the ecstatic and non-ecstatic phases are articulated in the two festivals lies in the way the festivals express politico-economic power. Although they meet the whole expense of the Bhadrakālī goddess festival, the net-owners as a collective force become prominent only towards the end of the festival, when they alone receive *prasāda* at the Bhairava worship. The net-owner's patronage is more visible in the Draupadī goddess festival. From the eleventh day, the *abhiṣeka* rituals, which they sponsor, are held everyday, and they have the privilege of carrying the Gaṇeśa's festival image around the temple every morning.

In addition to these ritual activities, the net-owner can more openly participate in the Draupadī goddess festival, directly displaying his economic status by, for example, donating firewood, or inviting dancers to come from Colombo. The Bhadrakālī goddess festival does not provide such occasions for display ; only on the last day can a net-owner provide a tractor for the procession.

To sum up, according to cosmological background, personal commitment and symbolism, the two festivals present more or less identical themes : controlled expression of the multiplex nature of the divine power of the goddesses, the acceptance of evil forces which are concomitant with the goddesses' suffering. At the symbolic level the main difference is that the Draupadī festival is universal, while the Bhadrakālī festival remains local. The differences in the village festival structure are mainly dependent on, but not solely reducible to, the role of the Brahman priest in the Draupadī goddess festival. This gives room for political forces to play in the festival.

Religion and Power

In the foregoing chapters I have dealt with the existential and cosmological meanings of votive and village festivals. They provide the villagers with important occasions for the renewal of life through symbolic death. Votive rituals are performed when an initial wish is fulfilled. The main idea is recreation of one's life through sacrifice. An active form of Bhadrakālī is brought in from the sea. The medium possessed by the goddess wanders around the village. The village as a whole is considered to be possessed by the goddess during the festival, as if it were attacked by an epidemic. But through a blood sacrifice, a new order appears, and the Bhadrakālī goddess festival extends the divine power of regeneration outside the temple, its purpose being the renewal of community. In the Draupadī goddess festival, a thousand devotees feel their own personal, existential renewal through firewalking, which is typical of ecstatic votive rituals, but the festival is also an occasion for cosmological recreation, as its reliance on the *Mahābhārata* clearly suggests. On the other hand, endless recreation by sacrifice creates an unchangeable stream of time, implying the ideological eternity of a given society. In a word both cosomological and personal dimensions are closely related to political functions. In this final section, I further delineate how power is represented and expressed through ritual.

Priest and Patron

Here I take up the theme of the relationship between the priest and the patron. This is part of the wider problem of the relationship between ritual power and politico-economic power, and of the nature of the authority constructed through rituals.

Recognising the dualism between status and power, or between religion, the ideology of purity and pollution epitomised by the Brahman priest, and the politico-economic domain, represented by the Kṣatriya king, in Indian society, Dumont argues that the former encompasses the latter. The dualism between the two domains is reproduced at the village level in the relationship between the Brahmans and the dominant caste (Dumont 1980 : 66-84).

What is clear from my analysis of the *maṇḍalābhiṣeka* in chapter 6 is that the patron symbolically follows the flow of power and is led to union with the divine being. True, the Brahman priest must maintain a high degree of purity and avoid pollution ; but when we shift the focus from purity and pollution to divine power, we find that the patron is symbolically as important and central as the Brahman priest. The chief priest only undergoes the first set of purificatory rituals, and remains outside the main flow of divine power. The main reason for the willingness of the man of power to invest his wealth in the *abhiṣeka* is that the rituals provide the place where he can publicly and legitimately demonstrate his politico-economic power. We need, however, to go beyond the vulgar functionalist view of rituals, as serving to reinforce solidarity and a given social order, and to investigate how rituals work at the symbolic level. In my view *abhiṣeka*, by placing the patron at the transcendental level, provides a mechanism for converting his secular power into religious power.

As far as the generation of divine power is concerned, the crucial acts of the *abhiṣeka* involve the destruction of sacrificial victims. It is this symbolic violence that enables the patron to transform himself and subsequently to legitimate his power. More importantly, the violence is symbolically aimed at the patron himself, as he is identified with the sacrificial victim. In other words, the legitimation of his power and establishment of his authority are achieved at the transcendental level through his own "death." More generally speaking, sacrificial rituals create an endless cyclical time of death and rebirth, thus removing the patron from historical time.

However, the very fact that his self-negation would lead to his removal from the world, and to the negation of worldly values, creates a fundamental contradiction between his continuous aspiration for transcendence through self-abnegation and his exercise of secular power in the world. Consequently he needs a priest, who specialises in controlling sacred power through his knowledge of *mantras*, and who can protect him on his journey into the sacred sphere. In other words, the relationship between the patron and priest can be characterised as an alliance with regard to the control and acquisition of untamed power, although such an alliance cannot get rid of tension between them, and there are local variations in their relationships.

Sacrificial rituals like the *abhiṣeka* which are presided over by a Brahman priest, serve to consecrate the man of power and legitimate the social order under his dominance, and to guarantee his prosperity. They make it appear as if *śakti*, which the man of power acquires through rituals, is the cause, not the result, of his wealth and worldly privilege. Hindu society is conceptualised through the production of divine power (its generation or introduction, and control) through ritual, this power then being represented as the source of creativity of the non-religious sphere. The real source of creativity is thus displaced. Aided by the priest, the patron has a virtual monopoly on the production of divine power and thereby consolidates his authority. The rituals can thus be seen as a manifestation of alienation. Surplus products are expropriated by the patron, and this enables him to hold rituals and accumulate divine power, which is then seen as the source of all creativity and material well-being or as life itself (Hubert and Mauss 1964 : 34). This is the inverted relationship between the production and consumption of power. But this is an analytical argument, in reality it is difficult to separate the secular sphere from the religious one, and participating in rituals is part of the political process, and they should not be considered as simply affirming the *status quo*.

Moving from the priest-patron relationship to the relationship between the dominant caste and the other, service castes, we have found that the Karaiyar caste, represented by the Hindu Temple Administrative Committee, collectively acts as patron of the village festivals and controller of the village temples, and allocates services to other castes. Even though not every village caste participates in the festivals, the above argument could extend to the relationships between the dominant caste and other service castes. The former monopolises both secular and divine power, while the latter hold only indirect access to them.[129]

Sanskritization Reconsidered

The close relationship between power and Brahmanical (Sanskritic) rituals is often argued in terms of Sanskritization. Sanskritization means the process in which relatively lower castes tend to imitate customs and manners of higher castes, especially Brahman caste. The concept was first proposed by Srinivas (1952 :30-31). At first he seems to consider cultural elements and the process is automatic, as everybody wants to raise his social status. Later he admits that economic or political conditions should be taken into consideration (Srinivas 1962 : 56-57). Furthermore, he emphasizes social differentiations inside a caste, which are caused by economic and political elements (ibid., 58 ; cf. Hartel 1980). According to him, a section of a caste obtains a new politico-economic power and then tries to adopt Brahmanical values and raise its status, either by involving other less powerful caste members, or by differentiating themselves from the rest of the caste as a new status group.

The development of the Draupadī goddess festival can obviously be seen as a typical case of Sanskritization, as historical changes since Brahman priests came to the temple, including the crucial tendency to pay homage to Pārtasārati, instead of Draupadī, suggest. What is at issue, in my view, is neither the raising of the caste status of the Karaiyar, nor the making of a new elite group. It is more of a process in which the net-owners have tried to acquire legitimacy and hegemony with the help of the Brahmanical rituals rather than seeing in them a cultural sign of higher status or prestige.[130] Srinivas considers Sanskritization in terms of caste status, and even when he later admits the political implications of the Sanskritic values (Srinivas 1989 : 63), he does not recognise fully the political function of the Brahmanical rituals such as *abhiṣeka*. Srinivas calls Sanskritic Hinduism a religion of Brahman, but I think it is a religion of power as well. In spite of its claim on transcendental values Sanskritic Hinduism could be more localised than has formerly been assumed, because local power structures are more closely involved in it than "ecstatic" Hinduism. This is at least the case with the Draupadī goddess festival. The above argument does not mean, however, that the Brahman priest is essential to rationalise the political functions of the rituals. Rather the various functions depend on how the rituals are performed (whether by priesthood or possession), and not who performs them (whether Brahman or not). Every ritual the Brahman conducts does not necessarily entail empowering a certain group. In fact, if the *abhiṣeka* patron is the village as a whole, then its political implications may be completely different.

In my concluding remarks, I must reiterate that although I have stressed the ideological functions of Hindu rituals and village festivals, I do not mean to suggest that the sole reason for their existence lies in these functions, nor that the villagers are totally blinded to reality and mystified by the message of the rituals. As for the non-political aspects of rituals, I tried to elucidate the existential and cosmological aspects of the festivals ; and, in relation to the limits of the mystifying function of the rituals, I have showed the dominant, inclusive, and yet hard-to-grasp nature of *bhakti*, and other instances of alternative readings of ritual activities. My attention to political functions and their articulations with cosmological and personal meanings of the rituals rather reflect my critical view of the main emphases in the anthropological literature on Hinduism.

NOTES

CHAPTER ONE

1. We should take the impact of colonialism on non-Western societies into account as well, because it artificially set the boundaries of the colonised societies, and controlled the interaction between them (Forster 1973 : 31).

2. This is not to say that it is only a straightforward structural-functionalist study of religion ; it pays due attention to some important concepts such as purity and pollution.

3. The following discussion is based on Srinivas (1952 : 214-15).

4. Cf. Radcliffe-Brown's Preface to Srinivas's monograph (1952 : vi-viii).

5. Cf. Leach's distinction between empiricist (functionalist) and rationalist (structuralist) approaches in social anthropology (Leach 1976a : 4). The shift from function to meaning is attributed to Evans-Pritchard's early works such as *The Nuer* (Dumont 1975 : 333-34), but the focus on the meaning became important in the 1950's.

6. "Our primary object is a system of ideas" (Dumont 1970a : 11).

7. Parry compares Dumont to Polanyi (Parry 1974 : 102-7).

8. Dumont's standpoint is, however, not consistent, and I will take up such an example in the next section. Certainly Dumont provides a general framework to understand Hinduism in his article, "Renunciation in Indian Religions" (1970b), but even here his emphasis on the importance of renunciation should be considered in its relationship with the caste ideology of purity and pollution.

9. The following discussion is based on Dumont (1986 : 460-64).

10. Although he does not claim causal relationships between the divine and the social orders, Harper's view may be also considered as a "correspondence theory of religion" in its wider sense.

11. In addition, Dumont's main theme of the separation between power and status in Indian society seems never to have occurred to Harper. This is partly because he conducted research in a village, where Brahmans formed a land-owning dominant caste.

12. See also Sharma (1970), who insists on the importance of the ideology of purity and pollution.

13. As has been discussed, Dumont himself is, however, inconsistent on this point.

14. Interestingly the importance of power in Hindu rituals was well recognised in such works as Abbott (1930) and Ayyar (1925), long before Dumont and Pocock (1959a). Ayyar uses a quasi-scientific adjective, "magnetism" rather than purity to explain the quality of the sacred objects (Ayyar 1925 : 28-29).

15. For a critique of ethnosociology in general, see McGilvray (1982 : 89-95).

16. "Man can also acquire and store up power through various means as Tapas (austerities), initiation, instruction as well as through the rites themselves. 'I do it through my Śakti.' is a reply I have had repeatedly. Śakti is not the same as ability. It always has the meaning of additional strength or power over and above man's natural capacity." (Diehl 1956 : 340, parenthesis mine).

17. See the last line in the above quotation, "Thus the Brahmans are both the most powerful beings and the most pure." Harper's continuum theory of Hindu socio-religious world can be considered as a forerunner of the monistic view of Hindu society. It should be noted that Harper carried out research in a Brahman-dominated village, as did Wadley.

18. Fuller aptly quotes Dumont and Pocock's view of divine power (Fuller 1979 : 698).

19. Cf. Burghart (1983 : 278) ; Pfaffenberger (1980 : 196-202). Burghart makes similar criticisms of functionalism, structuralism and ethnosociology : they all assume a single system in their analyses of Hindu society. Instead he proposes to consider Hindu society as consisting of more than one cultural system and focus on the interactions between them. He calls this approach intercultural analysis. Although I agree with his criticism of functionalism and other alternative approaches, his solution is, I insist, not satisfactory without referring to politico-economic factors which constrain these cultural systems and their interactions.

20. Stirrat criticises Evans-Pritchard's arbitrary systematisation of the Nuer religion (Stirrat 1984 : 200-201). Evans-Pritchard (1956) has to refer to the diffusionist approach, when some elements do not fit in with the religious "system" of the Nuer, by describing them as borrowed or foreign. Note that Stirrat's criticism is very similar to my criticism of Srinivas, whose view of rituals I took as an example of structural-functionalism. This also indicates some of the underlying similarities between the functionalist and the idealist approach to religion.

21. Compare Dumont's remark on the man-god relationship (Dumont 1986 : 456-57), in which he sees the master-servant relationship based on the caste system. Dumont's argument is exactly opposite to that of David. For David (and Harper), religious spheres provide an encompassing framework which integrates otherwise divided Hindu society. For Dumont , except for the purity-pollution ideology, they are a reflection of social relationships.

CHAPTER TWO

22. After huts (*kottu*)for fish-curing built in this place.

23. Given these close links between Cattiyur and Adipetti, I do not make a rigid distinction between them, for—especially in the religious field—few exist. For example, the Muttumāri goddess temple is located in Adipetti, but is considered as a village temple by the Cattiyur residents. I do not therefore always specify whether my data comes from a Cattiyur or an Adipetti villager, though some of the statistical data are presented separately.

24. The Munnesvaram myth explicitly states that to administrate the daily religious observances (priesthood) has a more meritious value than to found or renovate a shrine (kingship) (Somaskanta 1927 : 36-37), but even here the underlying principle is not purity, but the nature of service, that is, worship.

25. In addition to the members of the above castes, there are eight other Hindu households in Cattiyur, whose caste identities are either unknown or uncertain.

26. Another writer, Hiltebeitel, based on research in southern India, points out that the most important and traditional caste holding the Draupadī goddess festivals is Vaṉṉiyar (Hiltebeitel 1988 : 32-39). They are said to have been warriors of local kingdoms, and some moved to Sri Lanka in the fifteenth and sixteenth centuries. He presents an interesting theory that they brought the Draupadī cult to Sri Lanka. Although there is no evidence, it is plausible to consider that the present Karaiyar of Cattiyur may be the descendants of those Vaṉṉiyars.

27. A Dutch governor mentioned Cattiyur as a fair-sized fishing village in his 1767 journey (Falck 1963 : 58).

28. One of them was even reported in a daily Tamil newspaper (Corea 1965 ; cf. Raghavan 1961 : 82-83).

29. In one version Kamalakkanni was actually his own daughter.

30. Some add a Goldsmith and a Paṇṭāram family.

31. One version suggests that Kamalakanni was killed by a villager.

32. Officially the Cattiyur villagers are registered as Ceylon Tamil. Indian Tamils were brought from India in the nineteenth century by the British colonial government, and are living in the hill countries.

33. David reports that the Karaiyars in Jaffna contribute to a temple festival as importers of ritual objects unobtainable locally (David 1977 : 212), but I could not elicit such a claim.

34. To use David's term, the Goldsmith caste members are not "bound" to the dominant caste (David 1977 : 197).

35. Cremation is rare in Cattiyur, because it is expensive.

36. These differences are viewed in purely technical terms, and are not considered in terms of distinctive social groups, as reported elsewhere (Alexander 1982 : 25).

37. The season is called *kaccaṉ kāṟṟu* (windy season).

38. This season is called *vāṭaik kāṟṟu* (northern wind season).

39. The figure was obtained from the list of the donors to the restoration of the village Muttumāri goddess temple and was confirmed by the villagers. It does not mean, however, that there were fifteen net-owners in 1903. In the past joint ownership was not uncommon (cf. Stirrat 1975 : 159-60).

40. Later from 1970 to 1976 he operated beach seines on the Cattiyur coast.

41. Gunasekere attributes this to the prevalence of beach seine fishing (Gunasekere 1970 : 225-30, 247).

42. The average age is 28.4 years old (N=38). The average age of raft fishermen is 30.0 (N=53).

43. This is a general trend throughout the island (People's Bank Resarch Department 1983 : 6, Table V).

44. Only four owners in Cattiyur do not go to the sea : one of them is a *vaḷḷam* beachseine owner, two are government servants, and one is a fish trader.

45. I conducted my census from November 1982 to February 1983 : therefore, most villagers knew the UNP had been extended and unless they were committed SFLP or the Tamil United Liberation Front supporters, tended to declare their support for the UNP.

46. They comprise the sites of both vegetable and fish markets, four village temples Muttumāri, Kantacāmi, Bhadrakālī and Pārtasārati from the north, coconuts estates attached to the temples, one fishing point along the canal, and beach seine fishing grounds attached to the village.

CHAPTER THREE

47. One month is the normal case.

48. For similar arguments on the identities of supernatural beings, see Moffatt (1979 : 234) ; Pfaffenberger (1982 : 170) ; Ryan (1980 : 75-76).

49. It should be a first born male. Cattiyur villagers usually bury such a corpse in the homestead, rather than in the open burial ground, lest it be taken away by an exorcist.

50. A young man from Mannur committed suicide on the railway. His younger sister suggested that as he had taken off the amulet prepared by a local exorcist, an evil spirit attacked him and drove him to suicide.

51. Only a married man can become a medium or a priest.

52. Detailed analyses of the annual festivals and their symbolic relationships to economic activities are found in Logan (1980 : 175-384) and Reiniche (1979 : 41-78).

53. Fuller gives a systematic explanation of the Tamil calendric system (Fuller 1980).

CHAPTER FOUR

54. *Bhakti* derives from *bhaj* (sharing, partaking), and signifies an interpersonal relationship of devotion, love, respect and service (Dhavamony 1971 :

13-23).

55. For example, Brockington writes:

"Devotion, love to a god should be expressed in love for one's fellows, and transcend the barriers of caste and sex." (Brockington 1981 : 133)

56. Cf. Lele (1979) and Shulman (1984). By contrast, anthropological studies on the *bhakti*, sects, and religious movements in contemporary India, stress the anti-traditional, especially anti-caste, attitudes of such movements which they relate to changing circumstances such as urbanisation, or the development of capitalism. (cf. Pocock 1973 : 153-56 ; Singer 1972 : 158).

57. From *patti* or *bhakti*, and from *aṭi* or foot respectively.

58. Manual labour and service are important expressions of one's devotion (cf. Uma Shankari 1980 : 68-69, 135 ; Yocum 1982 : 173).

59. The singing of hymns is considered a typical expression of *bhakti* (cf. Uma Shankari 1984 : 182-83).

60. See chapter 6 for a further discussion on *mantra śakti*.

61. This is especially the case for those held by married women (cf. Logan 1980 : 205-6).

62. Though not common, a minor ritual (for example, just visiting a local temple) may be performed when a vow is initially made. Even if the wish is not completely granted, a votary might still perform a ritual to ensure his recovery. The distinction between wishmaking and thanksgiving can be blurred, as recovery may be delayed, or the vow may be for a long-term and general term, such as family prosperity. Cattiyur net-owners, for example, perform a ritual for a good catch in the coming fishing season and call it a votive rite. They also say that it should be repeated annually. In this case, the ritual for fulfilling the vow made in the past turns into the ritual for the future. In this wider sense, *neṟṟikkaṭaṉ* refers to the rituals performed at any stage of the vow (wishmaking, reassurance of deity's help and thanksgiving).

63. Besides these rituals, four men and three women participated in *akkiṉiccaṭṭi*.

64. In addition, the offering items of *arcanā* are identical to those of *homa* or fire sacrifice (see chapter 6).

CHAPTER FIVE

65. These original events are recited in devotional songs during the Bhadrakālī goddess festival in Cattiyur. On the inner wall of the new Bhadrakālī temple there are murals depicting these events, and the story of the emigration of Cattiyur villagers from India to Sri Lanka.

66. The motif is based on the myth of Mahiṣāsuramardinī, who killed the buffalo-demon, Mahiṣāsura.

67. Draupadī and Muttumāri are, however, not called *ūrkkāval*.

68. Bhadrakālī's relationship to the evil spirits is of the same nature as her relationship to cholera. The legend of the Munnesvaram Bhadrakālī temple reveals Bhadrakālī's fierceness. According to it, the owner of the temple once inadvertently

left his son behind in the inner shrine, and locked him in. A few hours later, the owner discovered that his son was missing and hurriedly came back to the temple. There he found Bhadrakālī's mouth red with the boy's blood. Since then, she has gained extraordinary power, and has attracted many devotees throughout the island. The temple is notorious for sorcery (*cēvaṉai* or *cūṉiyam*), and animal sacrifices were conducted there until recently.

69. This does not mean the deity of a kin group here, but Bhadrakālī's retinue of deities.

70. There was much tension in the village about the delay over the Bhadrakālī temple renovation. A special committee was set up, but its members were said to have stuffed their own pockets. Kataresan fell into trance when the *mahākumbhābhiṣeka* and *śaṅkhābhiṣeka* rituals were finally held to complete the restoration of the Bhadrakālī temple.

71. The Bhadrakālī goddess temple has no flagstaff.

72. The *cūrapuli*s are only allowed to enter the inner sanctum sanctorum during the festival time.

73. The priest was actually the usual priest, Kulantaivel, of the Bhadrakālī goddess temple, because the chief priest of the Muttumāri goddess temple was the medium in the festival.

74. Cf. Logan (1980 : 336-43) ; Good (1983) ; Reiniche (1979 : 66-75).

75. Cf. Beck (1981 : 114 n.38) ; Brubaker (1978 : 351-53) ; Fawcett (1891 : 269) ; Fuller and Logan (1985 : 105).

76. Bhadrakālī is said to be most powerful just before she sets out for the village borders. It was at this time that the medium started biting his own hands seriously, disturbing the festival the previous year.

77. The song consists of simple praises of Kālī and her pot.

78. On the relationship between *kummi* dance and female fertility, see Iyer (1957 : 77-78).

79. A cremation ground on the village border is called *cuṭukāṭu* or "a hot forest."

80. Women are not allowed to board beach seine boats, as they may start menstruating, and pollute it. Chewing a betel leaf or smoking at sea was also considered an offence against the goddess in the past.

81. But not all *ampā*s are religious (cf. Pusparajan 1976).

82. As we shall see, the theme of suffering goddess is apparent in the case of the Draupadī goddess festival (cf. Hiltebeitel 1988 : 265-66 ; Meyer 1986 : 223)

CHAPTER SIX

83. Anointing with fruit involves making a salad consisting of the types of fruit involved ; e.g. mango, banana, pinapple, jackfruit, by cutting them into small pieces, and then nibbing this onto the object.

84. The case I observed in Cattiyur went on for forty-three days.

85. Ayyar writes :

"There is also a popular belief that Lakshmi, the goddess of wealth, abides in certain materials and betel leaf is one of them" (Ayyar 1925 : 165).

86. Sometimes other substances such as medicinal herbs and a one rupee coin are added.

87. Diehl describes the thread wrapped around the pot as "sinews" of the body (1956 : 264).

88. A turmeric root is sometimes tied to the cord.

89. *Kāppu* derives from *kā* or "protect."

90. Collectively called *ōrmaram* in Tamil. They are twigs of *aracu* (*Ficus religiosa*), *ālam* (*Ficus bengalensis*), and *atti* (*Ficus racemoso*).

91. The *navadhānya* usually consists of *kaṭuku* (mustard), *nel* (husked rice), *tuvarai* (red gram), *payaṟu* (Bengal gram), *eḷḷu* (sesame seeds), *uḻuntu* (black gram), *koḷḷu* (horse gram), and another kind of gram called *kaupi.*

92. When the scale of an *abhiṣeka* is larger, he may use sesame seed oil, curd, and sugar cane juice in addition to the above items, sprinkle rose water, coat the idol with sacred ash, sandalwood paste, and vermilion powder.

93. Eichinger Ferro-Luzzi points out most of the substances for the bathing ritual are classified as "cool" ones (Eichinger Ferro-Luzzi 1980 : 730-32).

94. Cf. Knipe (1975 : 103). Although his interpretation of fire sacrifice is slightly different, Gray suggests the ladle used by the priest for the offering symbolises a phallus (Gray 1979 : 100).

95. I owe the concept of embodiment and disembodiment to Logan (1980 : 123-30).

96. Ryan tells a similar story from northern Sri Lanka :

"From the fire (of a fire sacrifice) the spirit (of the deity) travels through a thread to a *kumpam* and from the *kumpam* by thread to the statue of the deity in the inner sanctum sanctorum. Villagers liken the travel of the spirit along the thread to the passage of electricity along a wire. The thread is said to get very hot"(Ryan 1980 : 26, parentheses mine).

97. The distinction between *mantra śakti* and divine power leads to the criticism of Wadley, who considers that both power and purity are somehow identical (see chapter 1). Although *mantra śakti* may be held by the Brahman, the purest caste, divine power is not identical to it. The means (pure and cool substances and *mantra śakti*) for controlling divine power and the object of that control (divine power) are of a different nature.

98. This is in disagreement with both Babb's interpretation of *prasāda* and Fuller's criticism of it. Babb considers it as the impure leftovers of a deity and the acceptance of it as "respect pollution" (Babb 1975 : 55-57). According to Harper, respect pollution is polluting behaviour voluntarily undertaken in order to show respect to another (Harper 1964 : 181-85). Thus Babb sees the humiliating aspect in the food transaction at *pūjā*. Fuller criticises Babb on the grounds that a deity is not affected by the logic of the pure-impure ideology, but does not give an alternative interpretation to *prasāda*. Rather he casts doubt on the importance of *prasāda* (Fuller 1979 : 471).

99. Ideally the *yāgaśālā* is constructed outside the temple building.

100. It cannot be denied that at the *pūjā* worshippers undergo a more subtle

and less visible transformation than the patron at the *abhiṣeka*.

101. Cf. Courtright (1985 : 48). Sathasivam contrasts *homa* to worship : the former is Vedic, and oriented to the enjoyment of worldly pleasure, whilst the latter is Agamic, *bhakti* or spiritually aspirant toward god (Sathasivam 1979 : 166 ; cf. Varma 1956 : 445). Although his contrast is too schematic, we may well identify the differences between the first part of *abhiṣeka* and worship with those between *homa* and worship. Inden's analysis of royal *abhiṣeka* is also relevant here, as he recognises two sections of the *abhiṣeka, homa* and worship, with contrasting ideologies (Inden 1978 : 49).

CHAPTER SEVEN

102. During the period, woman keeps hair dishevelled. Thus keeping the hair dishevelled means that Draupadī will remain polluted until the death of Duryodhana. While women are menstruating, sexual intercourse is forbidden. She is therefore comparable to a virgin or a widow without husband. In South India, Draupadī is said to be fearful and thirsty for blood like Kālī during exile in forest (Hiltebeitel 1988 : 289-95). According to the notice of the Mannur Draupadī goddess festival, it is Draupadī who resists the compromise between the Pāṇḍavas and the Kauravas to avoid the war, and orders her husbands to fight to the last man. These facts suggest that Draupadī is not benevolent in nature and stays in a liminal state until the oath is fulfilled.

103. According to Hiltebeitel, the original cult started in Gingee in the fourteenth century (Hiltebeitel 1988 : 17). Today the Draupadī goddess festival is found in many places both in and outside India, but is usually confined to the areas of Tamil culture. Modder (1908 : 178-79), Nevill (1887) and Raghavan (1961 : 75-77) refer to the Draupadī goddess festival in Cattiyur.

104. Hiltebeitel points out two opposite kinds of nature in Draupadī in the *Mahābhārata*. One is the auspiciousness of Śrī or Lakṣmī, and the other the fierceness of Kālī (Hiltebeitel 1980 : 153 ; Hiltebeitel 1981 : 205 ; Hiltebeitel 1988 : 289-95 ; Hiltebeitel 1991 : 399-400). Draupadī's other name was Kṛṣṇā (dark lady), the name reminiscent of Kālī (black lady) (Biardeau 1976 : 235).

105. Hiltebeitel presents more detailed accounts and interpretations of Pōttirācaṉ (Hiltebeitel 1988 : 76-127) and Vīrabhadra (Hiltebeitel 1991 : 113-16, 409-29).

106. *Āṭi uccavam, āṭi perunāl* or *āṭi tilviḻā* are more commonly used by the villagers. All refer to the festival of the month of *Āṭi*.

107. The festival is conceived to be held for eighteen days by the villagers.

108. The number is identical with that of table 16.

109. But no margosa leaf is used, and there is no subsequent act of hanging the leaves on the fence.

110. This process was compared to that of charging a battery by villagers.

111. Lime is auspicious, and is of cooling nature.

112. Like the song of the *kummi* for Bhadrakālī, this song was composed by the singer's father. Although complicated by some references to the *Mahābhārata,*

the main themes are a worldly desire for plenty, children, and freedom from disease and other sufferings.

113. Divine feet often feature as object worthy of worship in devotional songs.

114. Not going beyond the Bhadrakālī goddess temple in the north (see fig. 3).

115. It is not clear as to why votive rites for Murukaṉ are held during the Draupadī goddess festival.

116. This is not the same well as the medium uses, which is inside the temple.

117. The Hindu Temple Administrative Committee charges ten rupees for the performance of a *pāṟkāvaṭi* and five rupees for the performance of a *pāṟcempu*.

118. Ritual whipping is reported at the Draupadī temples in eastern Sri Lanka (Cartman 1957 : 120), Tamilnadu (Biardeau 1984 : 20 ; Hiltebeitel 1991 : 28-30) and Singapore (Babb 1974 : 21-23). Babb notes that whipping is "to subdue violent manifestation of trance" (ibid., 21-22).

119. This story seems to have some similarities to the episode of Pōrmaṉṉaṉ discussed by Hiltebeitel (1988 : 333-47). In the fort Pōrmaṉṉaṉ keeps a box for worship which will guarantee the victory of the Pāṇḍavas for the fight with the Kauravas. But he declines to open the fort to the Pāṇḍavas, and Kṛṣṇa disguised as an old lady, enters the fort with Draupadī. Pōrmaṉṉaṉ falls in love with Draupadī, and gives the worship box to Kṛṣṇa on the condition that he can marry Draupadī. He actually gets to marry Yudhiṣṭira's sister, Caṅkuvati. On this occasion Pōrmaṉṉaṉ demands an extraordinary dowry, as Vīrabhadra does in the Cattiyur *Mahābhārata*. Recently Hiltebeitel presents similar stories about Vīrabhadra (Hiltebeitel 1991 : 409-29).

120. The guardian deities are said to have moved from the mounds to the four corners of the firewalking pit.

121. In the past a goat was sacrificed and its blood was sprinkled around the firewalking pit (Modder 1908 : 179).

122. This is highly reminiscent of the blood sacrifice which occurs at the Bhadrakālī goddess festival and reminds us that there used to be blood sacrifice at the Draupadī goddess festival.

123. For a similar idea, see the origin myth of *kāvaṭi* in chapter 4.

124. This seems redundant, as he is already in trance. A villager told me that the second one was for praying to Muttumāri.

125. However, strictly speaking, as women are excluded from the activity, "communitas" may need some qualification here.

126. Cf. Babb (1974 : 25) ; Hiltebeitel (1988 : 439-40) ; Reiniche (1979 : 176).

127. Frasca's analysis of a Draupadī festival in South India is based on a model derived from van Gennep's *rite de passage,* and he indicates its anti-structural nature (1990 : 167-78). Given that Hubert and Mauss's sacrifice model and van Gennep's model have similarities, it is not surprising that Frasca's account and my own also resemble each other. I have already indicated, however, that I am critical

of the idealised emphasis on "communitas" in the studies of village festivals.

128. Duryodhana can also be considered as a sacrificial victim : the circumstances of his death bear a striking similarity to the goat sacrifice at the Bhadrakālī goddess festival. He is a symbol of evil, and killed, though not by Draupadī, but by Bhīma, later to be accepted by her. This is the same pattern the village goat sacrifice takes during the Bhadrakālī goddess festival. Duryodhana is not, however, a victim on behalf of the village. The medium is. So the killing of Duryodhna is, like other votary acts, comparable to votive offerings of goats after the sacrifice of the village goat. According to the textual exegesis, the exile period of the Pāṇḍavas in the forest is *dīkṣā* (a liminal period in a scheme of classical sacrifice) and the battle between the Pāṇḍavas and the Kauravas is a symbol of immolation (Biardeau 1976 : 172, 207 ; Biardeau 1984 ; Frasca 1990 : 178-79). In Cattiyur, however, there are no rituals except for *arcanā* offering during the period and only the account of the war is retold in the festival. Such a displacement is, I think, due to the change of main figures from the Pāṇḍavas in the *Mahābhārata* to Draupadī in the village festival. As far as the Pāṇḍavas are concerned, the battle is the moment of sacrifice, but it would make little sense to consider this as the appropriate time for Draupadī's transformation.

CHAPTER EIGHT

129. Although more elaborate, my emphasis on the nature of the alliance between the Brahman and the Kṣatriya-like dominant caste resembles Dumont's original analysis of the relationships between the top two *varṇas* (Dumont 1980 : 66-72). Raheja has recently argued, based on the data collected from North India, that the dominant caste plays a central role in accumulating auspiciousness leading to village prosperity. At the same time they transfer sin to other castes including the Brahman in the form of gifts (*dān*) (Raheja 1988). She considers this view of the caste relationships to be different from the hierarchical model of Indian society, where the Brahman is, being the purest, at the apek of the hierarchical order. However, she fails to analyse how the Brahman members conceptualise their seemingly contradictory status.

130. My criticism of Sanskritization is close to Hardiman's (1984 : 213-19). Cf. Carroll (1977).

REFERENCES

Abbott, J. 1930. *The Keys of Power : A Study of Ritual and Belief.* London : Methuen.

Alexander, Paul. 1982 *Sri Lankan Fishermen : Rural Capitalism and Peasant Society.* Canberra : Australian National University Press.

Ayyar, P. V. Jagadisa. 1920. *South Indian Shrines.* Madras : The Madras Times.

————1925. *South Indian Customs.* Madras : The Diocesan Press.

Babb, Laurence A. 1974. *Walking on Flowers in Singapore : A Hindu Festival Cycle. Working Paper No. 27.* Singapore : Department of Sociology, Singapore University.

————1975. *The Divine Hierarchy : Popular Hinduism in Central India.* New York : Columbia University Press.

————1976. *Thaipusam in Singapore : Religious Individualism in a Hierarchical Culture. Working Paper No. 49.* Singapore : Department of Sociology, Singapore University.

Banks, Michael Y. 1960. Caste in Jaffna. In *Aspects of Caste in South India, Ceylon and North-West Pakistan.* (ed.) E. Leach. London : Cambridge University Press.

Barnett, Steve, A. 1970. *The Structural Position of a South Indian Caste : Koṇtaikkatti Vēḷāḷar-s in Tamil Nadu.* Thesis. University of Chicago.

Beck, Brenda E. F. 1981. The Goddess and the Demon : A Local South Indian Festival and its Wider Context. *Puruṣārtha,* 5 : 83-136.

Biardeau, Madeleine. 1976. Études de mythologie hindoue (IV) II : *bhakti* et *avatāra. Bulletin de l'École Française D'Êxtreme-Orient,* 63 : 111-263.

————1984. The *Śamī* Tree and the Sacrificial Buffalo. *Contributions to Indian Sociology* (*N. S.*), 18 (1) : 1-23.

Bloch, Maurice. 1977. The Past and the Present in the Present. *Man* (*N. S.*), 12 (2) : 278-92.

Brockington, J. L. 1981. *The Sacred Thread : Hinduism in its Continuity and Diversity.* Edinburgh : The University Press.

Brubaker, Richard L. 1978. *The Ambivalent Mistress : A Study of South Indian Village Goddess and their Religious Meaning.* Thesis. University of Chicago.

Burghart, Richard. 1983. For a Sociology of Indias : An Intercultural Approach to the Study of 'Hindu Society.' *Contributions to Indian Sociology* (*N. S.*), 17 (2) : 275-99.

Carroll, Lucy. 1977. "Sanskritization," "Westernization," and "Social Mobility" :

A Reappraisal of the Relevance of Anthropological Concepts to the Social Historian of Modern India. *Journal of Anthropological Research,* 33 (4) : 355-71.

Cartman, James. 1957. *Hinduism in Ceylon.* Colombo : M. D. Gunasena.

Christian, Jane M. 1982. The End is the Beginning : A Festival Chain in Andhra Pradesh. In *Religious Festivals in South India and Sri Lanka.* (ed.) Guy R. Welbon and Glenn E. Yocum. New Delhi : Manohar.

Clothey, Fred W. 1978. *The Many Faces of Murukaṉ : The History and Meaning of a South Indian God.* The Hague : Mouton.

——————1983. *Rhythm and Intent : Ritual Studies from South India.* Madras : Blackie and Son Publishers.

Cohen, Percy. 1968. *Modern Social Theory.* London : Heinemann.

Corea, Henry. 1965 *Maṇam puriya vanta maṟakkula maṉṉaṉ* (Tamil, Marakkulam king, who came to marry). *Tiṉakaraṉ,* 13 October.

Courtright, Paul B. 1985. On this Holy Day in My Humble Way : Aspects of *Pūjā.* In *Gods of Flesh/Gods of Stone : The Embodiment of Divinity in India.* (ed.) J. P. Waghorne and N. Culter in association with Vasudha Narayanan. Chambersburg (P. A.) : Anima Publications.

David, Kenneth. 1977. Hierarchy and Equivalence in Jaffna, North Sri Lanka : Normative Codes as Mediator. In *The New Wind : Changing Identities in South Asia.* (ed.) Kenneth David. The Hague : Mouton Publishers.

Dhavamony, Mariasusai. 1971. *Love of God according to Śaiva Siddhānta : A Study of the Mysticism and Theology of Śaivism.* Oxford : Clarendon Press.

Diehl, Carl G. 1956. *Instruments and Purpose : Studies on Rites and Rituals in South India.* Lund : C. W. K. Gleerup.

Dumont, Louis. 1970a (1957). For a Sociology of India. In *Religion, Politics and History in India : Collected Papers in Indian Sociology.* Paris : Mouton.

——————1970b (1960). World Renunciation in Indian Religions. In *Religion, Politics and History in India : Collected Papers in Indian Sociology.* Paris : Mouton.

——————1975. Preface to the French Edition of *The Nuer.* In *Studies in Social Anthropology* (ed.) Beattie, John and R. Lienhardt. Oxford : Clarendon Press.

——————1980. *Homo Hierarchicus : the Caste System and its Implications, Complete Revised English Edition* (translated by Mark Sainsbury, L. Dumont and Basia Gulati). Chicago : University of Chicago Press.

——————1986. *A South Indian Subcaste : Social Organization and Religion of the Pramalai Kallar* (translated by M.Moffatt and A. Morton, revised by the author and A. Stern). Delhi : Oxford University Press.

——————and David F. Pocock. 1959a. Purity and Impurity. *Contributions to Indian Sociology,* 3 : 9-39.

——————1959b. Possession and Priesthood. *Contributions to Indian Sociology,* 3 : 55-74.

Eichinger Ferro-Luzzi, Gabriella. 1981. *Abhiṣeka* : The Indian Rite that Defies Definition. *Anthropos,* 76 : 707-42.

Evans-Pritchard, Edward E. 1956. *Nuer Religion.* Oxford : Clarendon Press.

Falck, I. Willem. 1963 (1767). Diary of a Tour on the East and West Coasts. In *Travels in Ceylon 1700-1800.* (edited and translated by R. Raven-Hart). Colombo : The Associated Newspapers of Ceylon.

Fawcett, F. 1891. On Some Festivals to Village Goddesses. *Journal of the Asian Studies of Bombay,* 2 : 261-82.

Forster, Peter. 1973. Empiricism and Imperialism : A Review of the New Left Critique of Social Anthropology. In *Anthropology and the Colonial Encounter.* (ed.) Talal Asad. London : Ithaca Press.

Fortes, Mayer. 1953. The Structure of Unilineal Descent Groups. *American Anthropologist,* 55 : 17-41.

Frasca, Richard A. 1990 *The Theater of the Mahābhārata : Terukkūttu Performances in South India.* Honolulu : University of Hawaii Press.

Fuller, Christopher J. 1979. Gods, Priests and Purity : On the Relation between Hinduism and the Caste System. *Man* (*N. S.*), 14 : 459-76.

——————1980. The Calendrical System in Tamilnadu (South India). *Journal of the Royal Asiatic Society,* (1980), 52-63.

——————1984. *Servants of the Goddess : The Priest of a South Indian Temple.* Cambridge : Cambridge University Press.

——————1985. Initiation and Consecration : Priestly Rituals in a South Indian Temple. In *Indian Religion.* (ed.) Richard Burghart and Audrey Cantlie. London : Curzon Press.

——————1988. The Hindu Pantheon and the Legitimation of Hierarchy. *Man* (*N. S.*), 14 : 459-76.

——————and Penelope Logan. 1985 The Navarātri Festival in Madurai. *The Bulletin of School of Oriental and African Studies,* 48 (1) : 79-105.

Gluckman, Max. 1967. Introduction. In *The Craft of Social Anthropology.* (ed.) A. L. Epstein. London : Tavistock Publications.

Good, Anthony. 1983. A Symbolic Type and its Transformations : the Case of South Indian Pongal. *Contributions to Indian Sociology* (*N. S.*), 17 : 223-44.

——————1985. The Annual Goddess Festival in a Tirunelveli Village. *South Asia Social Scientist,* 1 (2) : 119-67.

Gray, John N. 1979. Keep the Home Fires Burnning : Sacrifice in Nepal. *Social Analysis,* 1 : 81-107.

Gunasekere, S. D. 1970. *A Study of the Social and Economic Geography of the Coastal Fishing Industry of Ceylon, two volumes.* Thesis. University of Wales.

Hardiman, David. 1984. Adivasi Assertion in South Gujarat : The Devi Movement of 1922-3. In *Subaltern Studies III : Writings on South Asian History and Society.* (ed.) Ranjit Guha. Delhi : Oxford University Press.

Harper, Edward B. 1963. Spirit Possession and Social Structure. In *Anthropology on the March : Recent Studies of Indian Beliefs, Attitudes and Social Institutions.* (ed.) L. K. Bala Ratnam. Madras : The Book Centre.

——————1964. Ritual Pollution as an Integrator of Caste and Religion. *Journal of Asian Studies,* 23 : 151-97.

Hartel, Bradley. 1980. Sanskritization and Westernization in Eastern U. P. : Some Survey Findings. *The Eastern Anthropologist,* 33 (4) : 335-51.

Hiltebeitel, Alf. 1980. Śiva, the Goddess, and the Disguises of the Pāṇḍavas and Draupadī. *History of Religions,* 20 (1-2) : 146-74.

——————1981. Draupadī's Hair. *Puruṣārtha,* 5 : 179-214.

——————1988. *The Cult of Draupadī Vol. 1 Mythologies : from Gingee to Kurukṣetra.* Chicago : The University of Chicago Press.

——————1991. *The Cult of Draupadī Vol. 2 On Hindu Ritual and the Goddess.* Chicago : The University of Chicago Press.

Hubert. H. and Marcel Mauss. 1964 (1899). *Sacrifice : its Function and Meaning* (translated by W. D. Hall). London : Cohen and Cohen.

Inden, Ronald. 1978. Ritual Authority and Cyclic Time in Hindu Kingship. In *Kingship and Authority.* (ed.) John F. Richards. Madison : University of Wisconsin.

Iyer, E. Krishna. 1957. *Bharata Natya and other Dances of Tamil Nad.* Baroda : the M. S. University of Baroda Press.

Kinsley, David. 1987. *Hindu Goddesses : Visions of the Divine Feminine in the Hindu Religious Tradition.* Berkeley : University of California Press.

Knipe, David M. 1975. *In the Image of Fire : Vedic Experiences of Heat.* Delhi : Motilal Banarsidass.

Lannoy, Richard. 1971. *The Speaking Tree : A Study of Indian Culture and Society.* London : Oxford University Press.

Leach, Edmund R. 1961. *Pul Eliya : A Village in Ceylon.* Cambridge : Cambridge University Press.

——————1976a. *Culture and Communication, the Logic by which Symbols are Connected : An Introduction to the Use of Structuralist Analysis in Social Anthropology.* Cambridge : Cambridge University Press.

—————— 1976b. *Social Anthropology : A Natural Science of Society ? (Radcliffe-Brown Lecture 1976)* London : The British Academy.

Lele, Jayanti 1981. The *Bhakti* Movement in India : a Critical Introduction. In *Tradition and Modernity in Bhakti Movements.* (ed.) J. Lele. Leiden : E. B. Brill.

Lévi-Strauss, Claude. 1953. Social Structure. In *Anthropology Today* (ed.) A. L. Krober. Chicago : The University of Chicago Press.

Logan, Penelope. 1980. *Domestic Worship and the Festival Cycle in the South Indian City of Madurai.* Thesis. University of Manchester.

Marriott, McKim. 1955. Little Communities in an Indigenous Civilization. In *Village India.* (ed.) M. Marriott. Chicago : The University of Chicago Press.

——————1976. Hindu Transactions : Diversity without Dualism. In *Transactions and Meaning : Direction in the Anthropology of Exchange and Symbolic Behaviour.* (ed.) Bruce Kapferer. Philadelphia : Institute for the Study of Human Issues.

McGilvray, Dennis B. 1982. Mukkuvar Vannimai : Tamil Caste and Matriclan Ideology in Batticaloa, Sri Lanka. In *Caste Ideology and Interaction.* (ed.) D. B. McGilvray. London : Cambridge University Press.

Meyer, Eveline. 1986. *Aṅkāḷaparmēcuvari : A Goddess of Tamilnadu, her Myths and Cult.* Wiesbaden : Franz Steiner Verlag.

Modder, F. 1908. *Manual of the Puttalam District of the Northwestern Province.* Colombo :

H. C. Cottle, Government Printer.

Moffatt, Michael. 1979. *An Uutouchable Community in South India*. Princeton, New Jersey : Princeton University Press.

Nevill, Hugh. 1887. Passing over Fire, to Draupadi and the Five Pāndavas. *Taprobanian,* 2 (2) : 58-60.

Oppert, Gustav. 1893. *On the Original Inhabitants of Bharatavarṣa or India.* Westminster : Archibald Constable and Company.

Parry, Jonathan P. 1974. Egalitarian Values in a Hierarchical Society. *South Asian Review,* 7 (2) : 95-121.

People's Bank Reserach Department (The). 1983. Fisheries. *The Economic Review,* 9 (3) : 3-16.

Pfaffenberger, Bryan L. 1980. Social Communication in Dravidian Ritual. *Journal of Anthropological Research,* 36 (2) : 196-219.

———— 1982. *Caste in Tamil Culture : The Religious Foundation of Sudra Domination in Tamil Sri Lanka.* Syracuse : Maxwell School of Citizenship and Public Affairs, Syracuse University.

Pocock, David F. 1973. *Mind, Body and Wealth : A Study of Belief and Practice in an Indian Village.* Oxford : Basil Blackwell.

Pusparajan, M. 1976. *Ampā : Essays on Fishermen's Folk Songs.* Jaffna (Sri Lanka) : Alai Literary Circle.

Radcliffe-Brown. 1940. On Social Structure. *Journal of the Royal Anthropological Institute,* 70 : 1-12.

————1952. Preface to M. N. Srinivas *Religion and Society among the Coorgs of South India.* Oxford : Oxford University Press.

Raghavan M. D. 1961. *The Karāva of Ceylon.* Colombo : K. V. G. de Silva and Sons.

Raheja, Gloria Goodwin. 1988. *The Poison in the Gift : Ritual, Presentation, and the Dominant Caste in a North Indian Village.* Chicago : The University of Chicago Press.

Redfield, Robert. 1956. *Peasant Society and Culture.* Chicago : The University of Chicago Press.

Reiniche, Marie-Louise. 1979. *Les dieux et les hommes : Études des cultes d'un village du Tirunelveli, Inde du Sud.* Paris : Cahiers de L'Homme.

Roberts, Michael. 1982. *Caste Conflict and Elite Formation : The Rise of a Karāva Elite in Sri Lanka, 1500-1931.* London : Cambridge University Press.

Ryan, Kathleen S. 1980. *Pollution in Practice : Ritual, Structure and Change in Tamil Sri Lanka.* Thesis. Cornel University.

Sathasivam, A. 1979. The Hindu Religious Heritage in Sri Lanka. In *Religiousness in Sri Lanka.* (ed.) John R. Carter. Colombo : Marga Institute.

Sharma Ursula M. 1970. The Problem of Village Hinduism : Fragmentation and Integration. *Contributions to Indian Sociology* (*N. S.*), 4 : 1-21.

Shulman, David. 1980. *Tamil Temple Myths : Sacrifice and Divine Marriage in the South Indian Śaiva Tradition.* Princeton : Princeton University Press.

————1984. The Enemy Within : Idealism and Dissent in South Indian Hinduism. In *Orthodoxy, Heterodoxy and Dissent.* (ed.) S. N. Eisenstadt, R. Kahane and D. Shulman. Berlin : Mouton.

Singer, Milton. 1972. *When a Great Tradition Modernizes : An Anthropological Approach to Indian Civilization.* New York : Praeger Publishers.

Somaskanta, P. M. 1927. *Śri Munnēsvara maṉmiyam.* Colombo : Co-operative Printer's Society

Srinivas, M. N. 1952. *Religion and Society among the Coorgs of South India.* Oxford : Oxford University Press.

——————1959 The Dominant Caste in Rampura. *American Anthropologist,* 51 : 1-16.

——————1962. A Note on Sanskritization and Westernization. In *Caste in Modern India and other Essays.* London : Asia Publishing House.

——————1989 The Cohesive Role of Sanskritization In *The Cohesive Role of Sanskritization and other Essays.* Delhi : Oxford University Press.

Stirrat R. G. 1975. The Social Organisation of Fishing in a Sinhalese Village. *Modern Ceylon Studies,* 6 : 140-162.

——————1984. Sacred Models. *Man* (*N. S.*), 19 (2) : 199-215.

Tamil Lexicon. 1982. Madras : University Press.

Turner, Victor W. 1957. *Schism and Continuity in an African Society.* Manchester : Manchester University Press.

——————1969. *Ritual Process : Structure and Anti-Structure.* Harmondsworth : Penguin.

Uma Shankari. 1980. *Sociology of Religion.* Thesis. University of Delhi.

——————1984. Brahmin, King and *Bhakta* in a Temple in Tamil Nadu. *Contributions to Indian Sociology* (*N. S.*), 18 (2) : 169-87.

Varma, L. A. Ravi. 1956. Rituals of Worship. In *The Cultural Heritage of India. Volume IV : The Religions.* (ed.) H. Bhattacharya. Culcutta : The Ramakrishna Mission Institute of Culture.

Wadley, Susan S. 1975. *Shakti : Power in the Conceptual Structure of Karimpur Religion.* Chicago : The Department of Anthropology, the University of Chicago.

——————1977. Power in Hindu Ideology and Practice. In *The New Wind : Changing Identities in South Asia.* (ed.) K. David. The Hague : Mouton.

Winslow, M. 1979 (1862). *Winslow's Comprehensive Tamil and English Dictionary.* New Delhi : Asian Educational Service.

Yocum, Glenn E. 1982. *Hymns to the Dancing Śiva : A Study of Māṇikkavācakar's Tiruvācakam.* New Delhi : Heritage Publisher.

INDEX